DIVISIONS OF PRE-HISTORY

MAN

AGE OF METALS		HOMO SAPIENS	MODERN MAN
NEW STONE AGE NEOLITHIC			
AZILIAN MAGDALENIAN SOLUTREAN AURIGNACEAN	NEANDERTHAL		COMBE CAPELLE
MOUSTERIAN			LE MOUSTIER KRAPINA WEIMAR
ACHEULIAN			STEINHEIM
CHELLEAN			HEIDELBERG
PRECHELLEAN			
			PILTDOWN

O P E

Neanderthal Man
Discovered 1856

EARLY MAN

DISCOVERY

EARLY MAN 36444

AS DEPICTED BY LEADING AUTHORITIES
AT THE INTERNATIONAL SYMPOSIUM
THE ACADEMY OF NATURAL SCIENCES
PHILADELPHIA, MARCH 1937

EDITED BY
GEORGE GRANT MacCURDY

INTRODUCTION BY
JOHN C. MERRIAM

ILLUSTRATED WITH
27 PLATES AND
54 TEXT CUTS

Essay Index Reprint Series

 BOOKS FOR LIBRARIES PRESS
FREEPORT, NEW YORK

STANDARD BOOK NUMBER:

8369-1184-9

LIBRARY OF CONGRESS CATALOG CARD NUMBER:

77-86770

PRINTED IN THE UNITED STATES OF AMERICA

DEDICATED TO THE

ACADEMY OF NATURAL SCIENCES OF PHILADELPHIA

IN COMMEMORATION OF THE

ONE HUNDRED AND TWENTY-FIFTH ANNIVERSARY

OF ITS FOUNDING

1812-1937

FOREWORD

ONE hundred years ago our knowledge of Early Man was almost as limited as was Neanderthal Man's knowledge of a future age of electricity. Prehistory has now become a science, a full-fledged branch of learning. Like all sciences it is international in scope and, as such, it demands international coöperation. This need for international coöperation has been, and is being, met in various ways. An important element is personal contact such as results when workers from all parts of the world meet in congress.

The first international congress *"pour les études préhistoriques"* met at Neuchâtel in the year 1866. When the Congress met in Paris the following year, the name was changed to *"Congrès international d'Anthropologie et d'Archéologie préhistoriques."* The following year (1868) the Congress met in Norwich and London. After 1868 the Congress did not meet annually; the fourteenth, and last, session was held at Geneva in 1912. In place of the old there are now two congresses: 1) International Congress of Prehistoric and Protohistoric Sciences, which met first in London (1932); the second session was in Oslo (1936) and the next will be in Budapest (1940). 2) International Congress of Anthropologic and Ethnologic Sciences, which likewise meets every four years; the first session was in London (1934) and the second will be in Copenhagen (1938). Both these congresses deal primarily with the Old World; for there was already a congress dealing specifically with the New World, viz., the International Congress of Americanists.

The International Symposium on Early Man, held in Philadelphia, March 17-20, 1937, to commemorate the 125th anniversary of the Academy of Natural Sciences of Philadelphia, was limited chronologically to early man, but it included early man of both the Old World and the New. Specifically the Symposium sought the following objectives:

1. To bring together a group of eminent world authorities on, and students of, prehistory.
2. Through papers read at the Symposium, to further the correlation of important new discoveries throughout the world.
3. Through special exhibits of specimens representing the major new discoveries, to facilitate the study and correlation of new data.
4. To stimulate coöperation among anthropologists, paleontologists, Pleistocene stratigraphers and prehistorians in furthering our knowledge of early man, his environment and his culture.
5. To make available in published form the results of the Symposium.

That the Symposium has succeeded in all its objectives, the following pages offer abundant proof. Much credit is due to those who came from distant lands, bringing with them rare original specimens, or casts of the same. The Symposium served especially to emphasize the relatively great rapidity with which our knowledge of Early Man is increasing. All students of prehistory the world over owe a special debt of gratitude to the Academy of Natural Sciences of Philadelphia.

GEORGE GRANT MacCURDY

May, 1937

CONTENTS

1. INTRODUCTORY REMARKS. BY JOHN C. MERRIAM. (READ MARCH 17, 1937) 19

2. A REVIEW OF THE STRATIGRAPHY OF JAVA AND ITS RELATIONS TO EARLY MAN. BY G. H. R. VON KOENIGSWALD. (READ MARCH 17, 1937) 23

3. THE NEAR EAST AS A GATEWAY OF PREHISTORIC MIGRATION. BY DOROTHY A. E. GARROD. (READ MARCH 17, 1937) 33

4. MOUNT CARMEL MAN. HIS BEARING ON THE ANCESTRY OF MODERN RACES. BY SIR ARTHUR KEITH AND THEODORE D. MC COWN. (READ MARCH 17, 1937) 41

5. LATE PALAEOLITHIC MAN IN NORTHERNMOST NORWAY. BY A. W. BRØGGER. (READ MARCH 17, 1937) 53

6. POLLEN ANALYSIS AS AN AID IN DATING CULTURAL DEPOSITS IN THE UNITED STATES. BY PAUL B. SEARS. (READ MARCH 17, 1937) 61

7. PLEISTOCENE LAND AND FRESH-WATER MOLLUSCA AS INDICATORS OF TIME AND ECOLOGICAL CONDITIONS. BY FRANK COLLINS BAKER. (READ MARCH 17, 1937) 67

8. MARINE PLEISTOCENE MOLLUSKS AS INDICATORS OF TIME AND ECOLOGICAL CONDITIONS. BY HORACE G. RICHARDS. (READ MARCH 17, 1937) 75

9. CERTAIN RELATIONS BETWEEN NORTHWESTERN AMERICA AND NORTHEASTERN ASIA. BY PHILIP S. SMITH. (READ MARCH 17, 1937)   85

10. EARLY MAN IN AMERICA: WHAT HAVE THE BONES TO SAY? BY ALEŠ HRDLIČKA. (READ MARCH 18, 1937)   93

11. FIRST PEOPLING OF AMERICA AS A CHRONOLOGICAL PROBLEM. BY HERBERT J. SPINDEN. (READ MARCH 18, 1937)   105

12. PLEISTOCENE GLACIAL STRATIGRAPHY OF NORTH AMERICA. BY PAUL MAC CLINTOCK. (READ MARCH 18, 1937)   115

13. CLIMATE AND EARLY MAN IN NORTH AMERICA. BY ERNST ANTEVS. (READ MARCH 18, 1937)   125

14. THE SIGNIFICANCE OF EARLY CULTURES IN TEXAS AND SOUTHEASTERN ARIZONA. BY HAROLD S. GLADWIN. (READ MARCH 18, 1937)   133

15. GEOLOGY OF THE FOLSOM DEPOSITS IN NEW MEXICO AND COLORADO. BY KIRK BRYAN. (READ MARCH 18, 1937)   139

16. THE FOLSOM PROBLEM IN AMERICAN ARCHAEOLOGY. BY FRANK H. H. ROBERTS, JR. (READ MARCH 18, 1937)   153

17. THE SIGNIFICANCE OF PROFILES OF WEATHERING IN STRATIGRAPHIC ARCHAEOLOGY. BY M. M. LEIGHTON. (READ MARCH 18, 1937)   163

18. THE PLEISTOCENE MAMMALS OF NORTH AMERICA AND THEIR RELATIONS TO EURASIAN FORMS. BY EDWIN H. COLBERT. (READ MARCH 18, 1937) 173

19. PLEISTOCENE AND POST-GLACIAL MAMMALS OF NEBRASKA. BY ERWIN H. BARBOUR AND C. BERTRAND SCHULTZ. (READ MARCH 18, 1937) 185

20. THE VERO FINDS IN THE LIGHT OF PRESENT KNOWLEDGE. BY E. H. SELLARDS. (READ MARCH 18, 1937) 193

21. THE PLEISTOCENE OF CHINA, STRATIGRAPHY AND CORRELATIONS. BY PÈRE P. TEILHARD DE CHARDIN. (READ MARCH 19, 1937) 211

22. PALAEOLITHIC INDUSTRIES IN CHINA. BY PEI WEN-CHUNG. (READ MARCH 19, 1937) 221

23. ADAPTATION TO THE POSTGLACIAL FOREST OF THE NORTH EURASIATIC PLAIN. BY V. GORDON CHILDE. (READ MARCH 19, 1937) 233

24. THE EVIDENCE OF THE DENTITION ON THE ORIGIN OF MAN. BY WILLIAM K. GREGORY AND MILO HELLMAN. (READ MARCH 19, 1937) 243

25. THE SIWALIKS OF INDIA AND EARLY MAN. BY HELLMUT DE TERRA. (READ MARCH 19, 1937) 257

26. THE ANTIQUITY OF MAN IN THE PACIFIC AND THE QUESTION OF TRANS-PACIFIC MIGRATIONS. BY DANIEL SUTHERLAND DAVIDSON. (READ MARCH 19, 1937) 269

27. DOMESTICATED PLANTS IN RELATION TO THE DIFFU-
SION OF CULTURE. BY E. D. MERRILL. (READ MARCH
19, 1937)   277

28. ON AUSTRALOPITHECUS AND ITS AFFINITIES. BY R.
BROOM. (READ MARCH 20, 1937)   285

29. ESKIMO CULTURES AND THEIR BEARING UPON THE
PREHISTORIC CULTURES OF NORTH AMERICA AND
EURASIA. BY KAJ BIRKET-SMITH. (READ MARCH 20,
1937)   293

30. ORIGIN AND DEVELOPMENT OF THE EARLY PALAEO-
LITHIC CULTURES. BY OSWALD MENGHIN. (READ
MARCH 20, 1937)   303

31. EARLY MAN IN JAVA AND PITHECANTHROPUS EREC-
TUS. BY EUGÈNE DUBOIS. (SUMMARY READ, MARCH
20, 1937)   315

32. EARLY MAN AND GEOCHRONOLOGY. BY GERARD DE
GEER. (READ BY TITLE, MARCH 20, 1937)   323

33. SOME OBSERVATIONS ON THE REMAINS OF A PLEISTO-
CENE FAUNA AND OF THE PALAEOLITHIC AGE IN
NORTHERN MANCHURIA. BY A. S. LOUKASHKIN.
(READ BY TITLE, MARCH 20, 1937)   327

34. THE CONFINS MAN. A CONTRIBUTION TO THE STUDY
OF EARLY MAN IN SOUTH AMERICA. BY H. V. WAL-
TER, A. CATHOUD AND ANIBAL MATTOS. (READ BY
TITLE, MARCH 20, 1937)   341

35. THE PLACE OF HOMO SOLOENSIS AMONG FOSSIL MEN.
BY W. F. F. OPPENOORTH. (READ BY TITLE, MARCH
20, 1937)   349

36. ON THE STONE AGE OF JAPAN. BY R. TORII. (READ
BY TITLE, MARCH 20, 1937)   361

ILLUSTRATIONS

DISCOVERY   *Frontispiece*

PLATE I   SKULL OF *Homo modjokertensis*   30

     II   THE NGANDONG SKULLS   32

    III   UPPER ACHEULIAN HAND-AXES OF LA MICOQUE
            TYPE   34

     IV   SKULL NO. V FROM THE LOWER LEVALLOISO-
            MOUSTERIAN LAYER OF MUGHARET ES-
            SKHUL   50

    V, 1   PLEISTOCENE FOSSILS INDICATING WARM WATER   76

    V, 2   PLEISTOCENE FOSSILS INDICATING COLDER
            WATER   76

     VI   SEA DEPTHS OF BERING SEA AREA   88

    VII   THE MELBOURNE SKULL   96

   VIII   DOUBLE ADOBE SITE   128

     IX   ORIGINAL FOLSOM POINT *in situ*   154

      X   VIEW OF DURST SILTS   170

     XI   PLEISTOCENE MAMMALS CONTEMPORANEOUS
            WITH MAN IN NORTH AMERICA AND EURASIA   174

PLATE XII   LATE PLEISTOCENE MAMMALS OF NORTH
            AMERICA AND EURASIA   178

      XIII   TERRACES EXPOSED IN THE WHITE RIVER VALLEY 188

      XIV   THE FORTY-FOOT TERRACES IN WHITE RIVER
             VALLEY   190

       XV   HEARTH PIT AND CHARCOAL LAYER   192

      XVI   DETAIL OF CANAL BANK   208

     XVII   SKULL OF EXTINCT WOLF (*Aenocyon ayersi*) 210

    XVIII   HEAVY TOOLS FROM KUNDA   234

      XIX   "HARPOONS" AND CONICAL ARROW-HEADS FROM
             URAL MOSSES   238

       XX   THE "DRYOPITHECUS PATTERN" AND ITS DE-
             RIVATIVES IN MAN   244

      XXI   FAMILY TREE OF THE PRIMATES   256

     XXII   A SKULL OF *Bison priscus*   330

    XXIII   THE CONFINS MAN   342

     XXIV   THE CONFINS MAN   344

      XXV   TORUS SUPRAORBITALIS OF NGANDONG VI, NGAN-
             DONG V, AND NEANDERTHAL MAN   350

     XXVI   NGANDONG SKULL VI IN NORMA LATERALIS   354

EARLY MAN

INTRODUCTORY REMARKS

BY

JOHN C. MERRIAM

President, Carnegie Institution of Washington

THE series of discussions and conferences on the beginnings of human history initiated here today is of unusual importance by reason of two exceptional conditions. First, the materials to be discussed are presented in person by distinguished investigators coming from some of the most important regions of the entire world; second, because the subjects are considered from a range of viewpoints making possible an unusually clear vision of conditions which obtained on the earth in these early stages of human history.

The coming together of investigators engaged with research in regions of especial interest scattered over the world makes possible a comparison of results of the highest importance at this stage in study of the earliest human history. Consideration of major problems from the point of view of geology, palaeontology, geography, climatology, general biology, anthropology, archaeology, and general distribution of organisms associated with man, enables us to develop a perspective which will be of great importance in all efforts to understand early human history.

It is difficult for any history to write its own beginnings. But fortunately the touch which every train of events shows with innumerable related or influencing features makes possible some increase in definition of the picture through study of these associated factors. So in the case of the beginnings of human history, contribution from many related subjects has given us invaluable data relative both to the story of man himself and to the setting or environment of man so important in connection with an attempt to visualize the initial steps in our history.

Not the least important of these contributions has been that furnished by a study of the general evolution of organisms in late geological time, including especially those forms which are most nearly related to man and out of which it is to be assumed that the human group would be derived if it be looked upon as the result of evolution rather than of special creation. Intensive studies on evolution of the higher groups of animals on all the continents has fortunately furnished us already with an extremely interesting picture of how life in these higher groups developed through the ages. This picture of the biological process as we find it operating through time is extremely important in connection with any consideration of the story of beginnings or early development of man.

Looking at the materials of this symposium from the purely palaeontological point of view, it is desirable to make record of the fact that the data which we have relative to early man and his history represent the most intensive and careful study that this aspect of science has been able to give. It is the palaeontologist's habit to subject every important fragment that can be discovered to the most careful possible study, with a view to interpreting the remains from every angle of vision. We should expect to find materials representing early man scattered and fragmentary as we go back in time. And we should also expect palaeontologists to bestow upon the materials obtained the most rigid scrutiny that this field of science permits.

With reference to the quantity of material obtained in study of earliest man, although it is true that collectively we have now a considerable group of specimens representing man of early time, we must appreciate the fact that even looking for a needle in a haystack, commonly held to represent the limit of difficulty, might be an easy task compared with the search for remains of early Pleistocene man taking the world as a whole. Or locating that elusive infinitesimal represented by the electron, may not represent a more difficult problem than the finding of determinable material of man from the first geological epoch in which his remains are known to occur. The development of techniques which have made possible first the location and next the determination of these materials is, in the judgment of those who have studied this problem, one of the important achievements of science.

In this field of research, as in all others, it is certainly proper, and perhaps desirable, to inquire regarding values which may ultimately be contributed through the information secured. It is easy to see how doubt may be raised concerning the human worthwhileness of investigations which have to do with fragments of human beings from a period so remote that there seems little touch with life of today. And yet there is reason to believe that the contributions of history which present early man with his peculiar characters and his strange setting have had a profound and far-reaching effect upon our conception of man and of his place in the world. The general environment in which man existed in past ages, with a different geography, different climatic conditions, and in the midst of a living world quite distinct from that of today—which presents man himself at a time when his physical characteristics and his intellectual effectiveness differed distinctly from man of the present day—these things collectively have had a deep and lasting influence upon our views concerning the nature of human kind.

There have been few contributions to knowledge influencing thought more critically than these discoveries relating to early man. This being the case, it is desirable that careful consideration be given, first of all, to the data regarding the history discussed as it will be presented by the distinguished investigators coming together at this Academy of Natural Sciences in Philadelphia. And it is important that ultimately we examine the meaning of these facts with relation to the present and future of the human world.

A REVIEW OF THE STRATIGRAPHY OF JAVA AND ITS RELATIONS TO EARLY MAN

BY

G. H. R. von KOENIGSWALD

Palaeontologist of the Opsporingsdienst van den Mijnhouw, Bandoeng, Java

IN 1890, Professor Eugène Dubois discovered in Trinil, in Central Java, the remains of the famous *Pithecanthropus*, also called the "Java Man." Since then, Java has become of special interest to scientists working on the problems of fossil man. This short address will give only a review of the latest results on the stratigraphy of the Pleistocene of Java, and its relations to early man.

Professor Dubois was the first to start excavations for fossil mammals in Java (1889-91). All the remains which he collected belong, in his opinion, to one and the same stratigraphic zone, to which he gave the name "Kendeng or Trinil Zone," and of "Pleistocene" age, according to his first publications. Later he changed his opinion and called this fauna "Pliocene."[1] In 1909-10 a German expedition under the leadership of Mrs. Selenka undertook new excavations in Trinil. They confirmed the Pleistocene age of Trinil. The fauna found by this expedition was, however, not as rich as that listed by Dubois. The significance of this fact will soon become apparent.

A new site of fossil mammals was discovered in 1922 in the bed of the Glagah River near Cheribon, Western Java. At this

[1] Dubois, E. "Das geologische Alter der Kendeng oder Trinil-Fauna." T. K. Nederl. Aardr. Gen. 25, (1908).

site *Mastodon* was found which does not appear in the large Dubois collection. This was the first indication that *different fossil faunas existed in Java.*

During the last few years the Geological Survey of the Netherlands East Indies has given special attention to Pleistocene formations. In various sites and horizons, in many more than we had expected to find, remains of fossil mammals were collected. The sites were mapped and investigated in collaboration with the geologists. This has enabled us to distinguish clearly several zones, each with stratigraphic guide fossils.[2] From these observations results the following stratigraphic sequence:

> Recent   — Zone
> *Sampoeng (Neolithic, but with extinct mammals)*
> Ngandong   — Zone
> Trinil   —   "
> Djetis   —   "
> Kali Glagah   —   "
> Tji Djoelang —   "
> Tji Sande   —   "

The names were chosen from type localities at which the zones were determined. Of these, the older layers are more or less folded; the last prominent tectonic movement in Java took place in the post-Trinil period.

In the Tji Sande zone we have the first traces of land mammals in Java, for in a coral limestone a tooth of *Aceratherium* was found. This may be taken as evidence of "the birth of Java," evidence also of its first land inhabitants. Our site is in Western Java, and it is significant that here are found the older mammal-bearing layers, while Central and Eastern Java remained submerged at that time, to become firm land only at a somewhat later date.

[2] v. Koenigswald, G. H. R. "Zur Stratigraphie des javanischen Pleistocän." De Ingenieur in Ned.-Indie, 1, (1934).

The Tji Djoelang zone has a typical Siwalik fauna.[8] Its characteristic mammal is *Merycopotamus*, the last of the *Anthracotheres*. Furthermore, we have *Hippopotamus*, pigs, antelopes and small cattle. Here also, we note the first appearance of *Stegodon*, belonging to a group of primitive elephants which is a typical fossil of the Javanese mammalian fauna, up to the end of the Pleistocene. This first *Stegodon* is, however, not sufficiently primitive to make it belong to a species of the lowest Pliocene. Such a view is supported by the simultaneous occurrence of *Elephas cf. planifrons*. Hence, this zone may be correlated with the Tatrot zone of the Siwalik series of India in which *Merycopotamus* also occurs.

The Kali Glagah zone shows many relations with the Tji Djoelang zone, but *Merycopotamus* is absent. The guide fossil is *Mastodon* (*Trilophodon*) *bumiajuensis* (v. d. Maarel).

In the Djetis zone, which is the most extensive in Central and Eastern Java, we have a much richer fauna: *Epimachairodus*, *Felis* and *Hyaena*; *Tapir*, *Rhinoceros* and a rare *Chalicotherium*; *Leptobos*; different antelopes; various species of *Sus*, *Hippopotamus* and *Cervus*; *Stegodon* and *Elephas*. Of *Elephas* we do not have sufficient material to allow identification of the species. As a whole the Djetis fauna is of typical Lower Pleistocene character.

In 1936 one of our native collectors found a human skull in the Djetis zone in Soembertengah, a small native village near Modjokerto, west of Soerabaja. The area is mapped by Cosijn and Duyfjes. The excavation in which the skull was accidentally found was only a little more than three feet deep. The skull (Plate I, fig. 1) is perfectly fossilized, and we are certain that it was found *in situ*, because the bone is so thin that it would have

[8] v. Koenigswald, G. H. R. "Die fossilen Säugetierfaunen Javas." Proc. Kon. Akad. Amsterdam 38, (1935). "Eine fossile Säugetierfauna mit Simia aus Süd-China." Ibid. 38, (1935).

been destroyed by any movement or rewashing.[4] The skull is only 138 mm. long, its thin bone and general characteristics prove it to be that of a child. Only the skull-cap is preserved; the facial part and the teeth are missing. The region of articulation with the mandible is typically human, so that we can be sure that this small skull is not that of an ape. The fontanelles are closed. In the case of a living infant they close usually at the end of the second year, when the skull is already much larger than our fossil skull. This seems to indicate that the fossil must belong to a human species with a small brain. A comparison of this fossil skull with that of a living child of equal length (Plate I, figs. 1-2) shows clearly that there is a remarkable difference in height and in the capacity of the brain case. Besides, the fossil skull presents certain primitive characters, namely: the incipient development of a post-orbital narrowness and of a flat occipital region.

The skull is too small to permit comparison with any recent and Neanderthal skulls, so it would be better to compare it with *Pithecanthropus*, which has a small brain and comes also from Java. The difficulty is that the Trinil skull-cap belongs to a full-grown specimen. It should be remembered that the characteristics in this skull (as in the skull of full-grown anthropoids) are developed only during growth. The difference between the skull of a human infant and a full-grown anthropoid is very remarkable, the anthropoid infant skull is relatively "human-like." From this it would follow that the skull of a young *Pithecanthropus* should have been much more human-like.

The difference in length between the two skulls is 45 mm. for the exterior part (due to the thick bones of the *Pithecanthropus* skull), but only 22-24 mm. for the interior part of the skulls. The height of the calvarium is 62 mm. in both specimens.

[4] v. Koenigswald, G. H. R., "Ein fossiler Hominide aus dem Altpleistocän Ostjavas." Proc. Kon. Akad. Amsterdam 3, (1936).

The relation of the infant's skull of Modjokerto to that of the adult skull of Trinil is very similar to that found in the La Quina skulls of Neanderthal man, since the La Quina infant and La Quina adult have the same weight of the calvarium, but differ in length only.

We have called this new fossil *Homo modjokertensis*, and in giving it a new species name two reasons may be cited. First, we have no teeth, and so the age of the child cannot be determined, which deprives us of any basis for comparison; and, second, it was found in a stratum older than that near Trinil, where *Pithecanthropus* was found.

We also use the name Trinil zone, but in a sense different from that of Dubois. Our Trinil fauna is exactly the same as that described by the Selenka expedition, for the animals of the Dubois list, which are missing here, belong really to an older level, namely, to the Djetis zone which Dubois did not recognize.

The Trinil zone shows *Hippopotamus* and *Stegodon* in a more highly developed stage. A large elephant is very similar to the Indian *Elephas namadicus*, perhaps even identical with it. Its presence proves the *Middle Pleistocene age of Trinil*, as H. F. Osborn and W. O. Dietrich first pointed out. The fauna is not very different from that of the Djetis zone, but *Chalicotherium*, *Leptobos* and *Epimachairodus* are extinct. Of antelopes we have only one species, *Duboisia*. There are fossil monkeys, and, of the anthropoids, a large orang (*Pongo pymaeus*). In a fissure located in the southern mountains we found, together with *Stegodon*, *Elephas* and a small Trinil pig, various remains of orang, gibbons, tapir and Malayan bear.

So, in the Djetis and Trinil periods some new faunal elements were added to the old, already existing, stock of "Siwalik mammals" in Java. These are orang, gibbons, tapir, and the Malayan bear. All of these animals exist, however, in the Pleistocene cave fauna of southern China (v. Koenigswald, Pei, Wang). Remains of *Stegodon* and *Elephas*, collected in Formosa and the Philippine Islands, suggest that this migration to Java took place from the north, and that the first Pliocene migration of the "*Siva-malayan*" fauna was completed by a second "*Sinomalayan*" immigration in early Pleistocene time.

Of human remains, Dubois found in Trinil a skull-cap, three isolated teeth and four femora, some of them very fragmentary, and in Kendeng Broeboes (east of Trinil) a small fragment of a mandible and a broken femur. In Dubois' opinion, all these different remains belong to the same species, but not all students of human ancestry agree with him. The first suggestion Dubois made after the find of the skull-cap was, that it belonged to a kind of chimpanzee ("*Anthropopithecus*"). Later, when he found the (first) femur, he chose the name *Pithecanthropus erectus*, which he regarded as a primitive human. He changed his mind a few years ago and now considers it as belonging to a giant gibbon (*vide* "Man," January 1937). But since *Sinanthropus* was found in China, which is quite definitely to be considered as a human being, and closely related to *Pithecanthropus*, we are sure about the hominid character of the latter. Weidenreich[5] has recently pointed out that *Pithecanthropus* is more advanced than *Sinanthropus*, and that the skull-cap of Trinil may even belong to a small female of the younger Solo man. It may, of course, be that *Pithecanthropus* came to Java with our sino-malayan immigration from China.

As for the three teeth from Trinil, the one lower premolar, small and absolutely human-like, differs greatly from the two upper molars, which are large and ape-like. They have already been compared with teeth of orang (Miller), but since we have discovered orang in the Trinil zone much more variable than the living orang, we can prove that these molars belong to this ape. The so-called "*Pithecanthropus* tooth" from Sonde, near Trinil,

[5] Nature, No. 3511, February, 1937.

collected by the Selenka expedition, belongs, without any doubt, to recent man.

There are substantial reasons for believing that the primitive skull-cap and the highly-developed femur do not belong to the same species of man. The latter shows, according to Ramstroem,[6] affinities to the man from Aurignac in France. But there are other traces of fossil man which belong apparently to a different species.

Two years ago, we found in the Trinil level the first stone implements.[7] These are small primitive points, scrapers and cores, in most cases only simple flakes. They are made of different silicified rocks, and are deeply patinated. They show a typical "Clactonian" (Plate I, fig. 3), some even a primitive "Levallois" technique. In comparing these with the very primitive implements found in China at Chou-Kou-Tien with the *Sinanthropus* remains, we are forced to conclude that our Javanese implements, from a typologic point of view, are much too advanced for as primitive a being as *Pithecanthropus*.

But there are not only these small flakes. Near the south coast of Central Java, not far from Patjitan, stone tools of old paleolithic type were discovered on terrace surfaces in 1935. Judging from the morphological character of the area, and from mammal remains found in a near-by fissure, and taking into account the age of similar stone implements in other parts of the world, it is quite probable that these implements, hitherto only known through surface finds, belong to the Trinil period.

Among the implements from Patjitan (Plate I, figs. 4-7), we find the same types of flakes as in the Trinil level, but in most cases they are much larger. Of special interest are true handaxes ("coups-de-poing"). Among them we have all types from

[6] In Werth, E. "Der fossile Mensch." Berlin, 1922.
[7] v. Koenigswald, G. H. R. "Early paleolithic stone implements from Java," Bull. Raffles Mus. Singapore. Ser. B. 1, (1936).

simple pointed pebbles, "rostrocarinate" and rostroid types to the typical Chelleo-Acheulean handaxes (Plate I, figs. 4-5). Some of them are very much rolled and waterworn and show varying patination. Apparently they belong to different levels. Classification of these implements and the geologic survey of this area has only just begun, and it is hoped that future researches will yield more detailed information.

The finding of these handaxes in Java was a great surprise. The farthest eastern point at which these implements were known until now, was Madras in India. De Terra[8] discovered tools of the same type in the Narbadda valley and in other localities in Northwestern India, together with the remains of fossil mammals of Middle Pleistocene age. It can be expected that the stone implements from Java will make for good correlations between the Pleistocene of Java and India. The manufacturer of these Java handaxes is possibly represented by the femur from Trinil belonging to an extinct human type of unknown affinity.

In 1931 the late Mr. C. ter Haar, member of the Geological Survey, mapped the high level river terraces along the Solo River, north of Ngawi, Central Java. Near Ngandong he discovered on a level 20 meters above the river, a site rich in fossil bones. Here the Survey started excavations, and more than 2,000 bones were found. The fauna includes *Stegodon*, *Elephas* and *Hippopotamus*, highly specialized, and recent species of rhinoceros, cattle and deer, but no antelopes. The guide fossil is an *Axis*-deer, in our opinion only a subspecies of the recent *Axis* of India and limited to this fauna. After this site, we have called these beds Ngandong zone.

In Ngandong, various remains of fossil men have been discovered: fragments of eleven skulls (Ngandong I-XI; Plate II) and two tibiae (Ngandong A and B). The skulls show a certain

[8] H. de Terra. "Cenozoic cycles in Asia and their bearing on human prehistory." Proc. Am. Phil. Soc., vol. 77, pp. 289-308, 1937.

PLATE 1.—1.—Skull of *Homo modjokertensis*, Djetis zone, Scembertengah near Modjokerto, Eastern Java.
2.—Skull of a Chinese child of the same length. Age 1½ yr. (Coll. Soerabaja). Figs. 1 and 2 same reduction. 3.—Flake, "Clactonian" technique. Trinil zone west of Trinil, Central Java. Natural size. 4-5.—Handaxes of Chellean type. (Bifaces) Patjitan. 6.—Point, made of a large flake. Patjitan. 7.—Round scraper or core.
Patjitan. Figs. 4-7 about ½ natural size.

variety, but belong to the same type. They are all heavy, with flat foreheads, supra-orbital ridges and a well-developed post-orbital narrowness. Ngandong man is more highly developed than Trinil man; he belonged to the group of Neanderthal man, and within this group *Homo neanderthalensis soloensis* shows the greatest affinities to the Rhodesia man from South Africa. Like him, the Ngandong skulls show the same remarkable, flat occipital region (similar to those of the anthropoids), but their supra-orbital region is not so bestial and heavy as in Rhodesia man. There is no reason why we should establish this fossil for a new subgenus (*Javanthropus* Oppenoorth). The relationship between Solo man and *Pithecanthropus-Sinanthropus* is uncertain as long as we have no teeth that might permit a comparison with the *Sinanthropus*-pattern.

Of Ngandong man, only fragments of skulls and two tibiae have been discovered, while all skeletal parts of the different animals associated with him have been found. All of the skulls have the facial parts missing and only two have a complete occipital region (Nos. VI and XI). All the others are damaged in the same manner (*vide* Plate II). A comparison with a skull, opened by living head-hunters for the purpose of eating the brain (Dajak; Central Borneo), provides an explanation: Ngandong skulls, too, were opened by man. Ngandong V shows clearly that this man was killed by a blow on the back of his head. In this manner we can explain the strange condition in which the human remains of the Ngandong site were found. It is an artificial assemblage, a kind of primitive skull-bowl, either accidentally lost at this locality as the remains of a cannibalistic meal, or deposited for a magic purpose. For some time Neanderthal man was known to have been a cannibal in Europe (Krapina; Ehringsdorf); now the same inference can also be drawn from the Ngandong skulls. In this respect it is noteworthy that genuine human skull-bowls are known from the Upper Pleistocene of France and Spain.

Only a few implements of Solo man are known. The stone tools are primitive, but the bone implements have been beautifully worked. A kind of axe was discovered, made of deer antlers, and a barbed spearhead of upper Paleolithic type confirms the Upper Pleistocene age of Ngandong.

The Pleistocene age of Dubois' Wadjak man, *Homo sapiens wadjakensis,* an australomorphic type of recent man (Pinkley), has, however, not been confirmed. A similar population lived in Java during the Neolithic period (Sampoeng cave).

These latest researches, therefore, indicate that Java was not as isolated a part of Asia as current opinion had it. The fossil mammals show relations with India and China. The occurrence of fossil man in the early Pleistocene of Java is a significant fact. The *Pithecanthropus* type, formerly known only from Java, has meanwhile been discovered in China and last year even in Africa (Kohl-Larsen). On the other hand, Rhodesia man, African type of Neanderthal man, has now also been found in Java. And the stone implements, too, show the same wide distribution of early human cultures. If one considers the enormous area between England in the north and South Africa, Portugal in the west, and Java, where Chelleo-Acheulean handaxe cultures were found, it would seem that Java was not isolated during the Pleistocene, and that the evolution of early man in this region followed the same lines as in other parts of the world.

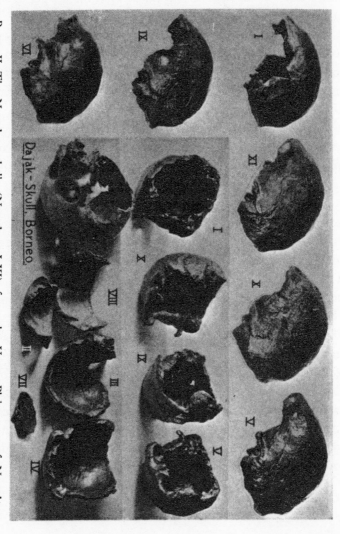

PLATE II—The Ngandong skulls (Ngandong I-XI) from the Upper Pleistocene of Ngandong on the Solo River, Central Java. In the lower photograph the skull-bowls are compared with a Dajak skull from Borneo, opened by head-hunters.

The fossil human skulls are in the collection of the Geological Survey. (Dienst van den Mijnhouw) of the Netherlands East Indies, Bandoeng, (Java).

THE NEAR EAST AS A GATEWAY OF PREHISTORIC MIGRATION

BY

DOROTHY A. E. GARROD

Research Fellow, Newnham College, Cambridge, England

REGARDED as a corner of the map, the patch of Asia known as the Near East seems very insignificant, but to the prehistorian it is a region of first-rate importance, since for him it is a possible highway of migration into Europe both from the Further East and from Africa.

Until comparatively recently, however, the rôle of the Near East in the Stone Age world has been largely a matter of speculation and hypothesis; to-day, as a result mainly of the work undertaken in the last eight years by the American School of Prehistoric Research, collaborating with the British School in Jerusalem and the Sladen Memorial Fund, by the Institut de Paléontologie Humaine of Paris, and by the Field Museum, we have a body of solid fact on which to build.

I can here only give a brief survey of the results of this work, and its bearing on the larger problems of prehistory. For this purpose the area studied can be divided broadly into three regions—the mountain country of the Zagros Arc, on the western frontier of Persia, the high land which to-day is the North Arabian Desert, and the coastal region of Syria and Palestine. I need not remind you that Mesopotamia proper, which is so rich in the remains of early civilisation, did not exist in Pleistocene times, when the head of the Persian Gulf lay close to where Mosul stands to-day.

I shall begin with the coastal region, because this has been most extensively worked, and so gives a standard of comparison for the other two. Our detailed knowledge of the Stone Age of Palestine begins in the Middle Pleistocene, with the Tayacian industry which lies at the base of two great Palestinian caves. All older stages are known at present from surface finds only as far as Palestine is concerned, and in Syria, from deposits whose date and relation to each other have not yet been worked out. It seems likely, however, that the Chellean, the earlier stages of the Acheulean, and the Levalloisian were all present in this region.

The Tayacian is an industry of small rough flakes, first identified in Western Europe, at La Micoque. In Palestine, as at La Micoque, it is followed by a late Acheulean, which passes upward into the true Micoquian with its lanceolate hand-axes. In the Tabūn Cave, at the western foot of Mount Carmel, the Micoquian layer is immensely thick, and has yielded more than eight thousand hand-axes, associated with an even larger number of flake-tools, chiefly scrapers, more or less in the Clactonian tradition, and closely resembling those from High Lodge. A particularly significant feature is the presence at a certain horizon within the Micoquian of a group of blades and blade-tools, including end-scrapers, burins and Chatelperron points, in marked contrast with the hand-axes and flake-tools with which they are associated. I suggest that these should be explained by contact between the Micoquian and a very early blade-culture, possibly ancestral to the Chatelperron stage of Europe, whose centre of dispersion theoretically lies somewhere in southern Central Asia.

In its general lines, apart from the presence of this group of blade-tools, the sequence at the base of the Tabūn is astonishingly close to that of La Micoque—in fact the relationship with Western Europe is far more strongly marked than with the corresponding stages in the neighbouring regions of Egypt and

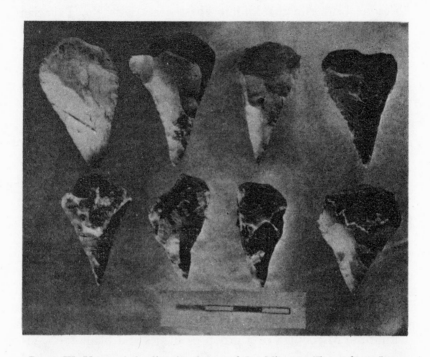

PLATE III—Upper Acheulian hand-axes of La Micoque Type, from Layer Ec, Mugharet Et-Tabūn (Cave of the Oven), near Athlit, Palestine. Scale in cm.

North Africa, in so far as these are known at present. I do not pretend to explain the exact significance of this, but it should be noted that Central Asia and the Far East lie outside the area of distribution of the hand-axe cultures, whose place of origin is now generally assumed to be Africa. If the Acheulean of Palestine, therefore, should prove not to be derived immediately from Africa it must almost certainly be regarded as a kind of backwash from Europe. I must add here that the evidence of fauna, as studied by Miss Bate, bears out the assumption that the Micoquian of the Near East is approximately contemporary with that of Europe, that is, it dates from the early phases of the Riss-Würm interglacial.

At Abbé Breuil's suggestion I have named the culture which follows the Micoquian in Palestine Levalloiso-Mousterian, to distinguish it from the true Mousterian of such European sites as La Quina, etc. This predominance of the Levallois tradition in the Middle Palaeolithic is in harmony with what we know of Egypt and East Africa, and points therefore to movements from the south-west during a long period; movements which, as we shall see, appear to spread into the two remaining areas with which I have to deal.

Judging once more from the evidence of animal remains the Levalloiso-Mousterian in all its stages appears to cover a considerable part of the Riss-Würm interglacial and the beginning of the succeeding glaciation. From its older levels comparatively abundant human remains have been obtained both by our own expedition and that of the Institut de Paléontologie Humaine. The description of these I leave to my colleague Mr. McCown, but I will note here that as a means of testing the theory of movements from Africa at this time it will be of interest to compare with the Mount Carmel and Nazareth men the human skull recently discovered by Dr. Kohl-Larsen at Eyassi in Tanganyika Territory, in a deposit containing a rather late Levalloisian industry.

The Levalloiso-Mousterian in Palestine is immediately succeeded by the blade-industries of the Upper Palaeolithic and these are predominantly of the type known in Western Europe as Middle Aurignacian. This culture, which in Palestine occupies nearly the whole of the Upper Palaeolithic sequence, is unknown in Africa. In view of its remarkable development in the Near East I would suggest that we are there not far from its centre of dispersion, which may possibly lie in Iran, or even further east. From Palestine and Syria the Middle Aurignacian spread into the Caucasus, but did not apparently penetrate into the South Russian plain, where an industry of Upper Aurignacian type held sway from the early stages of the Upper Palaeolithic. The route by which the Middle Aurignacian entered Europe must however have skirted the northern shore of the Black Sea, for the caves of the Crimea have yielded an Upper Palaeolithic sequence closely resembling that of Palestine.

When we come to the Mesolithic, the Palestine culture is a specialised microlithic industry which I have named Natufian. Its older stages are characterised by small carvings, usually of animals, in bone or stone. Pottery is absent, but the presence of flint sickle-blades with hafts of bone suggests that these people may have practised a primitive form of agriculture. I am pretty sure that the origins of the Natufian must be sought somewhere to the north of Palestine, perhaps in Anatolia; certainly it is not an Egyptian culture, though it does just penetrate into Egypt, where it occurs in the surface station of Heluan.

With the Mesolithic I close my survey, because although the Neolithic and Chalcolithic periods do of course come under the heading of prehistoric, these obscure and complicated cultures demand a paper to themselves.

I turn next to the third of my regions, the mountain country of the Zagros Arc. The very slender knowledge which we possess of this part of the Palaeolithic world is the result of an expedition undertaken jointly by the American School of Prehistoric Research and the Sladen Memorial Fund in the autumn of 1928, an expedition of which I had the good fortune to be the leader. In the caves of Southern Kurdistan we found the remains of two periods—a Levalloiso-Mousterian resembling the last stages of that industry in Palestine, and a blade-industry of Upper Aurignacian type with shouldered points and abundant small notched blades. The latter is quite unlike the Aurignacian of Palestine, but resembles the industry of Kostienki and Gagarino, and other stations of the South Russian plain. The presence of geometric microliths in the upper levels suggests, however, that the Kurdish industry is rather later than the Russian, dating probably from the very close of the Palaeolithic. Of any earlier Upper Palaeolithic industry in this region we found no trace, but our survey was limited to a very small number of stations. If the theory of an Eastern origin for the Aurignacian of Palestine is correct, we should expect ultimately to find that culture in the Zagros, most probably in immediate succession to the Levalloiso-Mousterian.

Our third region, the North Arabian Desert, has yielded only surface finds. The Field Museum Expeditions have collected a large amount of material from this area, and I have had the privilege of studying and describing this, but as it is still unpublished I can only touch on it briefly here. The oldest industry which can be identified with certainty is an Upper Acheulean closely resembling that of Palestine. So far this has been obtained only from the western fringe of the area, but it is probable that it has in fact a wider distribution, since in 1928 I picked up a hand-axe of Upper Acheulean type from the surface at Chemchemal in

Southern Kurdistan. The Levalloisian and Levalloiso-Mousterian are well represented in the Desert collection, and there are a few Aurignacian stations of Palestinian type, but so far no trace of the Natufian has appeared. In its place we find a number of unfamiliar industries, of uncertain age, but probably ranging from the close of the Palaeolithic to the Chalcolithic. No trace of these has been found either in Palestine or in Iraq, and it is possible that they may have penetrated northward as a wedge from the Arabian peninsula, a region up to the present unexplored by the prehistorian.

In an address to Section H of the British Association last summer I dealt with the blade-cultures of the Near East as part of a general study of the Upper Palaeolithic, and it will be useful at this point to outline very briefly the conclusions which I then reached, while insisting that they are merely tentative. In agreement with Peyrony I distinguished within the Upper Palaeolithic a first fundamental division between the cultures based on the blunted-back blade—such as the Lower and Upper Aurignacian and the Capsian—and the Middle Aurignacian with its predominance of steep and carinated scrapers and *grattoirs à museau*. Peyrony retains the name Aurignacian for the latter culture, and with this I agree. The blunted-back blade industries, however, he groups together as Perigordian, but I am not convinced that there is an evolutionary sequence from the Lower to the Upper Perigordian,—that is, from the Lower to the Upper Aurignacian in Western Europe. I have therefore preferred to call the former Chatelperronian, and the latter Gravettian, and to regard the Capsian as an independent culture, not directly related to the Gravettian, but possibly derived independently from the Chatelperronian by way of East Africa, where we find an almost typical Capsian in the so-called Upper Kenya Aurignacian.

In Western Europe the Chatelperronian, Aurignacian and Gravettian follow each other, and to some extent intermingle, giving the classic French sequence which for so long was used as a standard for the rest of the world. If we trace them back to their hypothetical centres of origin, however, we find them more or less segregated into provinces. First we have the Chatelperronian, the earliest identifiable phylum of the blade-cultures, already emerging in Lower Palaeolithic times in some as yet unidentified Asiatic centre, and making contact with the Acheulean in Palestine, and to some extent in East Africa. Ultimately it sends out a branch into East Africa to give rise to the Capsian, possibly another into North-east Europe to develop into the Gravettian, though it is not inconceivable that the latter has an independent origin. Meanwhile another stock, the Aurignacian, pushes westward and separates these two great provinces of the backed-blade culture. From the Aurignacian and Gravettian centres migrations then pour into Central and Eastern Europe along the southern edge of the ice-sheet, and cultures which in their homelands tend to remain distinct and exclusive succeed and influence each other, until at the extreme limit of their journey we get, as I have said, the familiar French sequence. Meanwhile along the fringes of the original provinces interpenetration necessarily takes place, and we find the Upper Gravettian filtering along the valleys of the Zagros Arc into Southern Kurdistan, and the Aurignacian penetrating northward into the Caucasus and the Crimea. The only stages of the Upper Palaeolithic of the West in which the Near East plays no part are the Solutrean, which apparently originates in Central Europe, and the Magdalenian, which arises as a specialised form of the Gravettian in Southern France.

To sum up: at the earliest stage for which we have detailed evidence, the Upper Acheulean, Palestine and Syria can be compared on general lines with Western Europe; in the Middle

Palaeolithic African influence predominates and apparently spreads eastward; with the Upper Palaeolithic Asiatic influence gains the upper hand, and persists into the Mesolithic. That is the main outline of events, as we see them at present; further discovery alone can modify the framework or fill in the details.

MOUNT CARMEL MAN
HIS BEARING ON THE ANCESTRY OF MODERN RACES

BY

SIR ARTHUR KEITH, F.R.S.

AND

THEODORE D. McCOWN

Research Fellow, American School of Prehistoric Research

THE ancient Palestinians upon whom we are reporting were discovered in 1931 and 1932 in limestone caves in the western slope of Mount Carmel. A little over a mile to the west across the coastal plain is the Mediterranean. Haifa lies fifteen miles to the north. Here the joint Expedition of the American School of Prehistoric Research and the British School of Archaeology in Jerusalem under the direction of Miss Dorothy Garrod worked for seven seasons, bringing to light a vast quantity of flint artifacts, providing a new basis for the Pleistocene palaeontology of the Middle East, and uncovering and preserving a unique collection of human fossils.

The sites from which come the human fossils with whom we are concerned now are the Mugharet es-Skhūl (Cave of the Kids) and et-Tabūn (the Oven), lying at the mouth of the Wady Mughara. Et-Tabūn is a huge, rather open cave and was filled almost to its top when excavation began. The total depth of the well-stratified deposit was 15.5 meters. There were no sterile layers; the occupation had been continuous from a time just anterior to the Palestinian Acheulean (the Tayacian) down to the end of the Levalloiso-Mousterian period. The human remains from this site come from two horizons. The middle-most

Levalloiso-Mousterian layer, Layer C, provided a nearly complete female skull and skeleton, and a massive mandible, undoubtedly male. The other remains are the fragment of the shaft of a right femur and a single molar tooth, both specimens having been recovered from the Acheulean deposits of the Tabūn. It is with the Levalloiso-Mousterian human remains that we are chiefly concerned.

The Mugharet es-Skhūl is a rock shelter and cave with an extensive terrace. The small cave from which the site takes its name played only a small part in the life of the site's inhabitants. The deposit averages two and a half meters in thickness; two-thirds of this archaeological deposit was extremely hard and refractory lime breccia. In this breccia, on the terrace, were found ten individuals, men, women and children. Five of these had suffered no important disturbance since the time of their interment and they provide us with much new information regarding the burial customs of early man.

The Skhūl and Tabūn fossil humans used the same kind of tools. The animal remains from the two caves indicate that the Skhūl people and the Tabūn people were contemporaries. In et-Tabūn the faunal sequence is remarkably full. Miss Dorothea Bate's careful analysis of the character and especially of the changes in the fauna indicates two things. First, that gazelle and *Dama mesopotamica* (the Fallow deer) were numerically most important. Secondly, her studies show that there was a shift in the proportions of *Dama* and gazelle; the moist climate of the earliest part of the Acheulean, with *Dama* most abundant, is replaced gradually by a climate drier and probably cooler, with gazelle the most common animal. Briefly we think that the evidence indicates quite clearly that the faunas, the industries and, most important, the people of the Skhūl and the Tabūn are pre-Würmian in time. Our people, therefore, lived in the latter half of the Riss-Würm interglacial period; by stressing the differences between the faunas of the Skhūl and of et-Tabūn, the

Skhūl people may be considered to be slightly later than the inhabitants of the Tabūn whom we find in Layer C. If, on the contrary, we emphasize the similarities of the flint industries and of the faunas we may consider the two groups of human remains to be contemporary.

The Tabūn and the Skhūl types of the Mount Carmel races provide us with some striking contrasts and some significant resemblances. Many of the physical features of the Tabūn woman are familiar to us: they are like those we meet with in the Neanderthal skeletons of Western Europe. Nor are the anatomical characters of the Skhūl type wholly unfamiliar: not a few of them are known to us in the skeletons of living native races or in the bones of the Upper Palaeolithic inhabitants of Europe. Hitherto there has been no convincing demonstration of the existence of a Neanthropic form of man before the time of the last Ice Age; a modern form of man of the middle Pleistocene, if we accept the shorter chronology proposed by one of us.

Our study of these fossil people has been made possible by the very liberal joint support of the American School of Prehistoric Research and the Royal College of Surgeons of England, both institutions sharing equally in the division of the material. For a variety of reasons we began our survey of Mount Carmel Man from the ground up, beginning with the feet and progressing systematically up the skeleton.

Let us turn our attention to the stature, the posture and the gait of these two types of humanity as revealed by their feet, their legs, the pelvis and the spinal column. One of the most striking features which distinguishes our two Carmel types is stature. The Tabūn woman with a femur length of 416.0 mm. had an estimated stature of just over five feet but her short, stout tibia (315.0 mm.) brings her height to half an inch less than five feet (1514 mm.), when we employ Pearson's formula for stature based upon combined femoral and tibial length. The Skhūl males have femora which vary from 518.0 mm. to 477.0 mm. in length.

Stature ranges from 1791 mm. (5'10½") to 1733 mm. (5'8").
The Skhūl women appear to have been short; 5'2" (1580 mm.)
is our estimate for the height of Skhūl VII. The medial convexity of the shaft, noted as a characteristic of the European
Neanderthal femora by Dr. Hrdlička, is to be observed in the
femora of the ancient Palestinians. In some of our specimens the
anterior convexity of the shaft is pronounced. Yet when we
examine the relative proportions which the articular extremities
form to the total length of the bone, both types of people are
modern. The absolute dimensions of the Skhūl men are comparable to those found among the tall Cromagnon males. The
femoral pilaster of the Skhūl males shows an immense development; in all the Tabūn specimens this feature is conspicuously
absent. The latter also are platymeric, the former pronouncedly
stenomeric, though both forms show a great degree of antero-
posterior flattening in the subtrochanteric region of the shaft.

The tibia revealed a similar story in many ways. At the extremes in the range of variability in our material we have the
massive and very long bones of the tall Skhūl men and at the
other, the short and stout tibiae of the Tabūn woman. Concerning the cnemic index, we find that most of the Skhūl tibiae fall
into the middle group between 65 and 70, as do Spy and La
Chapelle. Skhūl V, with an index of 63, is platycnemic, while
the Tabūn woman, with an index of 77 for her left tibia is
eurycnemic. In the proportions of the articular extremities to
the length of shaft both Tabūn and Skhūl types are modern.
Yet the former, in certain features of the knee joint, namely, the
"set-back" and inclination of the articular condyles, is reminiscent of the Neanderthalians, whereas the Skhūl people are not.

The posture and gait of the ancient Palestinians, as shown by
the two remarkably preserved feet—one of the Tabūn woman,
the other of Skhūl IV, a tall man—were modern. In neither of
these feet is there any trace of the condition which M. Boule
has described in the La Chapelle foot, a condition in which the

heel and foot are intermediate in certain respects between ape and man. The heels of our specimens are stout, compact, short and perfectly upright. In some details the Carmel feet retain traces of their anthropoid heritage; the tarsal element is short relative to the metatarsal, the middle phalanges of Skhūl IV do not show the reduction so common amongst modern races, the joint between the hallux and the first cuneiform retains the saddle-shaped anthropoid form more perfectly than do most modern feet but there was no greater mobility of the great toe; it was human in every respect. The transference of both size and power from the third to the second metatarsal has taken place in both feet. Lengths, breadths, the proportions of these to each other, the degree of arching of the foot, all vary, but within quite modern limits.

The remaining chief components of stature, posture and build of body are the pelvis and the vertebrae. Let us turn first to the pelvis. The chief conclusions which our study of the os coxae have lead us to formulate are that the anatomical details of the Skhūl type agree with those found in the pelvis of Neanthropic man, particularly the Cromagnon pelvis, rather than with those of the pelvis of Neanderthal man. Within the total assemblage of characters, however, we meet with a larger proportion of Neanderthal features than are to be found in any modern race. The woman from the Tabūn cave presents an altogether peculiar pelvic picture. Her pelvis differs not only from those of the Skhūl type but presents features, particularly in the conformation of the pubic bones, which have not been described before either in living or in fossil man. The nearest parallels to her pubic architecture is to be met with in the anthropoids, particularly the gorilla. In other respects her pelvis agrees with the Neanthropic rather than with the Neanderthal type, and yet Neanderthal features are preserved. We cannot think that her pelvic features are merely a manifestation of individual variability; they seem too sharply defined for that.

One of the facts which warrants our first consideration is the proportion of pelvic height to length of thigh. The absolute pelvic heights of the Skhūl people do not differ markedly from those of the Neanderthalians (Skh. IV, 218 mm.; Skh. V, 205 mm.; Neanderthal, 225 mm.) but the proportions in respect to femur length (Skh. IV, 42%; Skh. V, 39%; La Chapelle, 56%; Neanderthal, 51%) indicate a considerable divergence from the Neanderthals. The femur-pelvic width ratios show that the Skhūl type was not only short in the hips but relatively small and narrow across the waist as well. The Skhūl pelves in other features have distinct Neanderthal leanings, the great downward area for sacral attachment, the greater approximation of the ischial tuberosities towards the acetabulum, the massive development of the anterior-inferior iliac spine, and with this the deep groove situated on the lateral aspect of the spine, created by the outward extension of the upper margin of the acetabulum. Yet the Skhūl pelves are modern in the size of their acetabular cavity, not Neanderthalian.

The extraordinary features of the Tabūn pelvis are not its Neanderthal features, but its primitive anthropoid ones. The extreme length and plate-like form of the pubic parts are clearly evident. The true pelvis was very shallow. The sections across the horizontal part of the pubis again emphasize the anthropoid similarities. The differences which distinguish the Tabūn woman's pelvis are of such a nature and of such a degree that neither sexual nor individual variability can be held to account for them. They are differences of type—of race.

As we have seen, the Skhūl type is narrow-waisted while the Tabūn woman is relatively wide across the hips. The characters of the trunk, the thoracic girdle and the arms make fuller our story of the strange mosaic of physical traits which constitute the two Carmel types. The ribs of the Skhūl people vary from a condition found in Skhūl V which is very like that which prevails in the ribs of Neanderthal man to a state, best exemplified in the very complete series belonging to Skhūl IV, which is closer in form to the Neanthropic variety of rib than it is to the Neanderthalian. The Tabūn woman again exhibits traits like those found in Neanderthal man and others altogether peculiar to herself. She was barrel-chested, with horizontally-placed first to third ribs which made the top of the thorax dome-shaped. The Skhūl men were relatively narrow-chested with thinner and wider ribs than those of Tabūn I. Her ribs, especially the diaphragmatic ones, are very thick relative to their width.

Skhūl V, our tallest male, has a relatively well-preserved set of vertebrae, particularly the cervical ones. As with his ribs, so his vertebrae show many resemblances in detail to those few known and described for the Neanderthal race of Europe. The shortness of the spinal column is a Neanderthal feature, yet relative to their stature the Skhūl people were very short in the back, especially in the loins and the neck. Skhūl V with a cervical vertebral height of 55.7 mm., is much below the mean measurement for this feature in Europeans (68.4 mm.). Mobility seems to have been sacrificed to obtain strength and rigidity, this despite the slender character of the individual bones. Yet if we except the primitive features which these people share with the Neanderthalians of Europe we can find no sure evidence of the vertebral specializations, particularly in the lumbar region of the spine, which are attributed to the Neanderthal man. The Skhūl spinal column might well evolve into the modern form.

We have quite well-preserved scapulae from two of the tall Skhūl men and the important parts of the left scapula of the Tabūn woman. In absolute and relative size of bone the Skhūl examples are little different from modern bones; if anything, they are on the small side in relation to stature. It is when we come to study the detailed conformation of these bones, especially of the axillary border, that we at once notice certain significant features. The Tabūn woman bears on the dorsal margin of the axillary border the groove which M. Boule found in some

Neanderthal scapulae. At first glance the Skhūl scapulae—those
of Number V are the most perfectly preserved—seem to lack
this feature. The axillary border is very thick—a rounded massive bar. Closer examination, however, reveals a peculiar condition which is intermediate in character between the distinctive,
ultra-human Neanderthal condition and the unspecialized,
anthropoid state prevailing in the modern scapula. One of our
specimens—the scapula of a Sikh—which we have used for comparison with the ancient bones shows a degree of development
of the marginal groove very like that which we find in Skhūl V.
In contrast to this the coracoid process in the Skhūl type is definitely modern in form. The Tabūn woman, on the other hand,
shows distinctive, Neanderthaloid characters in this part of the
scapula.

Our attention is immediately taken by the extreme length and
slenderness of the humeri, particularly of the Skhūl people. The
females had less long arms but they were equally slender in
build, which brings to mind the Krapina examples.

The Tabūn woman has a relatively short humerus but the
proportions of the extremities to the length of the shaft link it
with the Skhūl type rather than with the western European
Neanderthals. Yet in its curvature, and the inclination of the
head of the bone, it is closer akin to the European Mousterians.

The forearm bones serve to distinguish the two types more
clearly. The bowing of the ulna and radius in the Tabūn woman,
with the resulting great interosseous space, is Neanderthal. The
Skhūl males have long and exceedingly straight forearm bones.
Skhūl VII—a small woman—in the size of her forearm bones, in
their curvature and in certain other features, tends towards the
Tabūn type. We may mention briefly that in the head and upper
part of the shaft of the Palestinian ulna we have a series of
changes, evolutionary in character and concerned with the finer
development of the powers of pronation and supination, which

bridges the gap between the condition preserved in the bones of
the anthropoids and that which prevails in modern man.

Our great fortune in having two nearly intact wrists and
hands—one of the Tabūn woman and the other of Skhūl IV—
we have utilized in studying the Pleistocene fossil hand fully
and, it may be added, for the first time. Skhūl V provides us
with another fairly complete, composite hand made up of right
and left bones, and with the addition of the fragmentary material from both sites we have been able to amass a comprehensive
body of information concerning this important organ. Here it
must suffice to say that the anatomical evidence from the carpus
alone allows us to distinguish between the Tabūn and the Skhūl
hand. The Tabūn woman stands nearer to what appears to have
been the Neanderthal form of hand, the Skhūl men to Neanthropic types, yet both the Palestinian types were closely related.

At this point the evidence which we have presented to you
concerning the skeleton of Carmel Man may be conveniently
summarized. We have attempted to make clear that the two
types are separable, the differences being due neither to sex nor
to the variation inherent in all living populations. Yet we are
impressed by the number of resemblances between the two
Carmel races. The Skhūl type is a mosaic of primitive features,
some of them to be met with in the Neanderthal remains from
Western Europe. The greater number of the type's physical
characters, however, are those which we find in the modern
races of man, the native races especially. When we examine
closely these neanthropic characters we see that of known races,
living or extinct, their closest analogies are the tall Cro-Magnons
of France and the Riviera. The Tabūn type possesses a curious
complexity of primitive and of specialized features in her skeleton. Shorter and stouter than the Skhūl type, one cannot but be
impressed by the slenderness of her bones and by the tendency
for the articular extremity-length ratios to approach the Skhūl
figures. The greater number of this type's physical characteris-

tics are primitive and not neanthropic. Of the known fossil types
of man, the Neanderthalians of Europe seem to be nearest akin
to the Tabūn woman.

Our studies concerning the details of the anatomy of the
teeth, the jaws and the skulls have not yet progressed as far as
with the other parts of the skeleton, but we may consider briefly
the evidence from them as it appears to us now. The teeth in
none of these ancient Palestinians show the degenerate, tauro-
dont condition of the roots which occurs in the molars of
Neanderthal man. The teeth in the adult palates and mandibles,
even the younger ones, are greatly worn and the crown patterns are difficult of decipherment. Fortunately we have part of
an unworn set from the maxilla of a Tabūn juvenile individual.
The primitive character of the cusp pattern is evident, and there
are many resemblances to the teeth of the youth from Le Moustier and to some of the Krapina teeth. The unworn permanent
teeth which we possess from the Skhūl cave belong to young
children: even so, the pattern, though primitive, is apparently
less definitely Neanderthaloid than the Tabūn examples.

The mandibles confront us with a most puzzling series of relationships. The Skhūl type with its upstanding ascending ramus
and the well-defined mental eminence contrasts very sharply
with the mandible of the Tabūn woman, which is chinless, with
a lowly corpus and backward sloping ramus. Miss Garrod discovered in the same layer with the Tabūn woman the massive
male mandible, Tabūn II. It exceeds in its dimensions all of the
Skhūl jaws and equals or even surpasses the Heidelberg mandible
in many measurements. There is an incipient chin, however. The
character of the damaged internal symphyseal area, as well as
other features, appears to link it to the Neanthropic Skhūl type.
It is a more primitive form to be sure, but more closely related to
these than to the Tabūn race.

The skulls of these Carmel people serve us very well in illustrating the peculiar nature of the Palestinian races. The skull of

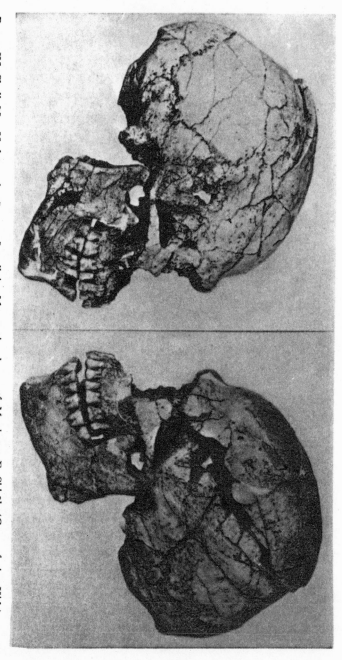

PLATE IV—Skull No. V from the Lower Levalloiso-Mousterian layer of Mugharet Es-Skhūl (Cave of the Kids), near Athlit, Palestine. (A) norma lateralis dextra: (B) norma lateralis sinistra.

the tall man, Skhūl V, is the best preserved. One notices the supra-orbital torus, the combination of facial and alveolar prognathism, the well-marked vaulting of the frontal and the parietals. Skhūl IX presents a somewhat different set of features, noticeably a greater length with relatively less height. The Tabūn woman's skull is more primitive than either of these, smaller, low and flat-topped. Skhūl IV, on the other hand, is low and flat-topped, though absolutely greater in nearly all dimensions than the skull of Tabūn I. None of them have the protruding occiput which is so noteworthy a feature of the European Neanderthals.

The variability in the measurements of all the Palestinians is remarkable. The cranial capacities are obtained by using Pearson's inter-racial formulae for the different sexes. In this point the Tabūn and Skhūl types are sharply demarcated; unfortunately we have no measurable female skulls from the Skhūl. The absolute measurements are less informative than the indices. Only one skull is more long-headed than the mean (about 74) for European Neanderthal man; the Tabūn woman approaches the upper limits of mesocephaly. Skhūl V is a low hypsicephal; the others tend in the opposite direction and with this goes a tendency towards tapeinocephaly. If we take the callotte height index as representing the proportions of the chief cerebral-containing portions of the skull vault, we discover that the Palestinian skull is close to the mean of 42.7 for Neanderthal man. Skhūl V is a notable exception: his index for these characters is 52, approaching those of some of the early Upper Palaeolithic inhabitants of Europe.

Let us now summarize our observations concerning this extraordinary group of people. The great physical variability of these ancient Palestinians is striking. The difference between the sexes is marked, not only between the Tabūn woman and the Skhūl men but also between the Skhūl females and the males. More striking even than this is the unexpectedly great variability in the Skhūl population. It is no exaggeration to say that if these individuals had been found in different sites at different times, and each one described by a different anthropologist or anatomist, we should have had a corresponding number of fossil races. Considered not in detail, however, but as a whole, the Skhūl individuals do form a well-marked type of humanity. Admittedly it is a variable one but in this fact we see significance. Morphologically the Skhūl type is intermediate between Neanthropic and Neanderthal man, yet the variations are mainly indicative of an evolution towards the modern types of man. In no essential point or complex of features can we exclude the Skhūl people from a position among the ancestors of the modern races. Of these modern varieties of man, the Skhūl type appears to be the most likely ancestor of the Cromagnon form of the prehistoric peoples of Europe. His physical characteristics are too well defined and he is too late in the Pleistocene to provide us with an ancestor for *Homo sapiens* in the widest sense of that term.

The Tabūn type, despite its undoubted kinship with the Skhūl type of humanity, is Neanderthaloid. At the same time, it differs in many significant particulars from the Western European Neanderthals and so far as the evidence permits, it seems to be more akin to the Krapina Neanderthaloids. The European Neanderthals are undeniably primitive; in addition to this they possess certain specialized anatomical traits which we believe must exclude them from the direct ancestry of modern man. The Tabūn woman we know to be chronologically earlier than the Western European Neanderthals, and her anatomy, though primitive, is less specialized. She represents an Eastern variety of the Neanderthaloid family. We believe also that she is probably closer to the form of humanity which was the parent of both the Palaeoanthropic and Neanthropic branches of mankind than is the case with her western cousins. If evolution is true, we should expect to find from time to time such a state of affairs as it has been our good fortune to discover in the Holy Land.

LATE PALAEOLITHIC MAN IN NORTHERNMOST NORWAY

BY

A. W. BRØGGER

Professor of Archaeology, Kongelige Frederiks Universitet, Oslo, Norway

Early man and Palaeolithic Man have no national land frontiers. The problems concerning them are international—of world
dimensions in fact. It is, therefore, of extreme importance now
and again to meet at an international center—like here in Philadelphia—where we find the appropriate environment for the
problems and, not least, the proper detachment.

Here is a map of Europe upon which you will see the more
important capitals marked: they have very little to do with the
ancient Stone Ages—they are shown here merely to give a geographical orientation. Making itself manifest in the wide European areas in the east, west and south, is, as is known, a wealthy
Palaeolithic Stone Age, but of late years finds have also been
emerging far in the north, quite up in the northernmost parts
of Norway—the area covered black on this map. These finds
have been made within the frontiers of the Kingdom of Norway
and it will perhaps readily be understood that we in Norway
are very busy indeed with them and, naturally, very proud. In
reality, however, they belong to international research, and it
was with this in mind that I have considered it proper to give a
short report regarding them to this international meeting. They
present peculiarities which, in any case, must be of interest to
palaeolithic research in general. May I first say a few words with
regard to how these finds came to light? It is quite a remarkable

story. Our Stone Age research in Norway has during the last generation been closely linked with glacial-geological research and then, naturally, the late-glacial and post-glacial periods in particular.

There is one man who in this sphere has contributed more than anyone else, Mr. Anders Nummedal, one of the staff at the University Collection of Antiquities, Oslo. He soon made himself at home with the circumstances appertaining to the Stone Age inhabitants and the ancient shore-lines, and, instead of letting the material reach us casually, went out in the field himself, looked for it—and found it! In this manner he has enriched our Stone Age with a large and highly important material. In the early twenties he suggested to me that he should travel to Finnmark—in the northernmost part of Norway—there to search for evidence of the ancient Stone Age. I encouraged him in this and in 1925 he began by spending his first summer there. Like the man with the divining-rod, he went straight to the sites of the finds and continued to do so for ten summers until 1934.

The first comprehensive treatment of these finds, written by Nummedal and Johs. Bøe, was put before the second International Congress of Prehistoric and Protohistoric Sciences held at Oslo in August 1936.

The sites of the stations are all along the sea-shore no matter whether they lie at the head of a fjord or on the open ocean. Altogether sixty find-sites are now known. The geographical delimitation is really interesting. It appears that to the west of the most western of these stations, not one single find has been made in spite of the most energetic investigations. Throughout the whole of the north-western area of North Norway, down to the Lofoten Islands, etc., there is not one of these finds. On the other hand, there is no doubt at all that related finds will be made in North Russia and Siberia, that is, in geographical regions of the same sub-arctic character as Finnmark.

The find-sites are what are termed in French archaeology *Stations de plein air*, not *abris* nor anything similar. The regions within which they lie still belong to some of the most desolate in Norway.

The Finnmark stations are defined by unilateral quantities of antiquities of stone—bone and horn not being found. Moreover, these habitations are without any stratigraphical character whatever; nor are organic remnants to be discovered, a circumstance due to the age-long action of natural forces, snow, ice and rain. This one-sidedness in the actual material also gives a certain one-sidedness to the cultural picture itself. We have to deal with a material very important as an archaeological type, but there is much to be desired where the cultural picture is concerned.

The raw material which these peoples of the Stone Age have used has been found on the spot and varies considerably in quality—most frequently being rather poor, when seen from the standard of European *éclat* (flint flake). The two best sorts of stone used are, on the one hand, a red-brown quartzite which gives quite good shapes after cutting, and, on the other, a "dolomite-flint" which, to some extent, one must admit to be quite excellent.

Dr. Bøe has made the rather important observation that, although habitations spread over a relatively limited area are concerned, there has been no question of any *transport* of raw material from one place to another. Each tribe used that which was available on the spot.

The habitations have therefore been chosen just as much out of regard for usable raw material for the production of utensils, as for the possibilities of capture and hunting in a wide circle around the place. The sites on the sea-shore indicate that marine capture was principally concerned, primarily the seal, and then fish and marine-birds.

As the material appears at present, it challenges, first and foremost, a purely archaeological evaluation. Dr. Bøe has done this in his great work and it is some of the results which I shall here attempt to define. First, of course, the starting point—the pebbles or the moraine block as the primary. The raw material is mostly loose stones from glacial moraines, and it is the utilization of these that gives the whole stone industry its character. We find here once more the large main lines of the palaeolithic industry in Europe, partly the utilization of the flake (French: *la lame*) partly of *l'éclat*. Developing from the two principal forms thus created come the individual special forms corresponding to the definite requirements of the particular utensil concerned. The heavy l'éclat industry may be considered the principal in the case of the Finnmark finds.

Quite a primary industry is encountered in the large double-edged stabbing utensils, both complete and incomplete, besides choppers and other implements. In addition there are large nuclei of éclats and ordinary nuclei of pebbles.

On a level with these are large éclats which, with a knowledge of the European palaeolithic industry, one may place as belonging to the well-known type-groups *clacton* and *levallois*.

As still being part of this coarser industry may be distinguished a series of scrapers, *racloirs*, which, for that matter, comprise one of the richest groups of utensils in the Finnmark finds; they occur on all sites and in many varied forms. Here is to be found, *inter alia*, a main group of large, coarse racloirs which resemble the type Absolon has termed *gigantholites* from Bohemia; further, a group of medium size, termed *véritables racloirs*, and a particularly typical group which may be included under the classical *Moustier*.

Points having many varied forms are a constant find at all habitation sites. On a number of them may be found delightful triangular éclats without secondary treatment but quite *Moustier* in character.

Particularly interesting is a series of points resembling the primitive specimens from Aurignacian, named after *l'abri Audi*. On the continent these belong mainly to primitive Aurignacian but also occur sporadically in later Magdalenian.

At several of the habitation sites *tranchets* are found more or less resembling those we find in Campignia, but which, moreover, are also proved in Moustier; they are presumed to be a representative type in South African palaeography, but there need be no direct, internal coherence, of course, between all these areas so different in time and place. It is rather that *tranchets*, as it were, automatically belong to the everyday *industrie lourde d'éclats*. In all probability these in Finnmark are "self-grown" and, in any case, they have no connection with the so-called "skivespalten" in the Danish kitchen middens.

A large group of the flake industry, comprised by the French term *burins*, is also present. This shows a series of forms from the simple and coarse without demonstrable *intention* towards the better formed kind as a result of an *adaptation intentionelle*. The groups determinable within these series show a clear and close relationship with Aurignacian.

Touched-up blades and flake-knives are found in large numbers and in many of them one will recognize a technique found in corresponding articles in Aurignacian. Some of them simply remind one of the so-called *points de Chatelperron*.

Finally, it may also be mentioned that we have knives and drills in various forms, scrapers of special shapes, scrapers of larger kinds and, lastly, quite a series of *microlites* found at most of the habitation sites. It is of significance that here, *inter alia*, arrow-heads really occur, having shafts of shapes we know from North German and Danish finds (Lyngby).

An analysis of all this utensil-industry—called by Dr. Bøe the *Finnmarkien*, analogous with Swiderien, Campignien, etc.—shows that we have to deal with ancient *industries d'éclats* which, in the main, end with Moustier in Western Europe, and have not been known in Scandinavia—at all events up to the present; but here are also elements from Aurignacian and similarly from Magdalenian. It is obvious that with these Finnmark finds we are in *a decided palaeolithic milieu*, but it must not be forgotten that here again there are various forms which, even if they are of ancient origin, also appear in later periods in the North.

The geological determination of the age of the Finnmark finds is primarily subject to the ice-conditions prevailing in the north during and after the last ice-age. Opinions in this respect rather differ but one thing seems definite and that is that the Finnmark finds must be later than the last fourth glaciation, according to de Geer's Chronology, at all events 12,000, but probably 15,000 years old.

The question of the area of the origin of these finds from northernmost Norway has also been exhaustively considered. Dr. Bøe has drawn into the sphere of his investigations comparative material from many regions, naturally French first and foremost, but also districts in the East, particularly Mähren. From North Russia, Siberia and China also come important series of finds which may claim connection. But in this respect we still know too little as investigations are so dispersed.

At the time these peoples lived on these harsh North-Norwegian coasts, the glaciers from the last after-glaciation period lay up in the fjords where, on the whole, the arctic conditions prevailing were such as those under which the Greenland Eskimo lives to-day. I therefore believe that if one is at all to be able to obtain any picture of these peoples in the north of the after-glaciation period, one must learn something of both the archaeology and present-day life of the Eskimo peoples. But I have no time to go into this question here and now. The sole observation I would much like to emphasize, however, is the great importance it would have if Knud Rasmussen's idea of international co-operation in respect to the arctic cultures could be realized. Thanks to the excellent Danish, Canadian and North American investigations of the last 10-15 years, we are now coming to know better and better the conditions along the arctic coasts of the North American continent, but the arctic coasts in Eurasia—Europe in Finland, Russia, with Siberia and the region to the Bering Straits in Asia—are very poorly known. It is with regard to these that work should be commenced.

The Finnmark finds as they now are provide excellent material for ordinary cultural-historical reflections which also help us to place them rather clearly. This is another matter, and there are just a few things in this respect I would, in conclusion, wish to indicate.

The utensil milieu we are in when dealing with the find I have discussed, characterizes itself fairly well—first by what it does *not* contain. This applies, for example, to the axe pure and simple —in the sense we see the axe in the history of humanity. The forms of *tranchets* found have nothing to do with the main requirements we connect with the axe.

It is different with the *arrow*. In the material available there are no arrow-points, with the exception of the very late forms which I discussed just now (Lyngby-Ahrenburg). We cannot conclude very much from this, however. We must reckon that, in bone and horn not preserved at these habitation sites, there may have been a series of the palaeolithic arrow forms we know, for example, from Magdalenian.

Judging from the material we really have, however, one thing at all events is clear:—that which characterizes the whole milieu of the Finnmark culture is the amount of *scrapers* found at all sites. This is just the very milieu of the arctic and sub-arctic. The hunting of certain animals which has played a predominating part—probably both the reindeer and the seal—has certainly formed the foundation upon which the existence of these hunting peoples has been built. Scrapers mean the preparation of hides in all forms and this in turn is but one single, but extremely important, link in the chain of the complete utilization of all large prey necessary for existence—food and fats, hides and clothing, raw material for utensils (bone and horn) and the satisfactory fulfilment of a number of minor requirements. They point to an existence founded upon the reindeer and seal.

In the stages with which we have to count in cultural-geographical development, this milieu is assigned a definite place. Nor do I believe in any "development" from here to any so-called higher stages of culture—just as little as it has at any time been proved that the Eskimo culture has assimilated into itself elements from domiciliary agricultural culture and thus changed the entire construction of the mode of existence.

To the study and research of these arctic and sub-arctic cultures of palaeolithic times I accordingly attach considerable importance as a link in general research in respect to the history of humanity itself.

POLLEN ANALYSIS AS AN AID IN DATING
CULTURAL DEPOSITS IN THE UNITED STATES

BY

PAUL B. SEARS

*Professor of Botany, University of Oklahoma**

T HE use of pollen analysis in dating cultural materials is a well-known procedure in the glaciated portion of Europe, where peat deposits are fairly abundant and have been systematically explored. Information regarding technique and results are available in papers by Erdtman,[1] Godwin,[2] and others.

Pollen analysis in North America is still in the exploratory stage. Its possibilities and limitations are not as yet widely understood. Therefore it seems advisable to present briefly some general information about it, to illustrate the use to which it can be put, to report its application in semi-arid regions, and, most important of all, to suggest means by which it can be made more serviceable to the archaeologist. In this connection, it should be emphasized that the progress of land exploitation is rapidly destroying valuable deposits which might be utilized for pollen analysis studies, so that scientific work ought not be delayed.

Pollen analysis is a method of studying the problem of past climates and vegetation as recorded by the stratification of wind-borne spores in organic terrestrial sediments. Organic remains which have accumulated *in situ* give a very localized picture of change; but the pollen which blows in from the adjacent forests or other plant communities presents a more general record. Conditions for the preservation of microfossils are most favorable

* Contribution from the Botanical Laboratories, University of Oklahoma. No. 48.

in peat and its associated deposits. These are particularly characteristic of cool, humid, glaciated regions.

The first essential in using these records for any purpose is to secure typical pollen profiles for whatever regions are to be studied. Such a profile is illustrated in Fig. 1. It records the varying percentages of pollen found at successive depths in a deposit in Minnesota. Study, both in Europe[3] and in North America,[4] has established the fact that regional profiles are quite characteristic and consistent.

Once these standard regional profiles are available, they have several direct applications.

(1) They afford a means of accurate correlation of archaeological material found at different places in the same deposit of peat, or in different deposits in the same region.

(2) They permit the correlation of remains found in association with thin and isolated peat strata, or of material which has small fragments of peat of unknown age adhering to it.

(3) Through their evidence as to climatic and other environmental change, they assist in the reconstruction of cultural conditions associated with artifacts.

Because peat deposits in the United States are generally exploited by drainage, burning, and cultivation, there has been little systematic exploration of them for cultural material. In Europe, however, where peat deposits are methodically worked, this is not true. Under such conditions definite cultural horizons with characteristic pollen percentages can be, and have been, established, thus exemplifying the first application above.[5]

To date, the most satisfactory application that has been made in the University of Oklahoma laboratory has been with reference to cultural material found by Professor Jenks of Minnesota at known levels in a peat deposit. Analysis of the deposit showed it to have the pollen profile characteristic for Minnesota, the most striking feature being a well-marked climax of oak some distance from the top, and believed to mark a warm, dry post-glacial climax of at least 3000 years ago. The cultural material lay well below this oak climax, as indicated in Fig. 1, and

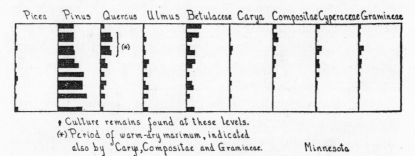

FIG. 1—Pollen profile illustrating fluctuations of pollen at different depths in a sedimentary deposit.

could therefore, with safety, be assigned an age considerably greater than 3000 years.

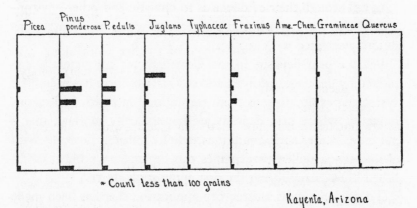

FIG. 2—Pollen analysis of canyon silts from Arizona.

The use of pollen analysis as a key to past environmental conditions has already been discussed by the author.[6] Suffice it to say that, while the events of early post-glacial climate are still obscure and no doubt confused by irregular edaphic conditions along the retreating ice front, there is fairly clear evidence of the post-glacial warm-dry maximum already referred to. This hypothesis is not without support from floristic and ecological sources.[7, 8] That such a climatic event would have significant effects upon primitive cultures with limited technical facilities at their disposal seems reasonable, and is the view taken by Raup[8] in recent studies on New England climatic history.

In Europe a precise chronology, through correlation of varve counts and pollen profiles, has been established. This task is not yet completed in North America.[9] Meanwhile a rough method of approximation has been developed by studying the rate of peat accumulation.[10] This has been made possible by attention to laminations found in peat and also by study of the depth of objects of known age. The rate of course varies with climate, and the record is not always continuous. Oxidized layers cannot be considered. For the Erie basin a conventional figure of about 25 years to the inch in peat older than 30 years has been obtained, while in the Wyoming mountains the figure is about 10 years to the inch. The importance of further work along this line, pending the development of a precise varve chronology, scarcely needs to be stressed.

In North America, applications of the method of pollen analysis are not necessarily limited to the glaciated area. The Spiro area, now under investigation by Forrest Clements near Ft. Smith, Arkansas, contains cultural remains of a high type, approaching the famous Hopewell. The Spiro mound itself was constructed from material excavated nearby, and the excavation has produced an artificial lake. The silt in this lake contains pollen enough to allow a profile to be constructed. By comparison of this profile with another obtained from an old cypress swamp near Little Rock, Arkansas, and by estimates based on the rate of silting, a maximum age of the order of 900 years was calculated for the mound. This agrees satisfactorily with Clements' estimate based on independent grounds. It must be emphasized, however, that our knowledge of the regional profile characteristics is far from adequate for this, as for many parts of the United States.

Not previously repor.ᴄu ᴜ the discovery, made in material furnished by Dr. Antevs, that pollen profiles can sometimes be obtained from silts deposited in canyons in the arid Southwest. Such a profile is shown in Fig. 2. The species of plants involved all have a sensitive relation to available moisture, and can ultimately be useful in tracing the course of environmental change. It must be emphasized, however, that no conclusions, either as to general changes or chronology, can safely be drawn from isolated profiles like the one presented here. Furthermore, no safe conclusions can be drawn for this region on the basis of pollen analysis alone. The erosion history of the entire region must be developed. Terraces and buried soils abound[11] and their relationships must be established as a necessary step in the application of pollen analysis of silt deposits.[9]

There is reason to believe, however, from preliminary observations of such terraces and buried humus layers along a number of the great rivers in the grassland states, that the effects of glacial changes are recorded far beyond the border of the ice, and that the erosion history of the middle and southwest can be developed in relation to chronological scales as they are worked out within that border.

It should be clear from the foregoing that the interests of archaeology can be served

(1) by methodical exploration of suitable peat deposits for cultural remains.

(2) by systematic prosecution of pollen studies throughout

the country until standard profiles of reference are obtained and the sequence of post-glacial events is determined.

(3) by thoroughgoing efforts to correlate these events with erosion and sedimentation, both within and without the glacial areas.

BIBLIOGRAPHY

[1] ERDTMAN, G. Pollen-statistics: A new research method in paleo-ecology. Science 73: 399-401. 1931.

[2] GODWIN, H. Pollen analysis, an outline of the problems and potentialities of the method. Part II. General applications of pollen analysis. New Phyt. 33: 325-358. 1934.

[3] CLARK, J. G. D., H. and M. E. GODWIN, and M. H. CLIFFORD. A bronze spear-head found in Methwood Fen, Norfolk. Proc. Prehistoric Soc. of East Anglia. 7,3: 395-398. 1934.

[4] SEARS, PAUL B. Types of North American pollen profiles. Ecology 16: 488-499. 1935.

[5] GODWIN, H. and M. E., J. G. D. CLARK, and M. H. CLIFFORD. Report on recent excavations at Peacocks Farm, Shippea Hill, Cambridgeshire. The Antiquaries Journal. 15,3: 284-319. 1935.

[6] SEARS, PAUL B. The archaeology of environment in eastern North America. Amer. Anthrop. 34,4: 610-622. 1932.

[7] GLEASON, HENRY A. The vegetational history of the mid-west. Annals of the Assoc. of Amer. Geog. 12: 39-85. 1923.

[8] RAUP, H. M. Recent changes of climate and vegetation in southern New England and adjacent New York. Jour. Arnold Arboretum. 17: 79-117. 1937.

[9] ANTEVS, ERNST. Dating records of early man in the southwest. Amer. Nat. 70: 331-336. 1936.

[10] SEARS, PAUL B. and ELSIE JANSON. The rate of peat growth in the Erie Basin. Ecology 14: 348-355. 1933.

[11] SEARS, PAUL B. and GLENN C. COUCH. Humus stratigraphy as a clue to past vegetation in Oklahoma. Proc. Okla. Acad. Sci. Vol. 15. 1935.

PLEISTOCENE LAND AND FRESH-WATER MOLLUSCA AS INDICATORS OF TIME AND ECOLOGICAL CONDITIONS

BY

FRANK COLLINS BAKER

Curator, Museum of Natural History, University of Illinois

The glacial advances and retreats of the Pleistocene Epoch profoundly affected all life, including the land and fresh-water Mollusca. Following an advance of the ice all life was killed or driven southward causing a commingling of arctic, subarctic, and temperate life south of the border of the continental ice sheet. During the warmer interglacial intervals this life again returned to the territory left bare by the retreating ice, only again to be driven southward by another ice invasion.

The reoccupied territory left bare by the ice was usually quite different in character from that previously occupied by the Mollusca and the new environments had a marked effect upon the development of the molluscan fauna. Climatic factors also contributed to the generally unfavorable conditions. These combined factors acting upon the inherent tendency to variation in this group produced marked changes in certain forms, causing new varieties and species to be evolved on the one hand and extinctions of certain forms on the other.

MOLLUSCA AS INDICATORS OF ECOLOGICAL CONDITIONS

Because of the hard shells of mollusks, which are easily preserved in nearly all kinds of earth deposits, these animals are better adapted for the interpretation of ecological conditions of the environment than are any other class of animals or of plants. A knowledge of the habitat relations of the existing species enables the student to make rather positive interpretations of the conditions which prevailed when the fauna of any fossil deposit lived. It is comparatively easy to know whether the habitat was a land surface, a lake, a river, a small stream, or a swampy territory. It is possible, also, to know whether the water was deep or shallow, clear, or with much sediment.

In the case of land forms it is possible to postulate tundra conditions, a forest habitat, a prairie region, or a locality where many small temporary ponds or swales abound. Some thirty years ago there was wide controversy concerning whether the ·loess deposits were of aqueous origin, and for several years the advocates of water and aeolian origin waged a wordy war.[1] The differences of opinion were finally reconciled by recourse to ecology, by which it was shown that the great majority of molluscan species buried in the loess were land shells which could not by any possibility have lived in water, and the few water species present were shown to live in ephemerous pools in the woods in which the land shells lived.

Another example of the use of ecological knowledge in the interpretation of fossil deposits is found in the study of old lake beds and the reconstruction of the history of the lake by a study of the strata laid down by the water body. Two notable examples of this kind of ecological study are known. One is by Dr. A. P. Coleman at Toronto, Canada, where the largest interglacial biota yet known has been discovered. Here are noted changes in habitat from land and river conditions to shallow lake and swampy conditions. In the second example, at Chicago, F. C. Baker[2] was able, from an examination of strata in the Chicago drainage canal, to reconstruct the entire history of the formation of Glacial Lake Chicago, and its descendant, Lake Michigan,

[1] Shimek, B., Bull. Lab. Nat. Hist., Univ. Iowa, V. 32-45, 1898.
[2] "Life of the Pleistocene," Chapters I-III, 1920.

showing fluctuations in lake level, changes from swampy to lake conditions, deep waters and shallow waters.

The ecological study of the Mollusca has been instrumental in determining the nature of certain geological deposits related to the Indian occupation of inland regions. Near Chicago, some years ago, a number of marine mollusks were found in the Calumet beach ridge southwest of Chicago Lawn in the Chicago region. These were southern species common in Florida and the Gulf of Mexico and not cold-water species of the northern part of the United States. Later research developed the fact that these shells were camp refuse of the Illinois Indians. Many such specimens were found in other places. Thus a seemingly difficult problem of geology was solved by the archeologist working with the conchologist. Had these shells been deposited by water they would have postulated a northern extension of the sea from the Gulf of Mexico, an impossible theory in the face of land elevations in northern Illinois during the Pleistocene Epoch.[3]

So, also, in the case of marine shells found abundantly in camp sites and in Indian mounds in the Mississippi Valley, once thought by many geologists to have been deposited by a late Pliocene sea from the south, are now known to be simply material obtained by the Indians of the middle west from natives of the coast, by barter. It is becoming increasingly important that deposits containing evidences of Man's occupancy be examined by the geologist and the zoologist to guard against false assumptions.

MOLLUSCA AS INDICATORS OF CLIMATE

Next to plant life, mollusks are good indicators of general climatic conditions. They should reflect many of the changes that have taken place during the advance and retreat of an ice sheet. With the beginning of an ice invasion the biota was slowly driven southward, the arctic and subarctic types crowding upon

[3] Baker, F. C., "Life of the Pleistocene," pp. 12-15, 1920.

the biota of a more temperate climate to the southward. This intrusion of one type of biota upon another must have continued until at the southern limit of the ice border there was a marked commingling of all climatic types that were able to survive. When the ice began its retreat and uncovered the glaciated territory there was a return of the biota and a reversal of the climatic types, the more boreal forms leading the way.

This oscillatory migration of faunas is plainly indicated in several deposits where the history of events may be clearly observed. At Toronto, Canada, the oncoming of the Wisconsin ice is shown by the variations of the biota in the different levels of the beds. The lowest beds contain a rich forest of coniferous and deciduous trees and a mollusk fauna of forty species, both plants and mollusks indicating a climate warmer than now prevails at Toronto, perhaps like that of southern Ohio and Pennsylvania. Above the warm fauna and flora, plants and mollusks occur indicating a much colder climate, like Labrador or Ungava, perhaps cold and wet.[4]

At Chicago, Illinois, the reverse types of life are found, the lowest deposits indicating a cold-temperate climate and the upper deposits a fauna of mollusks, largely river mussels, indicating a climate like that of central Illinois. These deposits picture the retreat of the Wisconsin ice. Taken together, the Toronto and Chicago deposits indicate the general nature of an interglacial cycle.[5]

Climatic change is also indicated in many other places, in fact, almost any fossiliferous deposit will show a fauna in places different from that now living in the vicinity. An inventory of a typical loess deposit in central Illinois frequently shows several species which are now found far to the north, in northern Minnesota, Michigan, and Canada, or to the west in the Rocky Mountain region. Such species as *Oreohelix strigosa iowensis*, *Discus*

[4] Coleman, A. P., Bull. Geol. Soc. Amer., 26, 243, 1906.
[5] Baker, F. C., "Life of the Pleistocene," Chapter III, 1920.

shimekii, Vertigo modesta, Columella alticola, and *Pupilla blandi* are foreign to the fauna of the Mississippi Valley at the present time, but are found abundantly to the north or west where the climate is considerably colder and drier. The species associated with these key forms are such as have a very wide distribution and are able to live in a rather wide latitude of temperature changes.

Other species are rare in the recent fauna of the middle Mississippi Valley but are more common in the north or east. Such are *Vertigo elatior, Vertigo gouldii, Vertigo morsei,* and *Vertigo pygmaeum.* Two species, *Vallonia gracilicosta* and *Carychium exile canadense,* are absent from Illinois but are common north and west of this area. All of these species are common to abundant in Pleistocene deposits. Stratigraphic studies of loess and other deposits usually show a transition from cold to warm temperate fauna, from bottom to top of section.[6]

A noteworthy feature of loess deposits of Early Wisconsin time (Peorian and Shelbyville) is the rarity of the large *Polygyra* land snails so abundant in the present fauna. In ninety-two deposits of Peorian age but eight species are found, *Polygyra multilineata wanlessi, Polygyra profunda pleistocenica, Polygyra profunda* (only two specimens), *Polygyra appressa* (one specimen), *Polygyra thyroides* (rare), *Polygyra hirsuta, Polygyra monodon,* and *Polygyra fraterna.* Only the smaller species are abundant. The same condition prevailed in twenty sections of Shelbyville loess examined. In the same region at the present time twenty-two species of Polygyra are found, many of large size. The maximum development of the genus Polygyra takes place in the warm temperate climate of the southeastern part of the United States and the small fauna of diminutive forms found in the loess of this region is indicative of a cold-temperate climate. Farther south, as at Natchez, Miss., a rich Polygyra fauna

[6] Baker, F. C., Journ. Paleont., 10, 72-76, 1936.

occurs in the loess deposits, including some large species absent from the more northern loess deposits.[7]

The Sangamon interglacial interval is believed to have been generally warmer than the preceding Yarmouth and Aftonian intervals. In support of this view it may be noted that the Poly-gyra fauna of the Sangamon is larger than that of any other interval and is also larger than any similar fauna found in the earlier Wisconsin deposits (Peorian and Shelbyville), and is comparable only with the existing fauna of this area. The forest beds of the Sangamon, especially in southern Ohio, bear a fauna of twenty-three species of this genus.

MOLLUSCA AS INDICATORS OF TIME

During the Pleistocene Epoch great changes took place in some of the animal groups and these changes, extinctions in many cases, indicate the passage of a long period of time since the Nebraskan ice sheet began its journey southward. This period of time has been variously estimated to be from one to five million years in duration. The groups most notably affected have been the mammals, of which seventy-four per cent are extinct, and the insects, of which nearly all recorded species are believed to be extinct.

With the Mollusca, however, the case is more difficult, since the majority of the species lived throughout the entire Pleistocene Epoch with but little change. Taking the group as a whole we find that among the Unionidae or river mussels sixty species and races have been recorded of which none are extinct and but little variation can be detected. Of the little pill and finger-nail clams, Sphaeriidae, sixty-five species are known with but two species extinct. Of the gill-bearing gastropods, sixty-five species and races have been identified, of which nine, or 13.8 per cent are extinct. Seventy-two fresh-water pulmonates are known, with six, or 8.3 per cent, extinct. Of the land snails (Pulmonata),

[7] Shimek, B., Amer. Geol., 30, 279-299, 1902.

one hundred and eight species and races have been recorded with twelve, or 11.1 per cent, extinct. From the entire Pleistocene Epoch three hundred and seventy species and races have been recorded in the glaciated area, of which twenty-nine, or 7.8 per cent, are extinct.

A study of complete stratigraphic tables of Pleistocene molluscan life brings out some interesting observations regarding the time element. Unionidae or river mussels were apparently not abundant in species in the glaciated territory during either the Aftonian or Yarmouth intervals. During the Sangamon interval, however, they were abundant. In Wisconsin time they show a gradual increase in number. The same may be said of the small Sphaeriidae mussels. Among the gill-bearing gastropods the number of species and races was small during the Aftonian and Yarmouth intervals but increased notably during the Sangamon interval. The same numerical superiority prevailed during Wisconsin time.

Of the eight species and races of gill-bearing gastropods believed to be extinct, *Valvata sincera illinoisensis* is known only from middle and late Wisconsin deposits and *Valvata lewisi precursor* is known from Yarmouth and Sangamon time and died out in late Wisconsin time. Of the little Amnicola genus, *Amnicola walkeri precursor* is known from Sangamon time and died out in late Wisconsin time. *Amnicola galbana, Amnicola mozleyi,* and *Amnicola greenensis* did not appear until middle and late Wisconsin time and disappeared in late Wisconsin or pre-recent time. The little *Pomatiopsis scalaris* appears to be a species confined to loess deposits and was not common until early Wisconsin time. Several aquatic species show a marked increase in form variation during middle and late Wisconsin time, which variation has not been observed in material from the interglacial intervals. Valvata and Amnicola show the greatest variation in this respect.

The fresh-water pulmonate gastropods also show an increase in variation as well as in speciation during Wisconsin time. Four of the supposed extinct species (*Stagnicola saskatchewanensis*, *Stagnicola bakeri*, *Fossaria glabana*, and *Fossaria anticostiana*) appear in late Wisconsin time, and two (*Planorbula indianensis* and *Gyraulus urbanensis*) are known as early as Yarmouth and Sangamon time. In two large families, Lymnaeidae and Planorbidae, thirteen and sixteen species respectively are known from interglacial deposits, while twenty-seven Lymnaeidae and twenty-five Planorbidae are known from Wisconsin time, a very large increase during the last glacial episode.

The land shell fauna of the Pleistocene is large and varied and contains fully eighty per cent of the species now living in the drift area. As in the other groups, the Sangamon interval contains more species than the previous Aftonian and Yarmouth intervals. In Wisconsin time the land shells do not show the same ratio of increase in species as do the aquatic forms. Many of the land species have lived continuously from Aftonian to the present time and a large number since Yarmouth time. During this time, however, twelve species and races have apparently died out and become extinct. Several of these are good indicators of time since they are found only in certain deposits of limited age. Thus *Vertigo hubrichti* and *Vertigo hannai* are known only from strata of Yarmouth age. *Polygyra hirsuta yarmouthensis* has only been seen from Yarmouth and Sangamon deposits. *Polygyra multilineata altonensis* occurs only in deposits of Sangamon age; *Oreohelix strigosa iowensis* is known from deposits of Yarmouth, Sangamon, and Peorian age. *Discus macclintocki* was common to abundant in Aftonian, Yarmouth, and Sangamon time and did not die out until the Shelbyville stage of early Wisconsin time; *Discus shimekii* is known from Yarmouth to early Wisconsin time. The *Succinea* genus contains several races which are believed to be extinct in their typical form, *Succinea ovalis pleistocenica*, *Succinea grosvenori gelida*, and *Succinea retusa fultonensis*. These races are found in all the interglacial intervals and died out in early Wisconsin time.

MARINE PLEISTOCENE MOLLUSKS AS INDICATORS OF TIME AND ECOLOGICAL CONDITIONS

BY

HORACE G. RICHARDS
Research Associate, New Jersey State Museum

In THIS paper we shall attempt to discuss the marine Pleistocene mollusks of the east coast of North America as indicators of time and climatic conditions. However, before doing so, it will be advisable to briefly outline the Pleistocene stratigraphy of the region.

Many of the earlier workers on the Pleistocene assumed that the sea level remained stationary while the land rose and sank. It has become clear and has been pointed out by numerous workers in recent years that the first part of this assumption is untenable, for the accumulations of the continental ice sheets must have withdrawn enough water to have appreciably lowered the sea level. Estimates of this lowering have varied greatly, but the more usually accepted figures for the lowering of sea level during Wisconsin time lie between two hundred and fifty and three hundred feet.

However, movements of the land must not be entirely ignored. There is a great deal of evidence to show that in Wisconsin time the weight of the ice depressed the land differentially. Upon the retreat of the ice, sea level rose and flooded the land. The land, in turn, rose, having recovered from the load, and the sea consequently withdrew. Abandoned shore lines of this late glacial sea can be seen ranging from several hundred feet above sea level in northern New England and the St. Lawrence Valley to only a few feet above sea level in southern New England.

A third factor to be considered is the diastrophic movement of the land independent of any effect of the ice. Such movements, while undoubtedly an important part in the Pleistocene history of many regions, have apparently played a relatively insignificant role in the late Pleistocene history of the east coast of Canada and the United States.

In brief, part of the region north of the Terminal Moraine appears to have been covered by a sea shortly after the retreat of the Wisconsin ice. Traces of earlier marine Pleistocene deposits have probably, in most cases at least, been destroyed by the action of the ice. South of the Terminal Moraine, there is little evidence of any warping of the land due to the ice. So, until it can definitely be shown that there has been movement of the land, marine Pleistocene deposits found near and above present sea level from New Jersey southward are best interpreted as of interglacial age, formed at a time of higher sea level than the present.

Let us now make a very hasty survey of the Pleistocene deposits of the east coast of North America, and see if the molluscan fossils in these deposits give us any indications of the climate prevailing at the time of deposition; we shall thus see if the molluscan evidence supports the geological history as previously outlined.

JAMES BAY

We shall start our survey in James Bay, the southern portion of Hudson Bay. James Bay today is brackish and contains a very small molluscan fauna. (Only five species were observed in the littoral or shallow water zones.) The Pleistocene fossils of the region, collected from bluffs along the tributaries of the Bay, up to elevations of three hundred feet or more, consist of numerous species that are now living farther north in the deeper, colder and more saline waters of Hudson Bay proper. In addition to the fossils from the river bluffs, worn shells of many of these

PLATE V, FIG. 1—Pleistocene fossils indicating warm water obtained from spoil banks of Intra Coastal Canal, Hyde County, North Carolina.

PLATE V, FIG. 2—Pleistocene fossils from James Bay indicating colder, deeper and more saline waters than now exist in the region. (For explanation see footnote[1] p. 77.)

same species are washed onto the beaches and were particularly noted on Charlton and Cary Islands, which lie about eighty miles north of the southern tip of James Bay. These mollusks (Plate V, Fig. 2), indicating a colder, deeper water, probably lived shortly after the retreat of the Wisconsin ice from the region, when James Bay was considerably deeper than at present, and extended some hundred miles south of its present limit. The release of the load of the ice caused the land to rise and the sea to withdraw to its present position.[1]

NEWFOUNDLAND

Certain parts of the island of Newfoundland are covered with a marine Pleistocene fossiliferous clay. The fossils are fewer in species than those from James Bay, and are all living off the Newfoundland coast today. Since in many places they overlie the till, they are probably also of post Wisconsin age. Some of the best material has come from the Bay of Islands region, on the west coast of the island.[2]

ST. LAWRENCE VALLEY

A marine clay is found throughout the entire St. Lawrence Valley from the Gulf almost to Lake Ontario. Molluscan fossils are often very abundant and are found up to about three hundred feet above sea level at Rivière du Loup and about five hundred feet above sea level at Montreal. In addition to the St. Lawrence Valley proper, this Pleistocene sea extended into numerous

[1] For fauna and bibliography see Richards, Horace G. "Recent and Pleistocene Marine Shells of James Bay." Amer. Midl. Nat., vol. 17, pp. 528-545, (1936).

1. *Astarte borealis* Schumacker.
2. *Pecten islandicus* (Müller).
3. *Leda pernula* (Müller).
4. *Astarte striata* Leach.
5. *Cardium ciliatum* Fabricius.
6. *Buccinum tenue* Gray.
7. *Macoma calcarea* (Gmelin).
8. *Saxicava arctica* Linn.
9. *Acmaea testudinalis* (Müller).

[2] For geology see especially: Coleman, A. P. "The Pleistocene of Newfoundland," Jour. of Geol., vol. 34, pp. 193-223, (1926). Daly, R. A. "Postglacial Warping of Newfoundland and Nova Scotia." Amer. Jour. Sci., ser. 5, vol. 1, pp. 381-391, (1921). For fauna see Richards, Horace G. "Pleistocene fossils from Newfoundland Collected by Expeditions from Princeton University." Amer. Midl. Nat., vol. 18, pp. 457-459, (1937).

branches, for instance up the Saguaney River to Lake St. John, up the Ottawa River to Ottawa, and south into Lake Champlain, extending as far south as Crown Point, New York and Chimney Point, Vermont. The fauna of the main part of this embayment is very rich and indicates a cold sea of some appreciable depth. Fifty-seven species are known from Montreal and about fifty species from Rivière du Loup, many of which are now restricted to waters considerably farther north.[3] The fauna of the Lake Champlain region in New York and Vermont indicates a shallow brackish sea with very few species, *Saxicava arctica* Linn., *Leda glacialis* Wood and *Macoma balthica* Linn. being the most common.[4]

These deposits are probably entirely of post Wisconsin age. The relieving of the load of the ice caused the land to rise and the marine waters, spoken of as the "Champlain Sea," to recede. The boreal character of the fauna indicates that the climate was still cold. In many places such as at Rivière du Loup, Quebec and Isle La Motte, Vermont, the marine deposits are interbedded with boulders and outwash, suggesting that there was still considerable ice in the region at the time that this fauna flourished.

"Folsom-like" points have been found in sand dune deposits in Vermont high above the shores of present Lake Champlain. It is possible that further study will be able to correlate this site with the "Champlain Sea" or with one of the high stands of the Glacial (freshwater) Lake Vermont, the ancestor of the present Lake Champlain.

NEW ENGLAND

Marine clays, similar to those of the St. Lawrence Valley, can be seen at several places in Maine and New Hampshire, where

[3] See Dawson, J. W. "Notes on the Post-Pliocene Geology of Canada." Canadian. Nat. Quat. Jour. Sci., n.s., vol. 6, (1871).
[4] See Goldring, Winifred. "The Champlain Sea." N. Y. State Museum Bull. nos. 239-40, pp. 53-94, (1922). Howell, B. F. and Richards, Horace G. "The Fauna of the 'Champlain Sea' of Vermont." Nautilus, vol. 51, pp. 8-10, (1937).

they overlie glacial deposits, presumably of Wisconsin age. The most complete faunas, obtained at Saco and Portland, Maine, indicate a cold sea and contain several northern mollusks not at present living off the coast of New England. Marine fossiliferous clays are found up to two hundred or more feet above the sea in Maine, indicating a considerable rise of the land brought about by the release of the load of the ice.[5]

Fossils from this same post glacial sea are also known from northeastern Massachusetts, but there appears to be no trace of any such sea south of the Cape Cod region.

An interesting collection of mollusks was found some years ago in subway excavations in the city of Boston by Shimer.[6] Certain of the species of the mollusks were said to be rare or absent in the Boston region today and were suggestive of the coast of Virginia. Remnants of a fish weir were found in the same deposit. Shimer concluded:

The remnants of the fish weir, excavated on Boyleston Street, give evidence of man in the Back Bay region of Boston, probably 2000 to 3000 years ago. He built this weir during a climatic period as warm as off the Virginia coast today.

The glacial and post glacial history of the Boston region is somewhat complex as indicated by the studies of Shimer, Crosby and others.[7] However, the significance of the warm fauna is somewhat uncertain. It may represent the warm "post glacial temperature maximum" for which there is some evidence in Europe; or it may merely represent a local warm sheltered cove,

[5] For Pleistocene mollusks of Maine see: Clapp, F. G. "Complexity of the Glacial Period in northeastern New England." Bull. Geol. Soc. Amer., vol. 18, pp. 505-556, (1908). Little, H. P. "Pleistocene and Post-Pleistocene Geology of Waterville, Maine." Bull. Geol. Soc. Amer., vol. 28, pp. 309-322, (1917).

[6] Shimer, H. W. "Post-glacial History of Boston." Proc. Amer. Acad. of Arts and Sci., vol. 53, pp. 439-463, (1918).

[7] See Crosby, Irving B. "Evidence from Drumlins Concerning the Glacial History of Boston Basin." Bull. Geol. Soc. Amer., vol. 45, pp. 135-158 (1934). Crosby, Irving B. and Lougee, Richard J. "Glacial Marginal Shores and the Marine Limit in Massachusetts." Idem, pp. 441-462, (1934).

for it is now known that many of the so-called warm species are living much closer to Boston than Virginia, in fact they can be found in Massachusetts waters.

Marine fossiliferous deposits thought to be older than the Wisconsin have been reported by several observers in the Boston area, for instance under the drumlins. While the interglacial age of these deposits has not been definitely demonstrated, and the mollusks reported are of little or no climatic significance, nevertheless at Sankaty Head, on the island of Nantucket, Massachusetts, there are deposits that clearly indicate a warm climate. The lower part of the bluff near the lighthouse contains a fauna with several species of southern distribution that are extinct this far north; the upper part of the bluff contains a colder fauna with several species of Arctic or sub-Arctic affinities which are also now extinct in the region. The lower deposit is probably of interglacial age, while the colder fauna at the top may indicate the beginning of a colder climate and the approach of a glacial stage. From studies and correlations on Nantucket, Long Island, and elsewhere, it seems probable that the Sankaty Head fossils (Gardiners-Jacob formation) date from the last major interglacial stage (Sangamon).[8]

LONG ISLAND

Pleistocene marine deposits are exposed on Gardiner's Island, off the eastern tip of Long Island. Two faunas are recognized, one (in the Gardiners Clay) indicating a climate similar to that of the region today, and another fauna, stratigraphically above the Gardiners (Jacob Sand) indicating cooler ocean temperature. The Gardiners clay is interglacial, probably the last, while the cooler Jacob is regarded as transitional between the mild interglacial (Sangamon ?) and the cold glacial stage (Wisconsin ?).[9]

[8] For fauna of Sankaty Head see Cushman, J. A. "Pleistocene Deposits of Sankoty Head, Nantucket." Pub. Nantucket Maria Mitchell Ass., vol. 1, no. 1, (1906).

[9] See MacClintock, Paul and Richards, Horace G. "Correlation of Late Pleis-

Similar fossils have been obtained elsewhere on Long Island, either in place or from water wells or excavations.

NEW YORK CITY

Excavations for subways, tunnels, etc., in the vicinity of New York City have yielded considerable data on the Pleistocene history of the region. For example, recent excavations for the Midtown Hudson Tunnel have demonstrated a considerable thickness of silts on top of the Wisconsin glacial drift in the Hudson River Valley. The fauna, consisting of sixteen species of mollusks, indicates cool marine or brackish waters with perhaps a slight transition to warmer conditions at the top of the deposit; these silts are best interpreted as post-Wisconsin in age.

In a few places in the New York area, traces of pre-Wisconsin marine fossils have been found. Sometimes underneath the Wisconsin drift, and sometimes incorporated within the till, we find fossils indicating a warmer sea. The most interesting evidence in this connection is the finding of coquina in the excavations for the Midtown Hudson Tunnel. This coquina resembles the coquina now being formed in more southern waters.[10]

SOUTHERN ATLANTIC COASTAL PLAIN

South of the Terminal Moraine, in other words from New Jersey southward, we find no evidence of post-Wisconsin seas on the present land. It is believed that in this region the land was not notably depressed by the ice and that the last invasion of the sea occurred in interglacial times.

The Pleistocene deposits of this coastal plain consist of a series of terraces with low bluffs or beach ridges at their landward margins. These terraces are apparently horizontal, and the series ranges from twenty-five to two hundred and seventy feet in elevation. While a marine origin for all has been postulated,

tocene Marine and Glacial Deposits of New Jersey and New York." Bull. Geol. Soc. Amer., vol. 47, pp. 289-338, (1936).

[10] MacClintock and Richards. *Op. cit.*, p. 329 and plate 2.

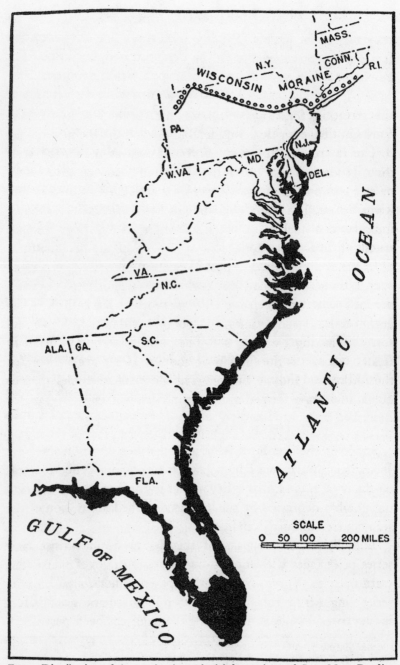

FIG. 3—Distribution of the marine interglacial formations of Cape May—Pamlico Age. Courtesy Geological Society of America.

only the lowest terrace (Pamlico with shore line at twenty-five feet elevation) can definitely be demonstrated as marine. The Pamlico terrace is remarkably horizontal from southern New Jersey to Florida, and marine fossils are found in the deposits of this terrace at a great many places; no marine fossils have been found in the deposits of any of the higher terraces.

The fauna of this terrace deposit (Cape May formation of New Jersey; Pamlico formation farther south) in all places indicates a temperature at least as warm as today and in many cases a warmer temperature, and is thought to date from the last major interglacial stage (Sangamon).[11] See Fig. 3 for map showing extent of the Pamlico sea.

In the deposits of the Cape May formation of New Jersey, such as those revealed by hydraulic dredging at Two Mile Beach, we find some fifteen species of mollusks that are extinct in this region today, but which are living in the warmer waters off the Carolinas or Florida. The remainder of the Cape May fauna of eighty-one species can be found in New Jersey waters today.[12]

In Maryland there is the famous Pleistocene locality at Wailes Bluff (Cornfield Harbor) on the Potomac River, which was described by Conrad as early as 1830. Here again the fauna indicates a water temperature slightly warmer than that of the region today.

Numerous similar localities could be mentioned in Virginia, North Carolina, South Carolina, Georgia and Florida. In all cases the fossils are found below the twenty-five-foot contour line, and in all cases the fauna suggests climatic conditions as warm as or slightly warmer than those prevailing in the same latitude today. This temperature difference, is, of course, less marked in Florida. For in Florida waters today we find a very

[11] See Richards, Horace G. "Fauna of the Pleistocene Pamlico Formation of the Southern Atlantic Coastal Plain." Bull. Geol. Soc. Amer., vol. 47, pp. 1611-1656, (1936).

[12] For fauna of Cape May formation see Richards, Horace G. "Marine Fossils from New Jersey Indicating a Mild Interglacial Stage." Proc. Amer. Philos. Soc., vol. 72, pp. 181-214, (1933).

rich marine fauna mostly of sub-tropical affinities, and a slight
rise in the temperature, while affecting considerably the fauna
of the region to the north of Florida, would probably affect very
slightly the fauna of Florida itself.

However, a few climatic changes in the fauna of Florida are
indicated by the shells. A fauna from a well at Delray (near
Palm Beach) studied by Vaughan[13] contains several species now
restricted to the Florida Keys and the West Indies.

The marine Pleistocene deposits of Florida equivalent to the
Pamlico formation are called the Anastasia formation, and consist largely of coquina. At Vero and Melbourne, Florida, this
coquina underlies the Melbourne Bone Bed where the "Vero
Man" was discovered some years ago.

If the coquina can be correlated with the Pamlico terrace, and
if it thus dates from the last major interglacial stage, as appears
probable from paleontological and stratigraphic studies, the
overlying Melbourne Bone Bed is either Wisconsin or younger,
most probably early post-Wisconsin.[14]

GULF COASTAL PLAIN

Sufficient work has not yet been done on the Pleistocene mollusks of the Gulf of Mexico Coastal Plain to obtain valid conclusions on the Pleistocene climate of the region. The marine shells
thus far collected from the Pleistocene of this coast—Florida to
Texas—are practically the same as those living in the Gulf of
Mexico today. On the other hand, a few Pleistocene fresh-water
mollusks from Mississippi and Louisiana do indicate a slightly
cooler climate than that of the region today. It is hoped that
further studies and correlations of the marine and fresh-water
Pleistocene deposits of this region will shed further light on the
Pleistocene climatic history of the Gulf Coastal Plain.

[13] See Vaughan, T. W. "A Contribution to the Geologic History of the
Floridian Plateau." Carn. Inst. Wash., Pub. 133, pp. 99-185, (1910).
[14] See Cooke, C. W. and Mossom, S. "Geology of Florida." 20th Ann. Rept.
Fla. State Geol. Surv., (1929). Richards, Horace G. "Studies on the Pleistocene
of Florida." Carn. Inst. Wash. Yearbook No. 35, pp. 323-325, (1936).

CERTAIN RELATIONS BETWEEN NORTHWESTERN AMERICA AND NORTHEASTERN ASIA

BY

PHILIP S. SMITH

Chief Alaskan Geologist, United States Geological Survey*

Students of the early migrations of man and animals have long recognized the mingling of Asiatic and American aspects in many of the forms that have come to their attention. Obviously the intermingling or close affinities of certain species or objects from the two continents do not require actual land connections for their accomplishment, because birds and salt-water fishes or animals might well pass unrestrictedly between the two under the existing conditions of separation. Present-day man with only his skin boats frequently makes the passage from parts of one continent to the other with little hazard. Could early man have done likewise? Necessarily the geologist can give only a partial answer to this inquiry, because it calls for knowledge of early man's mental processes which obviously the geologist does not possess. He can, however, assert with considerable positiveness that since Tertiary time at least the gap between the two continents in the northern part of the Bering Sea area has not been materially wider than the gap that now exists. The greatest submergence since the Tertiary in this general area of which there is evidence does not exceed 600 feet below present sea level. Submergence to this depth might have opened a new waterway less than 4 miles wide a few miles east of Bering Strait, but it

* Published by permission of the Director of the United States Geological Survey.

would not have widened the present Bering Strait perceptibly, because Cape Mountain, America, and East Cape, Asia, the limiting bastions of that strait, rise precipitously to elevations far above that level. Within the strait there are three rocky islands, the largest of which, Big Diomede, is 4 miles long and 1,759 feet high. Thus there is no broad unbroken expanse of water in the 56 miles that now separate the two mainlands. Instead, the longest stretch of open water is only 25 miles. This is of significance in trying to forecast early man's reaction to this natural gap. Standing on the highlands adjacent to Cape Prince of Wales, even in only moderately clear weather one can usually see plainly the outlines of Fairway Rock and the Diomedes midway in the Strait, and in clear weather the Asiatic coast from East Cape southward for miles is distinctly recognizable. It would therefore seem to require little more temerity for primitive man to have attempted to traverse this gap after he had acquired the art of constructing even crude watercraft than it would to make journeys of similar length along the coasts of his own continent. He would not have had to make a serious incursion into the realms of the mysterious unknown, for he would have long been familiar with the general appearance of these lands; nor would it have required navigating skill and aptitude, because his objective could have been in plain sight throughout the whole journey. Bering Sea and the Arctic Ocean in this region are devoid of strong tidal range—a diurnal tide of a foot being perhaps the average range throughout a considerable area. As a result early man would have been able to disregard tides in his wanderings there. True, during the open season there is usually a strong current flowing northward into the Arctic Ocean through Bering Strait. Such a current has doubtless existed as long as the contiguous lands have stood with their present configuration and might well have played a role in transporting, perhaps involuntarily, from one continent to the other persons or things. Probably few, if any, crossings in the immediate neighborhood of the strait have been made on drift ice except through accident, because there the ice is usually most broken up and in most active motion. Farther from the straits the ice is usually in larger fields and less mobile. To the south the big ice masses break up and disappear during the summer, but to the north the masses become more and more numerous until finally they form part of the great perpetual packs that make an almost continuous expanse of ice to the pole. Deliberate crossing from continent to continent on the ice was probably not early undertaken by man and was accomplished, if at all, to the north rather than in or to the south of the strait. Temperate-climate dwellers who think of vast fields of sea ice as almost insuperable barriers to migration should realize that in reality this is not a correct view. The ice surfaces allow fully as easy travel by sled or on foot as do the ordinary land surfaces, and near the margin of the ice or along leads through it there is almost always an abundance of animal life such as seal, walrus, whale, and fish that can be relied on for food or other uses.

In contrast with the nearness of the two continents at Bering Strait, at other places they do not lie close enough to each other to be intervisible. For instance, the nearest land tie between the two mainlands by way of the Aleutian and Komandorski Islands includes several gaps of more than 100 miles in width. Thus the distance from the Asiatic mainland to the nearest of the Komandorski group is 115 miles and from the easternmost point of that group to the westernmost point of Attu Island, the nearest island of the Aleutian group, is 175 miles. The overcoming of such distances necessarily requires far more seafaring skill and courage than does the crossing of the Bering Strait gap. Also, the Aleutian area lies far south of the zone in which extensive areas of sea ice form or reach during the winter, so that that means of ferriage is precluded at the present time, and so far as is shown by geologic records, was not available even during the greatest expansion of ice during the Glacial period. Strong treacherous currents characterize the waterways between the islands in the Aleutian group, and rugged water for small boats is to be expected in them at all times. Thus, crossing by this route would always be a precarious undertaking, calling for the exercise of exceptional seafaring skill and navigating ability.

It is not sufficient, however, to review the present conditions and to show that in places the two continents have stood for a long time about as near each other as they now are, because certain relations of present-day animals and plants require closer intercommunication, and one rightly wants to know whether or not at some not too remote time they stood closer together or were even actually land connected. Unfortunately, the geologist is not yet able to give positive answers to these questions. Evidence of former higher stands of the land bordering this sea is not now subject to direct observation in this area because such records are now covered by the sea. That certain parts of Seward Peninsula have stood higher in the recent past cannot be doubted in the face of the physiographic evidence of recent submergence of such embayments as the head of Norton Bay, Golofnin Sound, Imuruk Basin, Shishmaref Lagoon, Eschscholtz Bay, Selawik Lake, and Hotham Inlet. The amount of the subsequent downward movement at these places has not been determined, though evidently the more recent movements have not been great. In addition to this qualitative evidence the mining work in the vicinity of Nome has afforded some quantitative measure of subsidence. Near Nome excavations that have been made at places to a depth of 30 feet below the present sea level have penetrated old beach deposits formed when the land stood at least that amount higher with relation to the sea than it now does. It is true that none of these bits of evidence indicate much movement, but it must be remembered that they probably record

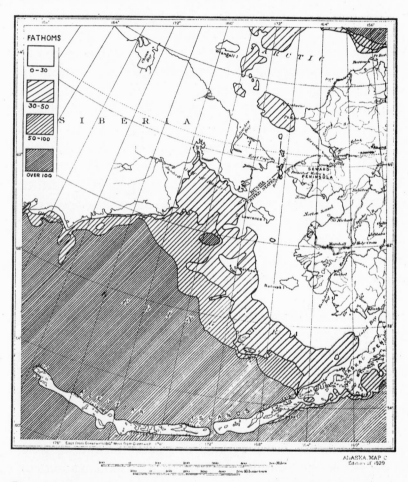

PLATE VI—Sea depths of Bering Sea area (on U. S. Geol. Survey base map).

only a small part of the total movement that has taken place, and furthermore, that even a small amount of uplift would profoundly modify the present relations between land and water in the northern part of Bering Sea and the southern part of the Arctic Ocean because of the extreme shallowness of those water bodies. The charts, showing the depths of these waters, indicate that there are tens of thousands of square miles of the floors of these seas that now are covered by water less than 200 feet deep and hundreds of thousands of square miles that are covered by water less than 600 feet deep. Such shallow depths obviously do not partake of the qualities of portions of true ocean basins but are rather to be regarded as slightly submerged margins of the continents. Plate VI illustrates the depths of water reported in various parts of Bering Sea and the Arctic Ocean, and shows that throughout much of the area covered by these water bodies within 500 miles north or south of Bering Strait the sea floor is a nearly featureless plain, practically all of which lies less than 100 fathoms below the surface and considerable tracts of it less than 30 fathoms. In fact, from the specific soundings recorded on the Coast Survey charts it would appear possible that a course could be laid out between the two continents where depths of water not to exceed 20 fathoms (120 feet) might be found. Movements of this magnitude would well be regarded by geologists as insignificant. Certain calculations based on the amount of water withdrawn from the sea to furnish the ice of the greatly expanded continental glaciers of the past, place the lowering of the seas of the globe due to this cause alone as perhaps equivalent to twice this amount. Thus, Daly,[1] summarizing his own and his predecessors' investigations, reaches the conclusion that the amount of water abstracted from the oceans to build the ice sheets of the latest Pleistocene stage would have lowered the

[1] Daly, R. A., "The changing world of the Ice age," pp. 11-12, 46-50. Yale Press. New Haven. 1934.

ocean level over the globe something like 85 meters (approximately 280 feet), and to build the ice sheets of the Pleistocene
at their maximum extent would have abstracted something like
105 meters (approximately 345 feet). These figures are based
on the assumption that the glaciers of the particular stage
analyzed reached their maximum extent contemporaneously
throughout the world—an assumption that, while not correct, is
sufficiently so for indicating the approximate scale of the phenomenon. Such removal of weight from over the ocean basins
and loading of the ice-covered land areas doubtless would have
also tended to cause some rise of the sea floors and consequently
further shallowing of the water bodies. Though it is not possible
to express the amount of these combined movements quantita-
tively, it is readily apparent that the result, if not offset by other
earth processes, would have been sufficient to form extensive
land connections between the two continents. Obviously, however, the mere sufficiency of a process to accomplish a certain
result is by no means to be accepted as demonstrating that it
actually effected that result.

Other processes equally competent to have brought about
land connections between Asia and America, and, not opposed
by any known evidence, might well be evoked by geologists.
Thus it is by no means unlikely that in the past there have been
broad warpings of the lands or sea floors produced by other
readjustments within the earth's crust which may have brought
above water level in this area parts of what is now the sea floor.
Indeed, warping of some of the old surfaces now above the level
of the sea has long been recognized in Seward Peninsula. Evidences of such movements are well recognized in some of the old
buried beaches at Nome which now are found scores of feet
above the elevation at which they were formed.

Despite the absence of tangible evidence of actual land connection there are thus a number of processes known to have

been active, any one of which might have brought about the relatively minor changes that would be required to make such connections. The geologist, therefore, reviewing such evidence as is available and bears on the subject, can hardly fail to believe that it is more likely than not that such connections have occurred. However, if land connections existed, it by no means necessarily follows that early man would have had incentives that led him to utilize these connections for migration. To one who thinks of Alaska as a land of perpetual ice and snow and who, extrapolating that concept back into the time when much of the eastern part of the northern hemisphere was glacier ridden, consequently postulates even more intolerable conditions then, this is perhaps a real difficulty. One who knows the real conditions, however, realizes that Alaska did and does present incentives for migration. Unlike most of Northern United States and practically all of Canada, in Alaska the glaciers of the Ice Age were restricted almost entirely to the mountain areas of the Alaska and Coast Ranges in southern Alaska and the Brooks Range in northern Alaska. None of these old glaciers deployed far into the lowlands beyond the fronts of these ranges, so that practically the entire central part of the Territory, an area several hundred miles from north to south and nearly 1,000 miles from east to west, at no time during the Quaternary was glaciated. This area, roughly about three-fifths of the Territory, may well have been a haven and place of refuge for animals and plants forced out from other regions by the growing ice sheets of the Pleistocene. Indeed it may even have connected with routes by which migration could at times have passed between the westward encroaching ice sheets of eastern North America and those originating in the western mountains of that continent. Very likely such connecting routes were at times cut off by the coalescence of the ice sheets from these two centers, but when open they must have offered many advantages over routes subject to the tempestuous waters of the ocean or the hardships of overland travel through forbidding mountain tracts. Thus, in Alaska there were several hundred thousand square miles that lay beyond the margin of even the extensive glaciers that originated in its mountains, so that in that area was an attractive and not a repellant land, and the fossil remains of its then existing flora and fauna show that it could well have supplied the wants of many migrant people passing through or dwelling within it.

EARLY MAN IN AMERICA: WHAT HAVE THE BONES TO SAY?

BY

ALEŠ HRDLIČKA

Curator of Physical Anthropology, United States National Museum

Extensive experience with human remains in the Old World teaches that whenever such remains approach or are of geological antiquity, that is when they are older than the present geological, climatic and biological conditions, they show, at least in some respects, more primitive features; and primitive features are such as approximate the parts concerned to their early human or prehuman conditions. Even the skulls of five to three thousand years ago, while in general much like those of the less cultured man of today, show collectively, it is now known, more especially in the teeth, the lower jaws and other facial features, distinctly less advanced characters. On the basis of this the physical anthropologist is justified to expect that American specimens of presumably geological antiquity should behave similarly. Such a demand might possibly be thwarted by a rare individual example, but certainly not repeatedly or even invariably.

The matter in America, however, is not so simple. It is complicated by the fact, less manifest perhaps elsewhere, that individual skulls of recent and even the present-day American aborigines not seldom show features that are more primitive, in instances even considerably more primitive, than the average in the white races. There are American skulls of recent date that are practically replicas of the Magdalenian and even of some of the upper Aurignacian skulls of the Old World and there are occasional skulls that in some of their characteristics remind one even of the Neanderthalers. Should such specimens be found under conditions suggesting geological age they could readily be taken on morphological ground as sustaining such a determination.

A few lines may here be useful as to the general status of recent American skeletal material. America in course of time received from Asia not one but several types of the yellow-brown man. These types, while presenting a basic racial unity, differ as widely in the form of the skull as do the various contingents of the white stem. Almost every shape of the vault of the skull that is found elsewhere in the world—barring alone the negro regions—is represented also in the American Indian. The variety ranges from extreme dolichocephaly to hyper-brachycephaly; from low to high vault; and through all the other as well as the intermediary shapes. There are further whole gamuts almost of variants in the breadth and length of the nose, the height, breadth, form and size of the orbits, development of the teeth and the jaws. And there is much variation in such characters as the supraorbital ridges, the suborbital ("canine") fossae, alveolar prognathism, and other features. There cannot but be expected, therefore, on the American continent great heterogeneity of cranial (not to speak of other) variants, and one or another of these not only may, but under the conditions must, resemble cranial types of older age, or of other parts of the world.

These facts are obvious enough to the expert, but regrettably they do not as yet constitute a part of the necessary mental outfit of all the younger workers in these lines and especially of those in collateral fields of scientific endeavor; which has resulted in serious errors and much unnecessary confusion. These conditions, moreover, are not as yet sufficiently clear to many of our colleagues abroad where matters differ, and this has led in the course of time to numerous disharmonies or misunderstandings.

All the preceding condenses into three recognitions of importance, so far as American aboriginal skeletal material is concerned; these are: 1) the justified expectation, wherever a claim of geological antiquity of such remains and particularly of the skull is concerned, of generalized, not merely localized, and repeated, not merely individual, primitive features; 2) the unreliability, with any single skull or skeleton, of whatever moderately primitive features they may present, as decisive criteria of antiquity; and 3) the impossibility of attributing any of the possible American cranial variants to non-American racial groups, particularly to those of other than the yellow-brown stem of humanity.

We may now pass in a brief review the skeletal remains on the American continent that since 1918 have been attributed to geological antiquity. All previous finds of this nature have been dealt with in Bulletins 33 and 52 of the Bureau of American Ethnology[1] and found wanting.

MAN AND MASTODON IN FLORIDA

All will recall the announcements in 1916 by Dr. E. H. Sellards, at that time State Geologist of Florida, of the discovery of ancient man near Vero, Florida. The original impressions, as in so many other instances, could not be sustained and had to be added to the already large category of plausible but non-proven cases.[2]

In 1923 and subsequent years new finds of somewhat similar nature began to appear near Melbourne, about thirty miles north

[1] "Skeletal Remains Suggesting or Attributed to Early Man in N. America." Bull. 33, Bur. Am. Ethn., Wash., 1907, 1-113. "Early man in South America." Bull. 52, Bur. Am. Ethn., Washington, 1912, 1-405.
[2] For details and literature see Jour. Geol., 1917; and especially Bull. 66, Bur. Am. Ethnol., 1918.

of Vero. Within three miles of the town of Melbourne three localities were found by a local man, Mr. G. L. Singleton, in which human relics were associated with the bones of extinct animals. Excavations on these sites were carried on first by Professor F. B. Loomis of Amherst, and later by Mr. J. B. Gidley of the National Museum. The lay of the ground, the deposits and the finds were described by Gidley and Loomis.[3]

The main locality where human remains were found was at the "Golf Club site, about two miles west of Indian River at Melbourne, on the east bank of the large drainage canal, and about 200 feet southwest of the club house on the Melbourne golf course. The surface of the ground here was underlain by eighteen inches to two feet of stratified deposits containing much vegetable matter and typical of the No. 3 bed of the Vero district. This bed was absolutely undisturbed until removed by the excavations. Below lay the No. 2 bed, which at this place was shown to be about five feet thick and to rest on the No. 1 bed."

A crushed human skull with its attached lower jaw was found here, in the upper part of bed 2. It was flattened horizontally as if it had been pushed down into the sand from above; and over it lay, "undisturbed, stratified material" of the No. 3 bed.

Dr. Gidley's conclusions were summarized as follows:

"From this reëxamination of the fossil-bearing stream deposits at Vero Beach, and this detailed study of similar deposits in the Melbourne district, which has furnished important new evidence, it may safely be assumed that man, although of modern type, reached Florida before the total extinction of the mammoths and mastodons. But that this arrival occurred far within Pleistocene time does not seem probable. Mammoths and mastodons are known to have survived in the Great Lakes regions up to the time of the formation of the swamp deposits which

[3] "Fossil Man in Florida," Am. J. Sci., XII, September 1926, 254-264.

PLATE VII—The Melbourne Skull. Fig. 1—Front view. Fig. 2—Side view. Fig. 3—Dorsal view.

followed the last retreat of the glaciers in North America, and it seems not improbable that a considerable remnant of the Pleistocene fauna survived the glacial periods in Florida and other localities of the southern and southwestern United States, and remained there after the great ice sheets had disappeared in the North. However this may be finally concluded, the present evidence as here interpreted seems to indicate quite clearly that the time of man's first appearance in Florida should be placed at a time much earlier than has hitherto been supposed, possibly early post-Pleistocene, and that these people seem to have preceded the Indians who built the mounds characteristic of the east coast of Florida."

The one find that needs to be critically discussed is the crushed skull of the Golf Club locality.

The skull lay within two and one-half feet from the surface, possibly not over two feet—the account is not quite precise in this respect. This may have no significance, but the suggestion can hardly be escaped that this would be just about the depth of an average Indian ground burial.

The skull was accompanied by "pieces of finger, arm and leg bones." In addition a clavicle lay in just about the position it would have occupied in the body (see Plate VII). Details about these skeletal parts are missing, and there is no photograph that would show their lay. The likelihood is that they represented what remained of a skeleton. This again rather suggests a burial.

The deposits above the bones are said to have been undisturbed. Such a conclusion is very risky in such deposits. Wide experience in excavation teaches that with many burials, Indian and others, after a few decades or scores or especially hundreds of years, all traces of disturbance disappear and that there may be even more or less of secondary stratification over the remains. Only where the pierced materials were sufficiently heterogeneous will signs of disturbance be permanent.

Mineralization of the bones is no safe criterion of antiquity; besides which the Melbourne bones are not mineralized to any great extent. The subject has been amply discussed in Bulletins 33 and 52 of the Bureau of American Ethnology. In many parts of Florida in particular, it is difficult to find human bones that have not suffered more or less of mineralization.

The fossil animal bones found near the skull were all single pieces or fragments, which makes it very probable that they were of secondary deposition and hence could not safely date the deposits in which they lay. Besides which there is always the question as to just when such forms really became extinct in the region.

The presence of arrow points, chips of flint and agate, and pieces of broken pottery in the same layer in which lay the golf course skeleton, speaks strongly for Indian origins.

The Melbourne skull finally, now reconstructed, though defective, is evidence enough in itself. It is the skull of an Indian male, of advanced adult age, undeformed, brachycranic, high, and, in general presenting the ordinary Florida mound Indian type and characters.

In view of all the above, it is difficult to see on what, legitimately, could be based any claim in the case of more than moderate antiquity.

HOMO NOVUS MUNDUS

In July, 1935, J. D. Figgins, for years now associated with claims of ancient man in the Southwest, published an article under the title of "New World Man,"[4] in which he described a skull from a skeleton found thirteen and one-half feet deep in the alluvial deposits in a bank of the Cimarron River, eight miles from Folsom, New Mexico.

[4] Proceedings of the Colorado Museum of Natural History, XIV, No. 1, 4 pp., 4 pl.

Later, in 1936, the skull was sent for examination to a number of American anthropologists, including the writer, and the results were published recently by Frank H. H. Roberts.[5] The gist of their conclusions follow:

Hooton: "Crania resembling this specimen are to be found in the Southwest among the Utes and other tribes, and I am of the opinion that skulls of this general type occur sporadically in series of American crania from various parts of the country."

Hrdlička: "There is only one possible conclusion, which is that the Figgins skull is that of an American Indian of a somewhat inferior type but of a type the elements of which are rather common in certain parts of California and other regions."

Shapiro: "I find no justification for setting up a new species in which to house this skull. It does not fall outside the range of American Indians."

Woodbury: "In the Paiute crania of Nevada and Utah "the same characteristics that distinguish *Homo novus mundus* are present although perhaps to a slightly less pronounced degree. There is a striking similarity between them."

"Pleistocene" Man in Southern California

In *Science*, December 4, 1936 (507-8), A. O. Bowden and I. A. Lopatin, of the University of Southern California, announce the discovery of a "pleistocene" human skull near Los Angeles. The specimen, with other bones of the skeleton, was unearthed by PWA workers in excavations for a storm drain from Los Angeles to the sea, "from a gray sandy clay resting immediately upon gravel some 13 feet below the surface." There were seemingly no other specimens with or near the bones, but "about 1000 feet from the site where the human remains were found, several bones of a large animal (mammoth) were discovered." The fact that the human bones and those of the mammoth were

[5] *American Antiquity*, 1937, II, 172-7.

found in the same geological stratum, which a geologist of the University concluded to be Pleistocene, enabled the authors "to conclude that both the man and mammoth had lived at approximately the same time, i.e., at the closing of the Pleistocene Epoch."

The skull is defective, lacking the face and the frontal portion of the vault. It is mineralized. It probably belonged to a female well advanced in years. The authors have this to say about it: "In comparing this skull with other female skulls found in America it is seen that in breadth (132 mm.) and in basion-bregma height (131 mm.) it is rather close to the 'Basket Maker' cranium. The height-breadth index of the Los Angeles skull is considerable—99.24; therefore, it should be classified as acrocranial. On account of the damaged state of the Los Angeles skull it cannot be measured as to maximum length, but in all probability the skull is dolichocephalic. . . . The cranium exhibits no striking primitive features which would justify classification of its owner as a lower being. On the contrary, the brain box is decidedly human, and the individual is a representative of our species."

It is hardly necessary to add that the claim of the specimen to any great age, both from the geological and from the anthropological point of view, is rather slim.

THE HYPERDOLICHOCRANIC SKULLS OF THE SOUTHWEST

Since 1840, when Lund explored the caves of Lagoa Santa, in Brazil, there have been coming to light in South and later in North America,[6] exceptionally narrow, long, and high vaulted crania. Similar types have become known from the sambaquis of Brazil. Ten Kate, and in 1894 Diquet, found them in Lower California. In 1917-19 Van Valin found the type near Point

[6] See my "Melanesians and Australians and the People of America." Smithson. Misc. Coll., Wash., 1935, XCIV, No. 11.

Barrow.[7] I have mentioned its occurrence among the Delawares, the northeastern Algonkins, the Seward Peninsula, the northern and especially the Greenland and Labrador Eskimo. Since 1880 they have been known from Coahuila,[8] since the nineties from southeastern Utah.[9] Within recent years they have begun to appear from various parts of Texas[10] as well as northern Coahuila. At the latest (1936-7) they are occurring, and not rarely, among the Algonkin crania from along the Potomac.

This type of crania at first (Lagoa Santa) was regarded as very ancient, later on[6] as un-Indian. As a matter of fact it is a peculiarly American variant, at times of probably mutational origin, wide-spread over this continent, and either more or less recently extinct or reaching to our own times.

THE MINNESOTA MAN

The essentials of the find are concisely expressed by Professor Jenks, its sponsor, thus:[11] "On June 16, 1931, a human skeleton was found in Minnesota[12] within 'the Missouri and Mississippi drainage area in undisturbed glacial deposits,' documented by geological and historical evidence, whose morphology indicates an early primitive type of Homo sapiens. We believe this skeleton represents glacial man in America . . . an early type of Homo sapiens of primitive Mongoloid affinity."

The details of the find are not as clear as would be desirable.[13] The first information, from a supervisor of the work (June 18,

[7] Anthropological Survey in Alaska. 46th Ann. Rep. B. A. E., Washington, 1930.

[8] Coll. by Edward Palmer; described by Cordelia A. Studley, Ann. Rep. Peabody Mus., Cambridge, Mass., 1884, 233 et seq.

[9] Catalogue of Crania, U. S. Nat. Mus., 1931.

[10] Hooton (E. A.). Bull. Tex. Arch. & Paleont. Soc., 1933, V, 25-38. Stewart (T.D.). Am. J. Phys. Anthrop., 1935, XX, 213 et seq.

[11] "Pleistocene Man in Minnesota. A fossil Homo sapiens." By Jenks (Albert Ernest); with a chapter on the Pleistocene geology of the Prairie Lake Region by Geo. A. Thiel. 4to, Minneapolis, 1935, 197 pp., 89 illustra. Univ. Minn. Press.

[12] Westernmost part of the State, region of the Detroit Lakes.

[13] See essentials also in Am. J. Phys. Anthrop., Jan.-March No., 1937.

'31) reads: "The men working on highway number 30 have found two human skeletons in a new cut, one of which was 'shallow,' near the surface. The other was ten to twelve feet below the surface in 'clay silt.' It was not found until ripped out by the scraper. They believe there were a good many bones of the skeleton. With it they found a piece of bone, eight or ten inches long, with a hole in one end, and a shell which may have been used as a cup and which had two holes drilled in it. There were also other pieces of shell recovered."

Dr. C. R. Stauffer, a geologist sent out by Professor Jenks, reported thus: The skeleton in question came from the middle of the highway (No. 30). The road had been finished and in use for some time, but the clayey or silty material of this particular cut heaved a great deal during wet weather. It was therefore decided to plow a ditch along the center of the grade and fill it with gravel. It was during this process that skeleton No. 1 was unearthed.

The skeleton was dug out by the road workers and "all the men who were present agreed that the skeleton lay on the left side with the skull in the middle of the road, lying a little south of east and the remainder of the skeleton extending toward the west shoulder of the road. The face was turned somewhat upward so that the right part of the frontal was uppermost in the silt. The legs were bent slightly backward at the knees. The upper legs were just noticeably flexed forward at the pelvis. The right arm was bent at the elbow so that the forearm lay to the left in front of the vertebral column, and the upper arm was on top of the ribs and vertebrae. The left arm was beneath the ribs and practically straight beneath or just in front of the body. It was noted that the skeleton appeared to be lowest at the left shoulder, the legs lying slightly higher in the silt. It was estimated that the skeleton lay in the silt at a depth of ten inches below the grader blade, or about 3.3 feet below the road-bed."

For the further history of the find and the results of its study it is necessary, due to lack of space here, to refer to the originals. The conclusions of Professor Jenks derived by him from the study of the skeleton, were as follows: "The measured and observed morphological characters of this skeleton proclaim it to be a primitive Homo sapiens, of an early type of evolving Mongoloid, already prophetically suggesting American aborigines, especially the Eskimo, more than the present Asian Mongoloids. Minnesota Man represents a group of primitive Mongoloids living in west-central Minnesota at the time the ice of the last glaciation had retreated northward and westward only as far as the Big Stone Moraine, about twenty thousand years ago, in late Pleistocene time" (p. 177).

A painstaking comparison, point by point, of the Minnesota skull with a fairly large series of female crania of the Indian people who up to some decades ago roamed over the territory of its discovery, leaves no room for any uncertainty as to its type and hence its appurtenance. The type is the characteristic type of the Sioux, which differs substantially from that of other North American Indians; and the skull after the comparisons here recorded, which are seconded by the visual observations, could not possibly be attributed by any expert worker to any other people than the Sioux.

As a Sioux, however, the skull and skeleton cannot be assumed to be twenty, nor ten nor even a few thousand years old, for on one hand the vast Sioux region has not shown hitherto any sites or accumulations which could represent any such period, and on the other hand it could not be assumed, without overwhelming proofs to the contrary, that the same type of American man could have remained in the same limited territory for such thousands of years and that without a modification.

Just how the skeleton came to where it was found in all probability can never be determined; but the evidence of the completeness of the remains and their lay indicates more a regular burial than an accidental involvement in the deposits.

On the whole should a professional and experienced professional physical anthropologist be given the task of proving by its somatic characteristics the Minnesota skull and skeleton as ancient or even really primitive, he would have to give up in despair. The task would be impossible.

CONCLUDING REMARKS

After all the preceding, there appears only one possible answer that physical anthropology can give to the question posed in the title of this discussion. This is, that so far as human skeletal remains are concerned, there is to this moment no evidence that would justify the assumption of any great, i.e., geological, antiquity.

It is greatly to be wished that all our workers both in archaeology and anthropology, and also, if I may dare to suggest, in geology and palaeontology, might find the opportunity to spend at least a season in Europe, particularly in France, the home of earlier man of all periods, where his remains may be seen and studied to great advantage. Such a trip would constitute invaluable sound basis for future American experiences with which they undoubtedly from time to time will be confronted.

FIRST PEOPLING OF AMERICA AS A CHRONOLOGICAL PROBLEM

BY

HERBERT J. SPINDEN

Curator of Primitive and Prehistoric Art,
The Brooklyn Institute of Arts and Sciences

THIS paper reviews some of the general evidence on the peopling of America. It does not concern the origin of man, or his earliest culture, which admittedly belong to the Old World. Rather it concerns the transfer to America, via the Siberia-Alaskan bridge, of a racial division of Homo sapiens, or modern man, bearing the relatively advanced neolithic arts with the flint knife and the stone axe as accepted symbols. In other words, my thesis is that the red man was the first human to enter America, and that he had the contemporary civilization of nomadic hunting-and-fishing tribes of northern Europe and northern Asia.

There is nothing very startling in this thesis. Few persons now venture to argue that man reached America before the last glaciation. Once there were high hopes of validating sporadic stone tools of outwardly primitive types, reported from many localities, but not occurring in proper situations of geological antiquity. The battle for paleolithic American man, fought on the single basis of the typology of tools, without support from circumstances of deposition or from associated human bones below the present standards, was necessarily lost, and it seems unlikely that that battle can ever be refought.

Modern man first appeared in the Old World when the reindeer was browsing in the Pyrenees, and ice sheets covered a large part of Europe and a still larger part of America. Ice-free territory in northern Asia was probably not humanly habitable. Indeed, if we plot on a map the sites of lower paleolithic age, as well as those of the Aurignacian, Solutrean and Magdalenian stages of Old World human cultures, we find a consistent northern demarcation of the early human range in both Europe and Asia even when we pass into non-glaciated territory. This demarcation in itself rules out invasion of America till relatively modern times.

It has often been said that man is by nature a tropical or subtropical animal and that his entrance into the more rigorous climates was only made possible by clothing, shelter and other adaptations outside his own body. The farthest north definitely determined for a lower paleolithic culture lies about 54° north latitude, near the River Nidd in central England. In southern Siberia upper paleolithic remains occur a little beyond 50° on the Yenessei and at 53° at Mal'ta near the outlet of Lake Baikal. But the portal to the New World lies at the Arctic Circle beyond a no-proof barrier zone a thousand miles deep extending clear across the Old World. It is not until we come to the Maglamose culture phase of the northern mesolithic, when forests were reclothing old tundra zones and the ice was retreating rapidly, that we find proofs of man's invasion of sub-arctic territories.

Before an ice-free road to America can be hailed with any degree of satisfaction as a factor in the peopling of the New World, it must be shown that man was prepared to travel that road. Nor can we wisely infer that man's habitat extended to the Arctic foreshore until traces of his habitations, his tools, or his bones are discovered in high latitudes. I am aware that Menghin has postulated a northern bone culture but on theoretical rather than positive grounds.

During mesolithic time the stages of northern invasion are clearly documented. This advance covered Denmark and finally reached Esthonia and the Gulf of Finland, or let us say 60° north latitude, still well short of the Arctic Circle. We now find a really notable correlation of evidence collected by various sciences—changes in shore lines and in the character of Baltic waters, changes in the forest cover, changes in climate. Men now live a fishing and hunting life by forest and stream. Already hardy frontiersmen are pushing along the strandways of Jutland, Gotland and Norway as the Gulf Stream melts back the exposed glacial front. During the period of Ancylus Lake the Duvensee, Maglamose and Kunda phases, each reach a little farther north. New implements appear which lead upward to American Indian technology; but the road is still a long one to travel. We may safely reconstruct canoes from paddles, we have harpoons and fish hooks, bone daggers with side-hafted flints, long-toothed combs and a little amber jewelry. The axe is in process of evolution and whether its origin is placed in the Baltic area or in some more southern area it pretty certainly belongs to forest peoples.

In the Littorina time of the salt water Baltic the kitchen middens show a cultural stage which is transitional to the true neolithic with the crudest of stone axes. The full neolithic technology does not appear to have reached the Arctic till about 2500 B.C., if as early.

We should remember that the microlithic tools really have a wide dispersal in Europe, Asia and Africa. The Maglamose is but a special phase of a wide manner of human adjustment, which everywhere is pre-agricultural although the last southern phases of it may indicate the borderline of grain-gathering economy. Menghin is right, I think, in his insistence that one order of man's cultural evolution ended with the Mousterian and that the upper paleolithic and the mesolithic should be combined to

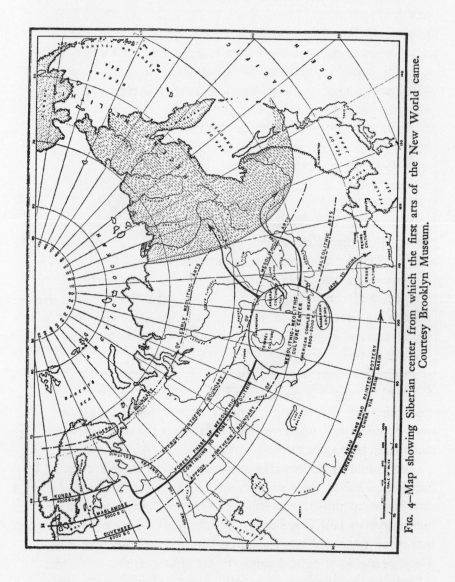

Fig. 4—Map showing Siberian center from which the first arts of the New World came.
Courtesy Brooklyn Museum.

make a second order. *Homo sapiens* was fitted to accept fresh tasks in social adjustment with the result that differentiation in his material and immaterial achievements became more pronounced. Miss Garrod says: "The Natufian, in spite of certain general features common to the great majority of microlithic industries, is definitely original, as indeed might be expected,.

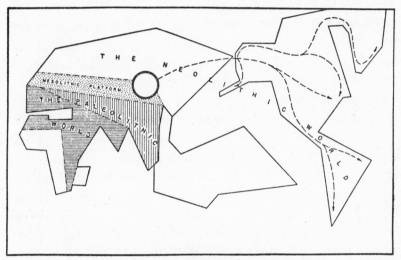

FIG. 5—Basic World Relations of Paleolithic and Neolithic Cultures. Courtesy Brooklyn Museum.

since by this time local differentiation all over the world is much more marked than in earlier periods."

Origin of the neolithic in connection with an agricultural complex in Egypt, Mesopotamia, etc., may call for earlier dates than those of the full neolithic for hunters and fishermen in high northern latitudes. But the peopling of America demands first of all the peopling of northern Europe and northern Asia. The classical setting is far removed from this purpose.

Socially speaking, neolithic arts mean sedentary life with leisure and specialized activities. Realistic and decorative designs

are used throughout the entire epi-paleolithic period to improve
the game supply and lay ghosts, and no great change is needed
to make the philosophy fit an agricultural regime. Hunter's
magic and maternity magic shift in part to agricultural purposes.
The cult of the dead, with cemeteries near villages, changes from
disease prevention and other contaminations to the idea of rebirth and rejuvenation. It is clear that the Indians carried to
America the animistic doctrine.

The time limits of the neolithic on the Mediterranean cannot
be understood as establishing maximum and minimum dates for
eastern Asia and perhaps the best point of attack on Far Eastern
chronology is found in the start of the Chinese bronze age.

In recent years there has been a remarkable advance in knowledge of early China, first concerning the occurrence of truly
neolithic art and secondly concerning the formation of the
Chinese national style in both pottery and bronze. At Anyang,
capital of the Shang Dynasty, a neolithic substratum has been
revealed. The painted pottery on this level shows little relationship to the white modelled pottery on the level of the earliest
bronzes. But a layer of plain black pottery separates the two and
very recently, according to Creel, deposits of this black ware
have been found at a new site which furnish evidence of transition leading up to the white ware with bronze age designs.

The existence of a Chinese neolithic stage was first demonstrated by Andersson in 1921—the now famous Yang shao culture with painted pottery in a bold primitive style. This was in
Honan; afterwards sites in Kansu and other provinces were explored and the material divided into early, late and middle, now
supplemented by a transitional style already discussed. Andersson isolated from ordinary household pottery a special mortuary
style which may take its patterns from those on antecedent
burial matting. Connections between these northern Chinese
wares and the pottery of Anau in Turkestan, Tripolye in south-

ern Russia and the Baltic passage graves seem fairly certain, the general time level of the western material being 2200-1800 B.C. in the *Chronological Table of Prehistory* of Burkitt and Childe. Andersson himself first suggested 2500 B.C. for middle Yang shao but Menghin reduced this to less than 2000 B.C. The bronze age at Anyang begins at about 1400 B.C. The rapid nationalistic evolution in northern China finds a parallel in the sudden blossoming of the sophisticated Maya art out of the naive products of the first American farmers on the Archaic level.

Although Japan was connected with the mainland during the Pleistocene period only one very doubtful paleolithic find has been reported and no mesolithic ones. On the other hand over ten thousand neolithic sites are listed as well as very numerous eneolithic and iron age ones. The eneolithic archeology marks an invasion from Korea; it is followed quickly by the iron age beginning about 200 A.D. Schnell shows that a demarcation through Lake Biwa in central Hondo puts ninety per cent of the neolithic sites on the old Ainu side.

Only neolithic remains are found in the Kuriles and Kamchatka, most of these being decidedly recent neolithic. Neither Jockelson nor Bergman could find paleolithic or mesolithic remains. Jockelson himself believed that the American Indians had entered the New World during an interglacial period but he admits failure to find evidence of early man in all of eastern Siberia.

Petri calls the earliest finds in the region of Irkutsk Magdalenian, using harpoon points for this determination. Recently the rather eccentric figurines of Mal'ta have been unearthed. Jockelson's general comment is: "This diversity of forms belonging to different stages of culture and occurring together appears to reveal a specific peculiarity of the Siberian paleolith, as the mixture of ancient and newer style comes forth in the excavations of many investigations."

Admitted typological mixture calls for datings on the latest ingredients. Examples of the mesolithic bone dagger set with flint flakes have turned up on the so-called paleolithic level—an instrument also documented from the Chinese-Tibetan border. Perhaps the early culture of southern Siberia is really part of a mesolithic platform established on the northern limits of the earlier human arts.

An ancestral culture of the American Indians exists in neolithic cemeteries along the Angara, outlet of Lake Baikal. At Kitoi, Rasputin and other sites, polished celts, chisels, knives and toggles mostly of nephrite are found in ancient shallow graves. Also there are harpoon points, fish hooks, needles, awls and spoons of bone as well as bone saws and daggers edged with flint, tools of chipped flint and objects of soapstone. There are grooved arrow polishers of sandstone, rubbed pebbles of ocher and ocher-stained skeletons. Also a little plain and basket-marked pottery is found as well as copper and sculptures representing fish.

The origins of this southern Siberian neolithic are pretty clearly in the west as is indicated by the distribution of comb-marked pottery in northern Europe, ocher graves in southern Russia, etc. From Lake Baikal region a water road along the Lena leads practically half way to East Cape. Other possible routes are by way of the Amur and the coast.

Turning to America we find everywhere neolithic remains at the bottom of the cultural series. Folsom and Yuma blades pretty clearly belong in this category showing a skill in chipping unequalled during the mesolithic.

General arguments sometimes used to increase American antiquity relate to food plants and the diversity of languages. But neither is conclusive. American food plants form a botanically independent group farther removed from wild types than food plants of Europe, Asia and Africa. More intensive breeding over a shorter period could have produced this effect under ceremonial controls. The accepted tree-ring calendar of the Southwest allows a thousand years for the evolution of eight or more segregated types of maize among the Tewa. In a much shorter period the Navajo forced maize to germinate when planted as much as thirty-two inches below the surface in dry stream beds with a little subflow.

As regards the language problem Franz Boas suggests that language capture has oversimplified the old conditions in parts of the Old World and the New. Far from the evidence supporting the idea that languages anciently of wide distribution have differentiated locally, it supports the contrary argument that several far-flung stocks have absorbed others by acculturation, with the old diversified condition maintained in sluggish areas. It only remains, then, on the linguistic side, to postulate that America was populated by tribes formerly occupying a deep sector of the Old World with its apex at East Cape, this population being already differentiated as regards speech.

In the halls of the Academy of Natural Sciences of Philadelphia is displayed new evidence on the extinction of great animals which survived the last glaciation. When did they die? I ask the paleontologists if they have a time scale, by which the last survivors of this pleistocene fauna can be dated, a time scale which has a presumption of accuracy equal to that reached by Old World neolithic chronology, more precisely by the date of the introduction of this culture into America. After all there are bones of elephants at Anyang in China and an extinct giraffe is pictured in a Mesopotamian bronze. Also some of the extinct animal remains from our own Southwest are remarkably well preserved.

I appreciate the part which geology and other sciences have played in the formation of sequences for man's early evolution. However, demarcation between an earlier vague chronology of human culture, based on the time scales of glaciologists and climatologists, and a later more precise time count of centuries or years resting on historical evidence and on far-reaching comparisons in art, falls more or less on the end of the mesolithic period and the beginning of the neolithic period in southern Europe, northern Africa and the Near East. Not that we actually find written history in southern Siberia where ancestral phases of the basic American Indian cultures can be located, but we do find neolithic archeology common to northern Europe and northern Asia, which can be dated by reference to antecedent or contemporary cultures in more southerly parts of the Old World, where truly historical chronology exists.

Our own West, from which the demands for twenty-thousand-years-ago Indians mostly come, when only four thousand years are available, may have acquired an inferiority complex on fresh-turned earth and fresh-cut trees which seeks an over-compensation in time through super-abundant antiquity for American archeology.

PLEISTOCENE GLACIAL STRATIGRAPHY OF NORTH AMERICA

BY

PAUL MacCLINTOCK

Professor of Geography, Princeton University

INTRODUCTION

Due to the fortuitous combination of several factors, it has been possible to establish rather confidently the glacial sequence in North America. The ice sheets radiated from four major centers. The intensity and extent of spreading from the different centers so varied at different times that the respective drift sheets and moraines overlap and cross each other. This facilitates correlation, particularly of the youngest, or Wisconsin, group of deposits. Glaciation of the Middle West took place on a plain which, within the United States near the margins of the drift sheets, acquired great deposits of drift with very little glacial erosion. The record of earlier glaciations, therefore, has not been entirely destroyed by subsequent invasions. Furthermore, the relatively soft sediments of the bed-rock in this same region have yielded abundant material to produce stout moraines and thick drift sheets. Finally, the Middle Western States have been cut by streams into steep-sided valleys, whose walls in many places lay bare the story of the Pleistocene glaciation.

Interpretation of interglacial deposits is one of the major concerns of the glacial stratigrapher. They consist of the weathering profiles of drift sheets, of loess sheets, of organic material, and of water-laid deposits such as stream, lake, or ocean. Of recent years, the profiles of weathering of drift sheets have proved to be exceedingly useful for correlation purposes. Loess sheets are being used to considerable advantage and should become of major importance when future study shall fix their stratigraphic positions and geographic distributions. The knowledge of the invertebrate fauna of the loess sheets is pretty full while that of the vertebrate fauna is making rapid progress. Study of the Pleistocene floras, however, has received comparatively little attention in America. The older interpretation that extensive gravel deposits, such as the Aftonian gravels, are interglacial in age has not been verified by more detailed investigations. They are now considered to be mostly of outwash origin and hence of glacial age. However, when sand and gravel deposits near the ocean contain warm water marine fossils, the evidence, of course, points to an interglacial age. Based upon these various phenomena, a current classification includes four glacial and three interglacial episodes.

4. Wisconsin	glacial	2. Kansan	glacial
Sangamon	interglacial	Aftonian	interglacial
3. Illinoian	glacial	1. Nebraskan	glacial
Yarmouth	interglacial		

NEBRASKAN

This, the earliest drift sheet, has been found below Kansan drift in Iowa and the adjacent parts of Illinois, Missouri, Kansas, and Nebraska. It emerges to become the surface drift in places in Missouri, Kansas, Nebraska, and Wisconsin. It is confidently recognized as one of the major units of the Pleistocene column because it is separated from the overlying Kansan drift by inter-glacial deposits, particularly gumbotil, which must have taken a very long time to form. (Fig. 6.)

Aftonian

This interglacial interval is recorded by thick soil profiles in-cluding gumbotil which in southern Iowa is 6 to 8 feet thick, also by peat deposits, by some stream-laid material, and by loess.

KANSAN

This drift sheet occupies a large surface area in Iowa and the adjacent parts of Nebraska, Kansas, and Missouri. An old drift sheet below the Illinoian drift of Illinois and Indiana, and emerging from beneath the Wisconsin drift in Pennsylvania and New Jersey, is believed to be Kansan in age. (Fig. 8.)

Yarmouth

Interglacial deposits of this age, lying between Kansan and Illinoian drift, are best known in eastern Iowa and south central Illinois. They consist of deep soil, including gumbotil 8 to 12 feet, peat, gravel, and loess. As judged by the thickness and perfection of the weathering profiles, this was the longest of the interglacial intervals.

ILLINOIAN

This drift sheet lies at the surface in Illinois, southeastern Iowa, southern Indiana and Ohio. A fringe of what is thought to be the same drift emerges from below Wisconsin drift in eastern Pennsylvania and northern New Jersey. (Fig. 10.)

Sangamon

This interval is marked by deep weathering of the Illinoian drift, by considerable erosion, by accumulation of peat and some fluvial deposits, and by the deposition of a widespread and thick blanket of loess. The interval was long enough for (a) the Illinoian drift to be weathered to a deep profile, including 5-6 feet of gumbotil on flat places; (b) the weathered drift to be considerably eroded; (c) a blanket of loess to be deposited unconformably on the eroded drift; and (d) the loess to be weathered to a mature profile before the onset of Wisconsin glaciation.

WISCONSIN

This, the last drift sheet, is naturally the most widespread at the surface. It extends from the Pacific to the Atlantic. But this

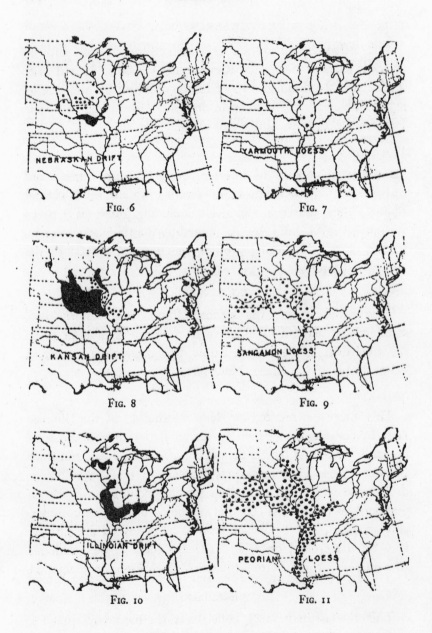

FIG. 6

FIG. 7

FIG. 8

FIG. 9

FIG. 10

FIG. 11

large area is not to be thought of as being covered by a single simple sheet of drift. Evidence from the distribution of moraines, from distinctly different characters of drift, and from the study of the routes of ice-transported materials, shows that the ice sheets were very lobate and that the lobes had complex histories; advancing, receding, overriding, etc., at different times and in different places. Furthermore, this glaciation started with ice radiation from the Keewatin center into northern and eastern Iowa. Following this, the active center of radiation became the Labradorian center with lobes pushing into central Illinois. Slightly later, ice from the area south of Hudson Bay spread southward and southeastward to override territory from central Ohio eastward that had not been previously covered by Wisconsin ice. And finally, dominance of radiation returned to the Keewatin center to spread the last of the Wisconsin drifts in Iowa and the Dakotas. It is upon this succession of events that a current classification of Wisconsin drift is established.

CLASSIFICATION OF THE WISCONSIN DRIFTS

5. Late Mankato (Gray drift)
4. Early Mankato (Red drift)
    Forest bed of Wisconsin
3. Cary drift
    Tazewell loess
2. Tazewell drift
    Iowan loess
1. Iowan drift

1. Iowan drift is a thin stony deposit in northeastern Iowa and southeastern Minnesota, and northwestern Iowa and southwestern Minnesota, of Keewatin derivation. (Fig. 12.)

2. Tazewell drift occupies a considerable territory in Illinois, Indiana, and Ohio. It is deposited as thick drift with a series of stout moraines both at its outer margins and within them. In Illinois for instance, there is the Shelbyville, Champaign, Bloomington, Normal, Farm Ridge, Marseilles, Minooka, and Marengo

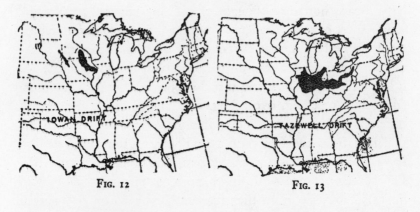

FIG. 12

FIG. 13

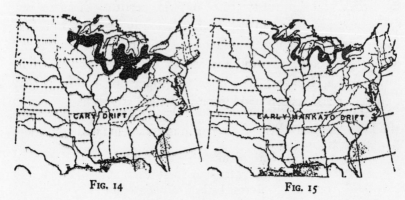

FIG. 14

FIG. 15

FIG. 16

moraines with gentle ground moraine between them. Some of the moraines are recessional moraines, but most of them are the end moraines of re-advances of the ice after what appears to have been considerable withdrawal. Tazewell drift is largely of Labradorian origin. (Fig. 13.)

3. Considerable erosion of the Tazewell drift was followed by reforming and re-advance of ice to deposit the Cary drift in Wisconsin, Illinois, Indiana, Michigan, and Ohio. The strongest center seems to have been the Patrician. This drift sheet, again, is marked by a series of stout terminal moraines interspersed with gentle ground moraine. (Fig. 14.)

4. Early Mankato drift is found in Wisconsin, Michigan, and Ontario. In eastern Wisconsin an important forest bed separates it from the Cary drift below. In Wisconsin this drift is red in color showing its derivation from pre-Cambrian iron-bearing rocks. (Fig. 15.)

5. The drift of the Dakota and Des Moines lobes comprises the Late Mankato. It is of Keewatin origin, is gray in color, and definitely overlies the red drift of Early Mankato age. (Fig. 16.)

LOESS SHEETS

Aftonian. Only a few places are known where loess has been definitely established to be of Aftonian age. But enough is known to conclude that there was a fairly widespread deposit of fossiliferous loess formed during this interval.

Yarmouth. Loess of this age is known from many places. Exposures in Nebraska, Iowa, and Illinois show that it was probably a widespread deposit at one time. A fauna of 18 species of typical loess fossils is known from Fulton County, Illinois.[1]

Sangamon. During this interval, one of the greatest sheets of loess was deposited. It is known to extend from western Kansas and Nebraska across Iowa and Illinois and well into Indiana. Its age is late Sangamon, for Illinoian till was weathered to gumbo-

[1] Baker, F. C. Trans. Ill. Acad. Sci., 1929, pp. 288-312.

til, and this in turn dissected, before the calcareous loess was deposited. However, it was not formed at the very end of the Sangamon interval because it was leached and weathered several feet before fresh Iowan drift, or Iowan loess, was deposited on it. It is characteristically a reddish brown color, which Lugn[2] has suggested shows it to have come from the Red Beds to the southwest. It is known as the Loveland loess from the type locality at Loveland in western Iowa. (Fig. 9.)

Iowan. A loess sheet lies upon the Iowan drift. Since no weathering of the drift took place before the loess was deposited, the latter is considered as having accumulated as the ice waned.[3]

Tazewell. In west central Illinois, Tazewell drift lies on Iowan loess but is itself mantled by fairly thick loess, designated as Tazewell loess. Beyond the outermost moraine of Tazewell age the two loess sheets form a single mantle of loess which as yet we have not been able to subdivide. This latter combination loess sheet has been known as the Peorian loess. It seems likely that as detailed work and techniques advance differentiation will become possible. In a few places, as in southeastern and west-central Illinois, it has been possible to distinguish an upper and a lower buff loess.

Peorian loess. This is the most widespread and thickest of the loess sheets. It extends in a great belt from western Kansas and Nebraska across Iowa, Missouri, and Illinois, and down the Mississippi to the Gulf. It ranges from over 200 feet thick in western Nebraska to a feather edge at the east, where it becomes lost in the soil profile. It is thickest not only at the west but also near the margins of the Iowan drift and near the major stream valleys of the region. (Fig. 11.)

[2] Lugn, A. L. Personal communication.
[3] There is some discussion of the significance of a pebble concentrate at the contact between till and loess, but it lies beyond the scope of the present paper. See Kay, G. F. "The Relative Ages of the Iowan and Illinoian Drift Sheets." Am. Jour. Sci., 5th Ser., vol. 16, pp. 492-518, 1928. And, Am. Jour. Sci., 5th Ser., vol. 21, pp. 158-172, 1931. And Leverett, Frank. "Loveland Loess; Pre-Illinoian, pre-Iowan in Age." Science, n.s., vol. 69, pp. 551-552, 1929.

Post-Peorian loess. In central Nebraska (Custer, Logan, and Lincoln counties) a three-foot black soil separates the buff Peorian loess below from slightly grayer loess above. The latter, in places, is from 50 to 100 feet thick. Whether or not this loess is of Tazewell age is still an open question.

LATE-GLACIAL AND POST-GLACIAL

In Europe, the Late-glacial episode, subdivided into the 1. Daniglacial, 2. the Gotiglacial, and 3. the Finiglacial, represents the time of deglaciation. During this episode, the single ice cap was progressively waning. The episode ended, according to Dr. de Geer, 6000 B.C. with the beginning of Post-glacial time. Unfortunately, the story of Wisconsin glaciation in North America was far less simple. As has been pointed out, the multiple centers of ice radiation acted at somewhat different times. Ice waned from central Illinois while it reached a climax in eastern Ohio, and waned from Ohio while it reached a climax in Iowa and Dakota. As a result, what would be called Late-glacial time in one area would be contemporaneous with glacial time in another. It might be contended that the duration of this overlapping may be a small fraction of the major period of deglaciation. But judging by the amount of erosion of valleys in north-central Illinois, about ten times as much erosion took place between Tazewell and Late Mankato time (i.e., while glacial conditions still caused the Great Lakes drainage to use the Chicago outlet at the Glenwood level) as has taken place since. If this line of reasoning be valid, Late-glacial time in central Illinois was long and important but was at least largely contemporaneous with glacial time in the Dakotas. "Late-glacial" still finds use in America if properly understood, but such a purely descriptive term as "Deglacial" might find an equally useful niche in terminology. During the later part of the Wisconsin, from the Cary substage, and for the rest of Late-glacial or Deglacial time, the history of the Great Lakes and the varve deposits of New

England furnish chronological landmarks by means of which events may be fairly well dated.

Post-glacial time in North America has as yet few correlation landmarks. The study of peat bogs seems at present the most fruitful line of investigation. Auer[4] finds that in southeastern Canada there was (1) a dry and warm period; (2) moist period; (3) a dry warm period; and (4) the present moister and cooler period. This corresponds well with the Post-glacial chronology found in the peat bogs of northwest Europe. Whether this chronology will be found applicable to other parts of North America remains to be ascertained.

PERIGLACIAL AND PSEUDOGLACIAL MATERIAL

Archaeologists have need for detailed interpretation of a group of deposits which have been rather neglected by geologists, particularly in America. These include periglacial material such as warp, structure boden, contorted ground, solifluxional material and all frost-heaved ground formed when virtual arctic conditions pertained. They include also materials formed under drier conditions, such as loess, loam, and ventifacts. And lastly, they include such deposits as slope wash and all types of alluvial accumulations. All of these types are to be interpreted along with an understanding of the soil profile so that mistakes in date and mode of implacement of artifacts may be avoided.

BIBLIOGRAPHY

Since it would be burdensome to list all the important papers which have been drawn upon, the reader is referred to the excellent bibliographies in "The Last Glaciation" by Ernst Antevs, Amer. Geogr. Soc., No. 17, 1928; "Das Eiszeitalter," by Paul Wolstedt, 1929; "Outline of Glacial Geology," by F. T. Thwaites, 1935; and the bibliographies of North American Geology by the U. S. Geological Survey.

[4] Auer, Vaino. "Peat Bogs in Southeastern Canada." Canadian Dept. Mines, Mem. 162, 32 pp., 1930.

CLIMATE AND EARLY MAN IN NORTH AMERICA

BY

ERNST ANTEVS

Research Associate, Carnegie Institution of Washington

CHANGES in climate deeply affected ancient man.

In Europe the development of the Pleistocene ice sheets and glaciers forced man to vacate the northern regions and the high mountains and to move to central and southern Europe, and perhaps to Africa and Asia. Also in Asia extensive ice caps and large glaciers compelled man to migrate southward and to lower elevations. The fall of sea level, which accompanied the accumulation of the ice, permitted man to occupy broad strips of former ocean bottom. When the conditions were reversed, the shrinking of the ice sheets induced northward and upward migrations of plants, animals, and man, and also landward movements ahead of the rising sea level. These processes and events accompanied each glacial epoch.

As for North America, man had to our knowledge not arrived before the last continental glaciation, called the Wisconsin. As the routes of spread led through Canada, which was glaciated from the Atlantic to the Pacific, they were blocked by ice barriers for long ages. If the successive culminations of the Wisconsin ice centers are correctly understood, ice barriers existed across western Canada roughly from 65,000 to 20,000 years ago with one exception.[1] Around 40,000 years before our time there was probably a break in the ice, a north-south extending corridor,

[1] Antevs, Ernst: Climaxes of the last glaciation in North America. Amer. Journ. Sci., vol. 28, 1934, pp. 304-311.

along the eastern foot of the Rocky Mountains and possibly another passageway on the plateau between the Rockies and the Coast Range. During the past 20,000 years there has been an open route. There is no conclusive evidence that man spread through the probable ice corridor 40,000 years ago, but he seems to have been here shortly after the final break in the ice barrier. It appears that when the last Pleistocene glaciers receded in eastern Asia, man followed the biota which took possession of the released land to the north and northeast. He crossed the then narrow Bering Strait on ice or in water crafts and diffused eastward to the Mackenzie Valley and thence southward.

Most of the oldest records of man in North America have been found on the Great Plains and in the southwestern states. Several finds taken from caves, desert basins, and river and lake deposits appear to date from the last part of the last pluvial or late-glacial. The doubts which I have expressed concerning the late-glacial age of the Minnesota man from Pelican Rapids have not been removed.[2, 3]

On this occasion I will consider early man in relation to climate as revealed by the place and mode of occurrence of the Lake Mohave culture of southern California and the Cochise culture of southeastern Arizona and adjacent New Mexico. Both cultures were recently discovered and are not described. The former was a hunting stage, the latter a food-gathering stage. Their relative age is not known.

The Lake Mohave culture, which is represented only by stone implements, includes dart points, knives, scrapers, choppers, gravers, drills, and retouched flakes.[4] It was discovered in De-

[2] Antevs, Ernst: "The spread of aboriginal man to North America." Geogr. Review, vol. 25, 1935, pp. 302-309. (See p. 305.)

[3] Jenks, A. E.: "Pleistocene man in Minnesota, a fossil Homo sapiens." Including G. A. Thiel: "Pleistocene geology of the Prairie Lake Region." Univ. of Minnesota Press, Minneapolis, 1936.

[4] Campbell, Elizabeth: "Archaeological problems in the southern California deserts." Amer. Antiquity, vol. 1, No. 4, 1936, pp. 295-300.

cember 1934 by Mr. and Mrs. William H. Campbell and Mr. Charles Amsden of the Southwest Museum in the basin of Silver Lake, the terminus of Mohave River, one hundred and forty miles northeast of Los Angeles. It has later been found by the Campbells in several basins that now lack water. I had opportunity to study the conditions of occurrence of the culture in December 1935 and in the spring of 1936.

Here only the occurrence in the twin basin of Silver and Soda lakes will be treated. This double basin once held a lake, called Lake Mohave,[5] which overflowed to Death Valley and somewhat lowered its outlet sill of bedrock. The artifacts of the ancient culture are confined to the beaches of the overflow levels. At Soda station chipped flints are embedded six to fifty-four inches in an old beach. Clearly, the artifacts are as old as Lake Mohave; and a dating of this lake is a dating of the culture.

The region is now a desert. The basins, though called "lakes", are normally dry and sufficiently firm to support an automobile. They are forbidding clay flats, devoid of vegetation. The growth outside the lake bottoms is predominated by the creosote bush. There are a few salty springs at and near the south end of Soda Lake. The local precipitation averages two to three inches a year. The evaporation would probably be four feet a year from a large water body.

However, Silver Lake is the terminus of Mohave River which rises in the San Bernardino Mountains sixty-five miles east-northeast of Los Angeles. In its upper course the Mohave is a perennial stream, but it is normally wasted in the desert and reaches its end basins only during floods. The average annual quantity of water that has passed through the canyon at Afton

[5] Thompson, D. G.: "The Mohave desert region, California." U. S. Geol. Survey Water-Supply Paper, 578, 1929. (See p. 563.)

into the four terminal basins during the fifty-one-year period
1883 to 1934 has been estimated at roughly 60,000 acre feet.[6, 7]

Ancient Lake Mohave was twenty-three miles long, three to
six miles wide, and at the beginning of the overflow forty feet
deep. If this lake existed at present more than 200,000 acre feet
of water would yearly evaporate from its surface. This is four to
five times the mean annual modern inflow to the Soda and Silver
basins. Lake Mohave also lost water by overflow and perhaps by
underground percolation. The existence of this large water body
therefore suggests a much wetter climate than now prevails.

During the postpluvial epoch, which comprises the past 10,000
years, the climate of the Southwest seems to have been relatively
dry, except for a stage at about 1000 B.C. which was moister
than the present.[8] This age was surely not wet enough to produce Lake Mohave. As suggested by earlier students of the lake,
it may date from the last pluvial period, the correlative of the
late-glacial, or age of ice waning, in the glaciated regions. In
California this pluvial seems to have culminated somewhat later
than did the last extensive mountain glaciation, that is between
25,000 and 20,000 years ago. As Lake Mohave overflowed, its
shorelines perhaps record not only the wettest stage of the
pluvial, but a considerable part of its duration. They were perhaps forming until some 15,000 years ago.

Since the artifacts under consideration are exclusively associated with the overflow levels of pluvial Lake Mohave, they
may be at least 15,000 years old.

Therefore, the ancient Lake Mohave people lived in a wetter

[6] Conkling, Harold; Rowe, W. P.; Gleason, G. B.; Kimble, J. C.; et al.: "Mojave River investigation." California Dept. of Public Works, Division of Water
Resources, Bull. 47, Sacramento, 1934. (See pp. 6, 7, 63, 75, 76.)

[7] Blaney, H. F. and Ewing, P. A.: "Utilization of the waters of Mojave River,
California." U. S. Bureau of Agric. Engineering, Division of Irrigation. Mimeo-
graphed Summary, August, 1935. (See p. 3.)

[8] Antevs, Ernst: "Pluvial and postpluvial fluctuations of climate in the Southwest." Carnegie Instn. of Washington, Year Book No. 35, 1936.

PLATE VIII—Double adobe site. At top and lower left, general views of arroyo wall; artifact-bearing sand marked by a cross. Lower left, mano *in situ*.

and cooler climate than prevails today. The lake, which had fresh water, could have been bordered by mesquites, cottonwood, willows, and arrow weed. In the neighboring hills there probably grew piñon and juniper. The local fauna surely included several rodents, antelope, quail, ducks, fish, and molluscs. Thus both plants and animals supplied food and other necessities in abundance. Obviously, the region was much more habitable than at present.

The Cochise culture was discovered by Professor Byron Cummings and field party in 1926 on Whitewater Draw at Double Adobe School, twelve miles northwest of Douglas in Arizona, and its significance was realized by Dr. Emil W. Haury and Mr. E. B. Sayles of Gila Pueblo in 1935. It consists of flat metates, small manos, various percussion-flaked stone implements, hammer stones, pestles, and hearths. It represents a food-gathering stage. The culture has been found by Haury, Sayles, my wife, and myself in sediments exposed by the modern arroyo cutting and also on and in beaches of lakes in now dry basins at several places in southeastern Arizona and southwestern New Mexico.

I will here confine myself to the original site at Double Adobe School. The given profile shows the sequence of beds in the fifteen-foot arroyo wall. The lowest exposed bed is a firm red clay which is eroded at the top. Above is a bed of sand deposited by the eroding stream. It is in this sand that the Cochise artifacts occur. These are found with hearth stones, charcoal of hickory and poplar (kindly determined by Dr. Ralph W. Chaney), and with fossil bones of horse. The presence of charcoal precludes redeposition. The sand is overlain by a cream-colored limy clay or marl with laminae which probably are varves (annual deposits). From the upper part of the marl Professor Cummings' field party removed the skull of a mammoth. Above is a bed of almost massive gray marl. The two marl beds are lake deposits. In the upper marl there is a stream channel four feet deep and thirty feet wide. Then follows a massive, gritless brown clay which extends for miles in the gently sloping valley. This clay was probably deposited from muddy water which worked in sheets down the grassy slopes to a meadow, or cienega, in the center of the valley, while the vegetation of the slopes acted as a strainer. Much of the material is undoubtedly soil. At other places on the draw, this cienega clay was eroded after its deposition. About one-half mile north of Double Adobe there is on the surface of the cienega clay a campsite with hearths and with potsherds dating, according to Dr. Haury, from between 900 and 1100 A.D. The cienega clay is overlain by a locally laminated yellow silt in which occur bones of domestic cattle. Cattle were introduced in Arizona, i.e. the Santa Cruz Valley south of Tucson, during the eighteenth century. In 1855 there were wild cattle in our general region. The course of Whitewater Draw was then marked by clay flats and water pools.[9] After 1872 white stockmen began to settle along the draw. By 1880 the herds increased greatly. As a result the country was quickly denuded of its natural grass cover, and the vegetation on the slopes became insufficient to retain the water and to check its flow after the occasional torrential rains, but the rushing water was abnormally concentrated in rills, gulches, and other fixed courses. Thus, Whitewater Draw began to cut its arroyo in 1884. The modern precipitation in the valley averages about fourteen inches. The climate is semi-arid and rather hot (mesothermal). The region is a semidesert. While the modern erosion is a consequence of overgrazing, the erosion in the past may have been due to drought which checked and destroyed the vegetation. This is the key to the profile.

Thus the lowest exposed clay indicates a moist or wet climate. The subsequent erosion and the overlying sand containing the

[9] Meinzer, O. E. and Kelton, F. C.: "Geology and water resources of Sulphur Spring Valley, Arizona." U. S. Geol. Survey Water-Supply Paper 320, 1913. (See p. 11.)

artifacts indicate a dry stage. The two marl beds mark a wet period. The later erosion signifies a dry stage, the cienega clay a moist age, the following erosion another dry age, and the top silt a slight moist stage.

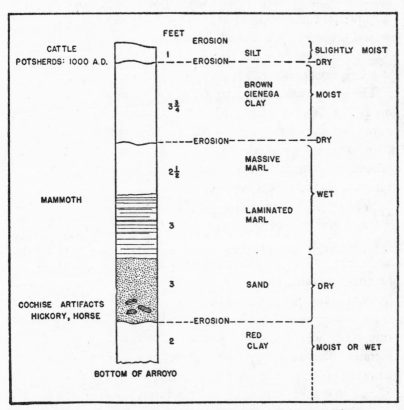

FIG. 17—Double adobe profile, and its climatic interpretation.

The pottery on the surface of the cienega clay shows that this bed was deposited prior to 1000 A.D. The mammoth skull in the laminated marl suggests that the lake beds date from the last pluvial period, the correlative of the late-glacial, for the mammoth seems to have become extinct during that age. The horse and the hickory in the artifact-bearing sand also suggest Pleistocene age. Hickory requires a moister climate than prevails in southern Arizona and now ranges from the mountains of northeastern Mexico and from eastern Texas eastward. Thus the Cochise artifacts seem to date either from a dry stage which interrupted the normal wetness of the last pluvial or from a dry age which preceded this pluvial. In any case, the artifacts may be considerably more than 10,000 years old, for the last pluvial seems to have prevailed roughly from 30,000 to 10,000 years ago.

The other mode of occurrence of the Cochise culture, namely on and in beaches of pluvial lakes, whose basins are now dry, strongly suggests that the Cochise people lived on these lakes.

In cienega clays in other valleys of southeastern Arizona occur implements which seem to have evolved from the Cochise culture and lead to recent cultures.

When the Cochise people camped on the Pleistocene Whitewater Draw the moisture may have been about as today, and the temperature a few to several Fahrenheit degrees lower. The vegetation in the valley undoubtedly included cottonwood, hickory, mesquite, creosote bush, yucca, and tule. Sycamores, live oaks, and junipers probably extended to lower levels than today along water courses and on hill sides. Mesquite pods and tule roots were probably the main products ground on the metates. The fauna may have included horse, mammoth, beaver, antelope, deer, rabbits, and wild turkey. It seems reasonable to assume that these and other animals formed part of the Cochise people's fare, but no projectile points have been found.

Such were the climatic and natural conditions which influenced the lives of two ancient peoples in the Southwest.

THE SIGNIFICANCE OF EARLY CULTURES IN TEXAS AND SOUTHEASTERN ARIZONA

BY

HAROLD S. GLADWIN
Gila Pueblo, Globe, Arizona

I THINK that there may be some justification for saying that this symposium may witness the rebirth of American archaeology. Ever since the beginning of the study of Man in the New World, investigation has been hindered by certain fixed beliefs which have minimized or destroyed the value of evidence which could not be reconciled with these beliefs.

With the discovery at Folsom by Barnum Brown, our mental attitude was liberated from these restrictions, and during the past ten years investigation has progressed to a point where today we are beginning to see Man in the New World against a background of respectable antiquity.

There remain, however, three tendencies as hang-overs from earlier habits of thought:

First, the general inclination to compare early American cultures with those of western Europe, and to classify our industries as Aurignacian-like or Solutrean-like.

Second, the refusal to grant antiquity to early American cultures when these fail to conform to European standards or techniques.

Third, the doubt which is cast upon the authenticity of ancient Man in America when it is found that our early men do not agree, as to physical type, with the better known early European types.

While such investigations in the New World are still in their infancy, it can already be said with assurance that no one ancient American culture in its entirety resembles any known European culture in its entirety. In addition to this failure to agree, there are some reasons for thinking that, in Late Glacial times, the respective economies of the Old and New Worlds were so different from one another that the cultures which these diverse conditions called forth were also fundamentally unlike. That this may have been true is suggested by the greater number of edible plants, roots, tubers, seeds, and nuts which were native to America. With such a wide range of vegetal foods easily available, it is possible, if not probable, that, in favorable areas, some ancient Americans depended more upon food-gathering and less upon hunting than their Old World contemporaries. This, in turn, makes it easier to understand how, in the southwestern United States, we are discovering the grinding tools, which one associates with a food-gathering economy, in horizons considerably earlier than was formerly thought to be possible. Regarded from this stand-point, future work may show that ground-stone tools were actually earlier in America than in the Old World.

That this southern food-gathering culture was not uniform throughout North America is demonstrated by a well defined division which seems to run from the vicinity of San Francisco Bay diagonally towards the southeast to the Gulf of Mexico.

To the south of this line are found the cultures which we know as Abilene and Edwards Plateau in Texas, as Cochise in southern Arizona and southwestern New Mexico, as Pinto Basin in the Californian desert, and the Coastal Cultures of San Diego and Santa Barbara counties in California. With few exceptions, all of these cultures include milling stones, and there seems to be some basic resemblances in their flint industries.

As a result of the work which Gila Pueblo has done in Texas

and Arizona, a collection of artifacts from the early cultures has been brought here and is now on exhibition. I will, therefore, not attempt to give any description other than to say that the horizons have been established by stratigraphy, that in the earliest levels artifacts were associated with the bones of extinct fauna and were laid down during a period when the climatic conditions were different from those of today, and that the dating of these cultures has been left to competent geologists for determination.

The resemblance of these southern cultures to one another is emphasized when comparison is made with those to the north and northeast of the dividing line.

From California to Maine, but almost exclusively to the north of the line from San Francisco Bay to the Gulf of Mexico, there is a culture characterized by the Folsom or Folsom-like industry. A few of these distinctive artifacts have been found in Arizona, southern New Mexico, and Texas; none in Mexico, Central or South America. That these two basic cultures were co-existent is shown by the influence which each exerted upon the other along the line of their meeting in Texas. That the southern culture arrived in America before the Folsom culture is implied by their geographical positions.

A second factor which has a direct bearing upon this problem is the distribution of a hyper-dolichocephalic type of man which, on the Texas Gulf Coast, in central and western Texas, and also in southern California, has been found in association with the southern food-gathering culture. This man has been said to resemble, in certain respects, the Lagoa Santa type from the caves of eastern Brazil and also the Punin man of Ecuador, a connection which not only indicates that the distribution was more or less confined to southern North America and northern South America, but which also concedes considerable antiquity to the type. Of possibly greater importance is the opinion expressed, at various times, by Hansen, Hooton, Keith, Oetteking, Sullivan, Ten Kate, and Woodbury, that various members of this human group bore a resemblance to the natives of Australia.

Turning now to the region lying to the north and east of this southern complex, we can consider the physical type of the people above the dividing line. While, as yet, we have no skeletal evidence on Folsom Man, we can say as a broad generality that, from the Pacific to the Atlantic Coast, human types occur which, although still dolichocephalic, were not as long-headed as those of the southern complex, nor did they possess the other physical characters which are considered as Archaic in the southern area. I do not mean by this that the northern long-heads were homogeneous; the region which they occupied covers most of the continent of North America, and there has undoubtedly been much mixing within the area, but it can be said, I believe, that there is a definable difference between the northern and southern types of dolichocephals.

Again admitting that there is, as yet, no archaeological association between this northern human type and the Folsom culture, it will be found that, if we plot the distribution of the one upon the other, the two factors will show a close conformity. This is particularly true in regard to Ohio where there seems to be a definite focus of the northern type of long-head, and from which 148 Folsom-like points have been reported, many more than from any other state in the Union.

Giving due recognition to the fact that there is probably a gap of many thousand years between the southern food-gathering-hyper-dolichocephalic complex and modern times, a surprisingly close correlation will be found to occur if we superimpose the distribution of this complex upon the area occupied by tribes of the Hokan family prior to the recent dislocation of the Siouan and Iroquoian peoples.

If now the northern complex be superimposed upon the region occupied recently by Algonkin tribes, a correlation is obtained which, as a triple complex, compares in value with that of the Hokan.

I submit these outlines to you for what they may be worth, but in conclusion I wish to draw attention to a few other points which I believe to be of importance.

It will be obvious that, both as regards culture and physical type, neither of these complexes can be profitably compared to any of the early cultures of Europe or western Asia.

In certain features, particularly those discussed by Nordenskiold, Wissler, and Dixon, a more favorable comparison can be made between the southern complex and the culture and physical types of Australia and some of the inner islands of Melanesia. To a lesser extent, but nevertheless suggestive, is a comparison between the northern complex and the culture and physical types of the islands off the east coast of Asia, from Japan to New Guinea.

This should not be understood as advocating any theory of trans-Pacific diffusion, since such movements seem to me to be highly improbable, if not impossible. There is, however, a suggestion that certain migrations, characterized by culture and physical type, which flowed eastward from Asia to Australia and Melanesia, had also representatives who found their way into the New World.

In view of the many observable differences between the Palaeolithic cultures of the Old and New Worlds, and also between the human types which were associated with these cultures, I venture to suggest that American archaeologists shall not rely too heavily upon Old World criteria or classifications in studying our ancient cultures or physical types, and that these factors be evaluated on their own merits, in the light of our own environment.

For those who wish to trace our ancient cultures to their Old World sources, I think that geographical propinquity and the many analogies of more recent times both point to eastern Asia as a profitable field of investigation. To be more specific, I would point to southeastern Asia as the possible home of an Old World Folsom industry, since it is there that we find many analogies with the culture which followed Folsom in North America.

GEOLOGY OF THE FOLSOM DEPOSITS IN NEW MEXICO AND COLORADO

BY

KIRK BRYAN

Associate Professor of Physiography, Harvard University[*]

INTRODUCTION

THE importance of the Folsom culture can hardly be exaggerated for not only do the characteristic points represent the maximum of skill by stone-working primitives, but the type is distinct and, so far as now known, unique. Furthermore the discovery came at a critical period in the development of archaeological thought. For many years there had been one attempt after another to prove great antiquity for man in America. One alleged find after another had been made and many, alas, had been demonstrated as mistaken or even fraudulent. As a result archaeologists became expert in discrediting "finds" purporting to show the existence of ancient man. The rejection of any such claim became more or less automatic. Opinion was crystallizing into a dogma to the effect that man is a very recent immigrant into North America. It was held that the Amerindian, in a hunting stage but with stone implements of Neolithic aspect, was the sole immigrant, although it was admitted that he entered in successive waves of slightly diverse physical and cultural types.

The discovery of Folsom points in association with the bones of extinct bison reported by Figgins and Cook[1] in 1927 and con-

[*] Published with the permission of the Smithsonian Institution.

[1] Figgins, J. D., "Antiquity of Man in America," Nat. Hist., vol. 27, pp. 229-239, 1927. Cook, H. J., *Ibid.*, pp. 240-247, 1927.

firmed by the masterly excavation of the site by Barnum Brown[2] changed the entire aspect of the problem. Here at last was the material evidence of a pre-Amerindian culture. Effort since that time has centered on tracing the extent of this culture, on distinguishing other cultures having somewhat similar stone technique, and on the search for new sites.[3] The problem offering the greatest difficulties is that of the age of the Folsom culture, which can be attacked from the standpoint of typology and also of geology. The latter method offers some chance of a solution, but for the present is much handicapped by the lack of an established and general chronology of Pleistocene and post-Pleistocene time in Western North America. Studies made at the original Folsom site in New Mexico and at the Lindenmeier site in Colorado are the result of the continued interest of the Smithsonian Institution in this problem and have been made at their instance and at their expense.

ORIGINAL FOLSOM SITE

The original discovery of Folsom points was made in a little valley called Dead Horse Gulch on the east flank of Johnson Mesa about twelve miles east of the city of Raton, New Mexico, and fifteen miles west of the village of Folsom, from which the name of the culture is derived. The little valley lies just under the crags of Johnson Mesa and leads down into larger and larger valleys in the Shoemaker Ranch to a main stream valley that flows eastward toward the town of Folsom.

The little valley is tributary to a larger, but also small, valley to the north. Both have flat grassy floors fifty to one hundred feet wide, and are bordered by terraces about twenty-five feet high, cut on the Cretaceous shale bed rock. An arroyo, or gul-

[2] Brown, Barnum, "Folsom Culture and its age," with discussion by Kirk Bryan, Geol. Soc. Amer., Bull. 40, pp. 128-29, 1929.
[3] Summarized in Roberts, F. H. H., Jr., Smithson. Misc. Coll., vol. 94, No. 4, pp. 1-10, 1935.

ley, recently cut in the flat floor has worked headward into the northern valley and left the southern undissected. The wall of this gulley gives a perfect section of the deposits forming the floor of the southern gulch, and in this wall, about four feet below the surface, the bones of bison were found. As excavated by Barnum Brown in 1928, this level showed the skeletons of about twenty-three bison, with associated Folsom points. Both occurred in undisturbed ground, as witnessed by me and others in 1928 and as recorded by Roberts.[4] The conclusion must be accepted that *Bison taylori* and the men who made the points were contemporaneous. Mr. Brown has pointed out that the large number of bison skeletons at one place, only partly disarticulated and with all bones present except tail bones, indicates that the animals were surrounded, killed, and butchered. He has emphasized particularly the absence of tail bones, for in the skinning of most animals "the tail goes with the hide." The finding of one point imbedded in the clay between the rib bones is a strong corroboration of this theory.

The material in which the bones were found is a clayey alluvium containing lenses of dirty gravel composed mostly of thin sandstone plates. It differs from material now being deposited in similar valleys only in having small limey concretions.

The age of this valley fill can best be understood if the local physiographic history is reviewed. The lava flows of Johnson Mesa rest on a smooth erosion surface of considerable antiquity, probably Tertiary in age. Stream systems which dissect this surface were probably developed in the Pleistocene. The first stream system on the east side of the Mesa appears to have developed broad open valleys. Remnants of these valley levels now form benches and spurs one hundred and fifty to two hundred feet above present stream grades. Stream grades were then lowered and new valleys (No. 2) were cut below the level of the

[4] Roberts, F. H. H., Jr., *Idem.*

older and broader valleys (No. 1). At this time, lava was poured from Mount Roberts, a volcano on the south flank of the main valley and four or five miles southeast of the site. It overflowed remnants of the earlier (No. 1) valley and filled the younger (No. 2). The lava dam thus formed has been cut through and the lake that may have formed behind it has been drained and its deposits removed. Again, stream grades were lowered by fifty to one hundred feet and a new inner valley (No. 3) was formed. The previous valley (No. 2) is represented by spurs and terraces fifty to one hundred feet high. The process of stream lowering again took place and the present valley (No. 4) was eroded below the No. 3 valley which is represented by terraces twenty-five to thirty feet high. A local basaltic lava poured from a terrace remnant of the No. 2 valley onto the valley floor of the No. 3 stage.

The present inner valley (No. 4) has everywhere a flood plain which, in localities downstream from the site, forms broad meadows. The stream has recently cut an arroyo ten to twenty feet deep in this flood plain. Downstream, near the Shoemaker ranch house, the material of this flood plain is loose and sandy and seems no different from the flood-plain deposits of other New Mexico streams which contain the relics of the Pueblo Culture. If one follows this flood-plain deposit upstream he passes without apparent break into the material containing *B. taylori*, the only differences are the increased clay content, which seems to be due to smaller volume of the stream, the limey concretions and scattered charcoal. The charcoal may be entirely of natural origin and the record of a local forest fire or it may be derived from the fires used by Folsom man to prepare the meat after the "kill." The concretions are the only physical evidence of a greater antiquity of the flood-plain deposits in the headwaters as contrasted with the downstream areas. It is possible that several cycles of alternate filling and erosion have occurred in this valley since the stream system attained essentially the present grade. The preservation in one of the valleys of one or more of the older flood-plain deposits is not impossible although a relatively rare contingency. The drainage from part of Johnson Mesa which during wet weather pours over the rim in falls was diverted from the little valley containing the site between stages No. 1 and No. 2 in the development of the valley system. Thus the little valley has a somewhat greater size than is proportionate to its drainage area. This circumstance may have been the deciding factor in the preservation of this remnant of an older valley fill.

The development of the valley system of this area through four successive stages doubtless required all of Pleistocene time. The late valley fill may be as much as one thousand years old. An older valley fill or flood-plain deposit containing extinct bison would be older. How much older is not indicated. On the ordinary criteria used by geologists it would be considered Early Recent or very Late Pleistocene.

THE LINDENMEIER SITE

The Lindenmeier site at which Dr. Roberts[5] has now been excavating for three field seasons is located on the escarpment marking the boundary between the High Plains and the Colorado Piedmont. This locality near the Wyoming-Colorado line is on the contact between two nearly flat-lying Tertiary formations, the sandy Arikaree and the tuffaceous Brule. This contact is marked by a spring zone which is of importance in the physiographic development of the area and also in attracting to this place the camps of Folsom man.

The Colorado Piedmont is a great area of relatively low land

[5] Roberts, Frank H. H., Jr., "A Folsom Complex, etc." Smithson. Misc. Coll., vol. 94, No. 4, pp. 1-35, 3 figs., 16 pls., 1935. "The Folsom Complex in American Archaeology." Paper in this volume.

at the foot of the Rockies, below the High Plains surface, developed by the incision of the South Platte and its tributaries. The Cache la Poudre is the principal tributary of this area and its northern tributaries are responsible for carving the existing escarpment of the High Plains. The little valley of the Lindenmeier site drains to tributaries of Boxelder Creek, a tributary of

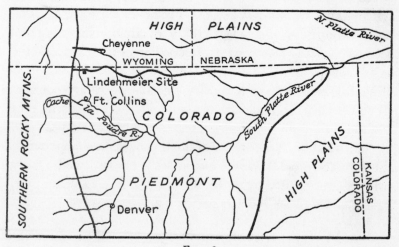

FIG. 18

the Cache la Poudre, and owes many of its peculiarities to the contest for headwater areas between these minor tributaries.

The Tertiary Brule tuff-clay and the Arikaree sand and gravel once overlaid the whole of the Piedmont area, from which they have been stripped from the unlerlying soft, shaley Cretaceous rocks in successive episodes of erosion, which have given rise to the present topography. Complexities arise by reason of the numerous pauses in the process. As the South Platte lowered its grade, each tributary was also lowered. With stabilized grades, the Platte and its tributaries cut broad plains until the process of valley widening was interrupted by renewed lowering of the Platte River.

Since Pliocene time the grade of the South Platte River seems to have been lowered five or more times. At each lowering a gravel-capped terrace was left as an indication of the episode. The intervals between lowerings were so great, judging by the broad valley surfaces that have been developed, that the major part of Pleistocene time must have been involved. The long sequence of events recorded in these terraces will not here be reviewed. It is obviously important that a chronology of the whole of Pleistocene time be established for the South Platte and each tributary. This task has been undertaken by Mr. Louis L. Ray, under my direction, but only preliminary results are now available. The higher and earlier terraces record events not immediately involved in the question of the antiquity of Folsom man and description of these terraces and events is here omitted. The lower and younger terraces obviously belong to very Late Pleistocene or Recent time and are directly related to the Folsom culture.

The little Lindenmeier valley (Fig. 19) owes its form to successive piracies between the headwater streams tributary to Boxelder Creek. Only so much of the history of these drainage changes is here given as is necessary to explain the form of the valley and the existence of the Folsom deposits. The valley has an east-southeast course which was attained in the fourth stage below the High Plains surface. Previous to that time drainage in this area had been southeast and thus more directly into Boxelder Creek. As the valley developed in this new position its floor lay just below the contact of the pervious Arikaree and the impervious Brule, locally a compact white tuff. Water moves through the tuff along joints and by capillarity in its fine-grained pores. Water emerges at the base of the Arikaree in only a few places as definite springs. Usually it emerges through the capillaries of the underlying tuff so that there result large areas of springy ground covered with rushes, sedges and other water-

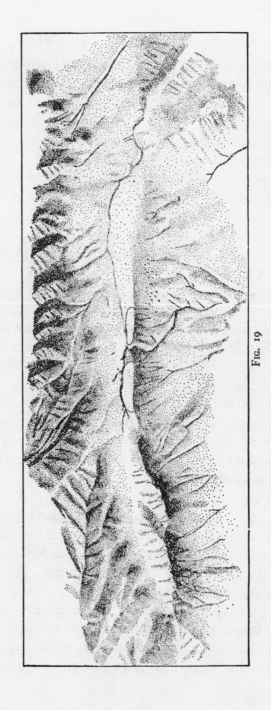

Fig. 19

loving plants. Springs, particularly in the broader valleys give rise to great swampy meadows. When the Lindenmeier valley was in this stage (No. 5), its floor must have been relatively wet and swampy and it must have resembled the area around the present Branigan Spring three miles northeast, or the large meadow in the drainage of Spottlewood Creek which has an area of about thirty acres.

A cross section (Fig. 20) shows that the southern slope of the valley once extended farther south than now. It was cut in the white tuff, and on the slope dark earth accumulated partly from the decay of swampy vegetation and partly from the débris of camps.

Immediately above the culture layer there is a rubble of particles and fragments of tuff which reaches a thickness of about twelve to fourteen feet near the center of the valley. This material has been carefully recorded in detailed sections by Dr. Roberts in his paper of 1936. Some change occurred by which the moist condition of this valley slope no longer existed and fragments from the higher slope accumulated as a side hill wash. This condition can be explained by the next succeeding event, a lowering of the ground water table by piracy. The streams working headward from the south and having a more direct course to Boxelder Creek and the Cache la Poudre had, during this interval, been attacking the south wall of Lindenmeier Valley. Their grades began to be lowered in the 6th stage and with this lowering the ground water was diverted although the surface waters still flowed down the valley to the east. As a camp site and location for a hunt, the valley lost its principal attraction, the grassy floor and slopes. The spring broke out in the flat to the south, leaving the valley dry. An episode of erosion also occurred by which the accumulations of débris ("A" in Fig. 20) in the valley were excavated. Again sedimentation occurred and a new deposit ("B" in Fig. 20) of sand and gravel lying largely to the north of the old, was formed. This is barren of Folsom or other cultural remains.

The last lowering of grade (stage 7) took place as the streams on the south lowered their grades, and surface waters of Lindenmeier Valley were diverted and poured over the southern rim of the valley to form an abrupt gulley forty to seventy feet deep which is a marked feature of the site.

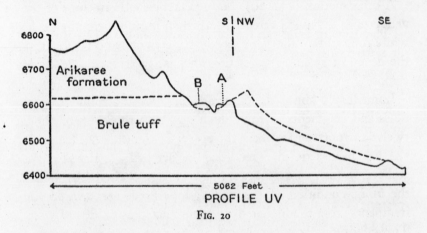

PROFILE UV

Fig. 20

The mere recital of this history indicates that the culture layer is relatively old. It is eroded on the south and buried to the north under twelve to fourteen feet of accumulated material, reexcavated and again buried. However, to place these events in a chronology requires even more elaborate study, which is in progress under the auspices of the Smithsonian Institution. The culture layer was formed in stage 5 of the sequence at the site. The valley floor, if traced downstream, becomes a terrace about twenty feet above stream grade and one of a series of terraces on the minor tributaries of Boxelder Creek and Cache la Poudre River. From this circumstance arose the hope that the local chronology could be fitted into a larger chronology, and this paper may be considered as a preliminary report on such an investigation. It seems possible that these terraces and specifically stage 5 can be traced downstream thirty miles to the Cache la Poudre and that the equivalent terrace can thence be traced up the Cache la Poudre eighty miles to the glacial cirques. It seems probable that the terraces might be so related to the moraines of the last glaciation in the mountains as to afford a correlation. This task has been assumed by Mr. Ray, and I present very briefly his most important results.

The twenty-foot terrace of the Lindenmeier site if traced downstream appears to be the thirty-foot terrace of the Cache la Poudre and the South Platte rivers. Additional evidence that the thirty-foot terrace is critical is gained from numerous Folsom finds at Kersey on the South Platte. Here Folsom artifacts occur in a sandy slope graded to the terrace. Although relations are obscure, it appears that Folsom man occupied the site when the river flowed on the grade of the thirty-foot terrace. The location seems to have no advantage as a campsite with the river at its present grade and location, whereas with the river on the thirty-foot grade, the site appears ideal for a hunter's camp.

This terrace is tentatively correlated with a twenty-five-foot terrace in the mountain section of the Cache la Poudre River. Above it are a fifty-foot, a ninety-foot and still higher terraces (see Fig. 21). Below it are a ten-foot and six-foot terrace which are unrepresented at the Lindenmeier site unless they may be related to the most recent fill. ("B" in Fig. 20.)

The Cache la Poudre Canyon has two well-defined moraines, one at the locality called Home and also on its tributaries at Chambers Lake, Corral Creek and Long Draw. The Home Moraine by reason of its relatively fresh till, the preservation of its topographic features, and its position within the canyon is attributed to the Wisconsin glaciation. The upper moraines, of the Corral Creek stage, probably represent a readvance of the ice marked by what was probably a long halt. Above the moraines of the Corral Creek stage there are no well-defined moraines but a plain of pitted outwash gravels below the now empty cirques.

The position of these terraces is shown diagrammatically in Fig. 21. The terraces conform to the grade of the stream. Evidence for their existence is scarcer in the steeper portions of the river—the canyon sections—but there is no question of their existence and essential continuity.

As shown by Fig. 21 the ninety-foot terrace ends at the Home Moraine. It appears, therefore, to represent the climax of the Wisconsin glaciation in this area. The fifty-foot terrace ends at the Corral Creek moraine and is correlatable with a late stage of the Wisconsin. The twenty-five-foot terrace extends to the outwash area above the moraine and seems to be the time equivalent of late stage of glaciers just previous to their final extinction. The existence of lower terraces in this locality indicates, however, that there were still later minor episodes in the history of the final waning of the glaciers.

It would be premature to attempt to evaluate the time intervals represented by the lower terraces. Even the stages of retreat of mountain glaciers in the West are still too little known for one to be didactic about the significance of the Home and Corral Creek stages. If the usual interpretation is placed on this record, it would be fair to say that the Corral Creek moraine represents a time after the climax of the Wisconsin and that the pitted outwash upstream from it represents a time well within the glacial retreat.

Correlation of the twenty-five-foot terrace of the Cache la Poudre whose date is thus tentatively fixed with the period of formation of the little valley (stage 5) of the Lindenmeier site is subject to the error of work carried over a distance of over one hundred miles. The date thus arrived at is also tentative. Subject to these limitations, however, the work has been more successful than at the original New Mexico locality. We can

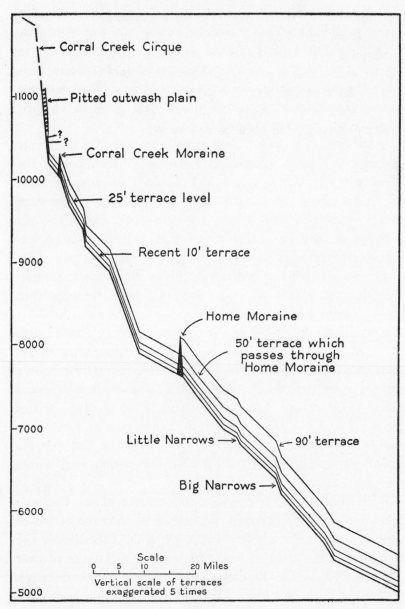

11000

Corral Creek Cirque

Pitted outwash plain

?
?
Corral Creek Moraine

10000

25' terrace level

Recent 10' terrace

9000

Home Moraine

8000

50' terrace which
passes through
Home Moraine

7000

Little Narrows →

90' terrace

Big Narrows →

6000

Scale
0 5 10   20 Miles

Vertical scale of terraces
exaggerated 5 times

5000

FIG. 21

conclude that Folsom man flourished during a time when glaciers, somewhat larger than now exist, still lingered in the mountains, and when, by inference, the climate was somewhat cooler and wetter than now. Changes in climate that have since ensued have caused alternate erosion and deposition on many minor streams so that, except in favorable places, his culture strata generally have been carried away.

THE FOLSOM PROBLEM IN AMERICAN ARCHAEOLOGY

BY

FRANK H. H. ROBERTS, JR.

*Archaeologist, Bureau of American Ethnology,
Smithsonian Institution*

THE so-called Folsom problem has assumed an important place in American archaeology during the last decade. It is outstanding in popular interest and in scientific circles is regarded as significant. This is due to the fact that it is closely coupled to the question of Early Man in the New World. At several places in New Mexico and Colorado implements have been found in association with bones of extinct animals and in deposits suggestive of geologic antiquity. These discoveries help push the date of occupation farther back into the past and have encouraged renewed consideration of the length of time that Man has been in America. The more important sites where such finds have been made are those near Folsom, between Clovis and Portales, and in the Guadalupe Mountains in New Mexico; and at the Lindenmeier Ranch and Dent in Colorado.

The first in the series—that which gave its name to archaeological remains of the type—is on a small intermittent tributary of the Cimarron River about eight miles west of Folsom, New Mexico. It was discovered in 1925 by local residents of Raton, New Mexico, and reported to J. D. Figgins, then director of the Colorado Museum of Natural History, at Denver. Bones sent to the museum showed that the remains were those of an extinct species of bison and of a large deer-like member of the Cervidae.

Prospects for fossil material were so promising that the Colorado Museum sent a party to the site in the summer of 1926. Parts of two finely chipped projectile points were recovered from the loose dirt during the excavations. Near the place where one of them was picked up a small triangular piece of stone was found embedded in the clay surrounding an animal bone. This fragment was left in the block of earth and sent to the laboratory at Denver. When the dirt was carefully cleaned away from the stone it was noted that it was of the same material as one of the points. Close examination showed that it was actually a part of the point as the two pieces fitted together. This indicated a definite association between man-made objects and an extinct bison. Mr. Figgins was greatly impressed by the find and reported it to a number of archaeologists, but the information was skeptically received in most quarters and he was given little encouragement.

The Colorado Museum again sent a party to Folsom in the summer of 1927 and had the good fortune to find additional points. One of these was noted before it was completely uncovered and work was stopped. Telegrams were sent to various institutions inviting them to send representatives to view the point *in situ*. Dr. Barnum Brown of the American Museum of Natural History, New York, and the writer responded. The point was embedded in the matrix between two bison ribs—in fact it has never been removed from the block which is now on exhibit in the museum at Denver—and there was no question but that the association was authentic. The writer returned to Raton and telegraphed to Dr. A. V. Kidder, then associated with Phillips Academy, now with the Carnegie Institution of Washington, and urged that he also visit the site. Dr. Kidder arrived two days later. That winter Dr. Brown, Dr. Kidder, and the writer reported on the finds at the annual meeting of the American Anthropological Association at Andover, Massachusetts. In

PLATE IX—Original Folsom Point *in situ*, Colorado Museum of Natural History photograph.

spite of the convincing nature of the evidence, most of the anthropologists continued to doubt the validity of the discovery.

The American Museum of Natural History and the Colorado Museum cooperated at the site in 1928. Dr. Barnum Brown headed the expedition. Additional bison skeletons were found with accompanying points and numerous specialists—archaeologists, paleontologists, and geologists—went to check the evidence. Consensus was that the finds were a reliable indication that Man was present in the Southwest at an earlier period than formerly supposed and that they constituted one of the most important contributions yet made to American archaeology. Most of the critics of previous years became enthusiastic converts and endorsed the Folsom materials. At the conclusion of his work Dr. Brown stated that the sediments overlying the bone bed belonged to the close of the Pleistocene and placed the remains at the end of that period. Some of the experts supported this opinion. Others believed that the site should be considered early Recent rather than Pleistocene and there the matter rests today.

The points associated with the bison bones differed from the ordinary types scattered over that portion of the Southwest. They were laurel-leaf shaped blades and were characterized by a longitudinal fluting on each face. In addition there was a secondary chipping along the edges that bespoke a highly developed stone-flaking technique. They became known as Folsom points.

The second important New Mexican area contains several sites. It lies approximately one hundred and sixty miles southeast of Folsom, between Clovis and Portales, not far from the Texas-New Mexico boundary. The sites were reported to Dr. E. B. Howard in the summer of 1932. He visited the area at that time and returned again the following November when a road construction company, digging for gravel, exposed a layer of bluish clay containing quantities of animal bones and signs of human occupation. As a result of that inspection Dr. Howard planned a series of investigations for the summer of 1933. This began as a joint undertaking of the Academy of Natural Sciences of Philadelphia and the University of Pennsylvania Museum. Later in the season Dr. John C. Merriam, president of the Carnegie Institution of Washington, visited the excavations and became so enthused over the prospects that he arranged for the California Institute of Technology to send a party, under Dr. Chester Stock, to cooperate in the work. Dr. Howard returned to the sites in the summer of 1934 in company with Dr. Ernst Antevs who studied the physiography of the region in an endeavor to date the sites. Dr. Howard again led a party to the Clovis sector in the summer of 1936. This was a joint project of the Academy of Natural Sciences of Philadelphia, the Carnegie Institution of Washington, and the University of Pennsylvania Museum.

The area is part of the Staked Plains, the old Llano Estacado of the Spanish explorers. In this district the flatness of the terrain is broken only by sand dunes rising along the edges of shallow depressions. These dry basins occur in a series that extends in a general east-southeasterly direction about midway between Clovis and Portales. Evidence points to a former period of heavy precipitation. At that time the basins were more or less permanently filled with water. Subsequent desiccation reduced them to mere water holes. They eventually dried up entirely and were filled with drift sand. Recent wind and water action have left them in varying stages of erosion. The sand has been whipped up into dunes along the northeastern borders of many of them, exposing a hard bluish-gray deposit. These constitute what are known locally as "blowouts." In some the bluish layer has been cut down to a harder, underlying stratum of caliche leaving shelves or benches around the edges of the basins and "erosion islands" scattered through the middle. Excavations in these shelves and islands yield animal bones, stone artifacts, some bone tools, charcoal and ashes. Many of the bones show the effects of fire. In numerous cases there is a definite association between the bones and man-made objects. The bones represent an extinct species of bison and the mammoth. Hence there is little question but what in this region man was contemporary with both animals. Camel and horse bones are present in lower levels antedating the human period.

Implements found there comprise projectile points, various kinds of scrapers, rough-flake knives, knives, blades, gravers, and bone tools of unidentified function. The projectile points are significant because many are comparable to the fluted examples from the original Folsom quarry. Others do not have as pronounced channels and some do not have the feature at all. The latter correspond to a much disputed form called the Yuma. The presence of the fluted forms is an indication of some cultural relationship between the makers of these implements and those from the Folsom pit. The meaning of the so-called Yuma specimens is not clear. They may belong to the Folsom implement complex, but it is possible that they represent trade objects from another complex. This is still to be determined.

Geologic evidence indicates that the blue-gray stratum in the Clovis region was a lake deposit, probably laid down when temperatures were lower and there was much more precipitation. These conditions have led Dr. Antevs to conclude that the time represented corresponds to the end of the Pleistocene period, his pluvial stage, dating back 12,000 to 13,000 years in this particular district.

At Burnet Cave in the Guadalupe Mountains, southeastern New Mexico, Dr. Howard found a fluted point in association with bones from an extinct bison and an extinct muskox-like bovid. This association in itself was indicative of some antiquity, but there was further significance in the fact that it occurred in a stratum underlying Basket Maker material. The latter belongs to the oldest definitely established horizon in the culture-pattern sequence of the Pueblo area in the Southwest and dates back some two thousand years. The point and the bones unquestionably are much older as they were in a hearth four feet below the bottom of the Basket Maker level.

The Lindenmeier Site is twenty-eight miles north of Ft. Collins, Colorado. It was discovered in 1924 by A. L. Coffin and his father, Judge C. C. Coffin. During the decade from 1924 to 1934 the judge, his son, and a brother of the judge, Major Roy G. Coffin of Colorado State College, visited it intermittently and collected specimens. From the beginning of their finds they recognized that the points were different from the ordinary arrowheads, so abundant in the region, but were not aware of their true significance until 1931 when they learned that they were Folsom type. Most of their material was gathered from the surface. A few implements were scratched out of the soil, but there was no attempt at extensive digging. The site was brought to the attention of the Bureau of American Ethnology, Smithsonian Institution, in the summer of 1934 by Major Coffin. As a result of a series of letters from the Major, the writer went to Ft. Collins in September. The owner of the land, Mr. William Lindenmeier Jr., gave permission for a series of investigations and preliminary prospecting was started. This first work was continued through October and into November. Most of the digging was confined to a deep pit in an arroyo bank where there was an exposed layer containing bones and artifacts, although some excavations were made at other portions of the site in an effort to determine its extent.

In 1935 two large trenches were dug across the portion of the site lying south of the deep pit in the ravine. This was done to reveal a complete cross-section of the deposits overlying the specimen bearing stratum and to determine the source of the objects found in the deep pit. Trenches were also dug through a portion of the area near the location of the original Coffin finds. A bone pile comprising remains from nine individual bison, *Bison taylori*, was uncovered. Further work carried on at this location in 1936 revealed the remains of a feast or barbecue. The carcasses of the animals, those found the previous year and others included in the new material, had been dismembered and cooked at the scene of the kill. Many bones were charred and several projectile points recovered from the debris exhibit the effects of fire. In addition numerous implements of various kinds were associated with the bones. Further interest was added by the fact that several foot bones from the camel, probably *Camelops*, were with the implements. Excavations made near the previous year's trenches yielded ample evidence of human occupation. There were traces of surface fires, quantities of debris left by the makers when they chipped the implements, and numerous broken and unfinished tools. No signs of habitations have been found, however.

During the summer of 1935 the Colorado Museum of Natural History also conducted excavations at the Lindenmeier Site. These consisted of a series of fifteen test pits spaced at intervals across the site, approximately at right angles to the line of the main trenches of the Smithsonian party. One of these test holes, west of the large trenches, penetrated the artifact bearing stratum where there was a concentration of material. With this as a starting point an area thirty by thirty feet was excavated. This pit yielded most of the specimens obtained by the Denver group. The material thus secured adds to the general fund of information on the site.

Approximately two thousand stone implements and a few ornaments, two of carved bone, as well as bones from animals have come from the excavations. No human skeletal material has been found. The general complex of implements consists of characteristically fluted points, snub-nosed scrapers, side scrapers, end scrapers, a variety of cutting edges, drills, gravers, chisel-gravers, rough-flake knives, fluted knives, large blades, sandstone rubbing stones, and a few bone tools, probably punches or awls. Most of the stone artifacts are chipped or flaked—there are no polished tools—and show that the lithic component in the material culture was primarily a flake industry. Only a few tools of the core type were found. These were mainly hammers and choppers.

Dr. Kirk Bryan of Harvard University has been in charge of geologic studies of the site and conclusions concerning its age must come from him. Evidence from the digging shows that the occupation level was once an old valley bottom which subsequently was filled in by the wearing away of bordering ridges. At the present time it suggests a terrace above an intermittent tributary to a series of streams that eventually join the South Platte River. This effect has been produced by erosion of the ridges which once bordered the valley on the south. At the time of occupation the valley bottom was dotted with bogs and marshy places. The makers of the implements camped on the slopes above these meadows.

The find at Dent, Colorado, which lies some sixty miles southeast of the Lindenmeier Site, consisted of mammoth skeletons and two large fluted points. This association is in agreement with that at Clovis. The digging was done by a party from the Colorado Museum of Natural History.

From evidence now at hand a broad generalization of the Folsom problem would be as follows: No human remains have been found and, so far as his physical characteristics are concerned, Folsom man is still an unknown person. There is no information on the type of shelter he may have used. On the other hand it seems obvious that he was a typical hunter depending entirely upon game—mainly bison but occasionally the mammoth and a stray camel—for his maintenance and sustenance. He no doubt supplemented his preponderant meat diet with wild seeds and "greens" but did not cultivate his own vegetal food. From information gathered at two sites his age has been placed at the end of the Pleistocene or possibly the beginning of the Recent period. Conclusions about the status of the Lindenmeier Site are still in the formative stage.

Mention should be made of the distribution of the fluted-type points. They have been known for a long time and variations of the form have been found from the Rockies to the Atlantic, from southern Canada to the Gulf of Mexico. The type is represented in collections in numerous museums and in at least one case has been called by another name, the Seneca River point. It did not attract particular attention until the finds at Folsom. This was largely because most of the examples were surface finds and without definite significance. There are two main classes of fluted points. One is represented by the Folsom specimens. The other is a larger, more generalized one embodying most of the characteristics but not exhibiting the same degree of skilled workmanship in their manufacture. The latter have the wider distribution. The question is whether all should be called Folsom points or if there should be some designation that does not carry the implication of equal age. H. C. Shetrone of the Ohio State Museum has suggested that they be termed Fluted Points as a class and the various forms then be more specifically designated by place names such as Folsom, Clovis, Lindenmeier, etc. This proposal has considerable merit and if adopted would remove much of the present confusion.

The significance of the fluted points occurring east of the Mississippi River is an open question. There is no evidence to suggest their possible age or place in the main archaeological picture. The vast majority are surface finds and although there are several centers—notably in Ohio, Tennessee, southern Virginia, Georgia, and western New York—where they are found in comparatively large numbers nothing has come to light which would indicate their relationship to the cultural remains present in those areas. The fact that the eastern examples bear a striking resemblance to those in the west does not make them of equal antiquity. They may represent the survival of a highly specialized and efficient implement in later horizons. The individuality of the form, however, and the apparent absence of the type from the recognized cultural complexes in the east is considered by some as a manifestation of its age. Also, from the standpoint of its wider distribution some are prone to believe it older than the western examples, basing their conclusions on the theory that the greater the distribution the older the type. Until examples are found in undisturbed deposits and in association with fauna comparable to that in the west no definite statements can be made. Only additional work will solve the problem.

THE SIGNIFICANCE OF PROFILES OF WEATHERING IN STRATIGRAPHIC ARCHAEOLOGY

BY

M. M. LEIGHTON

Chief, Illinois State Geological Survey

Oₙₑ very important line of inquiry in dating a deposit containing evidences of early man *in situ* is an examination of the profile of weathering in the upper portion of the deposit, and if there are any superjacent materials, their degree of weathering should also be observed. This is a part of stratigraphic archaeology.

The term "profile of weathering", as used here, is synonymous with the term "soil profile" as used by pedologists. The former, however, is preferred because the term soil has been otherwise employed, and is still popularly employed, in a sense quite different from that in which pedologists use it today.

"Profile of weathering" is a term applied to all of those clearly recognizable subdivisions of the weathered zone, as seen in a vertical or nearly vertical geologic section. The natural physical and chemical characteristics of these divisions are due to processes operating through sufficient geologic time to leave their impress, and they reflect the climatic, topographic, and vegetative environment in which the deposit has existed. In the early stages of the cycle the profile also reflects to more or less degree the characteristics of the parent material.

The late Dr. K. D. Glinka, Director of the Agricultural Institute of Leningrad, appears to have been the first to call attention to the detailed characteristics of profiles of weathering, or soil profiles as he called them, as a result of a very extended study

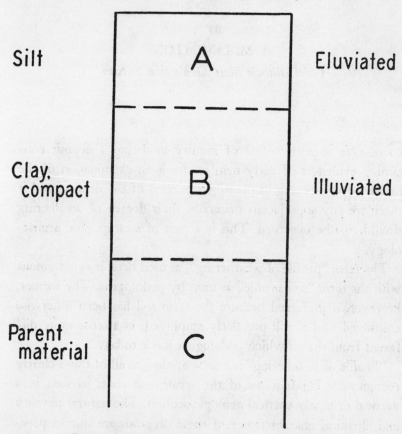

Silt   A   Eluviated

Clay, compact   B   Illuviated

Parent material   C

FIG. 22—Idealized diagram of Glinka's soil profile.

of the soils on the widespread youngest glacial drift-sheet of Russia.[1] Briefly it may be said here that he recognized the following subdivisions, beginning at the top: a surficial material

[1] D. Glinka, "Die Typen der Bodenbildung, ihre Klassifikation und geographische Verbreitung" (Berlin: Verlag Gebrüder Borntraeger, 1914).

(A, eluvial, in Fig. 22) from which, either by chemical or mechanical means (probably both), more or less material has been removed or eluviated; beneath this, a subzone (B, illuvial, Fig. 22), into which the clayey material has been introduced chemically or mechanically; and beneath this, the parent material (C, Fig. 22). His A includes the humus-charged silty material, as well as any non-humus silty material, that lies above the denser, more compact, and plastic B (when wet). Glinka also pointed out, among other things, that vegetation as well as climate had its effect upon the nature of the profile.

This classic work was followed by similar studies by pedologists and geologists in this country, particularly under the stimulation of the late Dr. C. A. Marbut, in charge of the Soil Survey Division of the Bureau of Soils, United States Department of Agriculture, who had had the opportunity of field conferences and observations in Russia.

Much work had already been done by geologists in this country in determining what chemical changes take place in producing weathered zones, either from solid rock or from glacial drift, but not until Kay[2] pointed out that the gumbotil on the Kansan drift of southern Iowa was derived from normal glacial till by advanced chemical weathering *under broad, poorly drained flats*, did geologists or pedologists give much attention to the effect of topographic environment in producing such materials in weathered zones. This was a distinct step of progress. Later MacClintock and the present author began to apply Glinka's philosophy to the interpretation of the weathered zones on various drift-sheets in Illinois. This work resulted in the recognition of an equally significant product, silttil, a counter-

[2] G. F. Kay, "Gumbotil, a New Term in Pleistocene Geology," Science, New Series, Vol. XLIV (1916), pp. 637-38; G. F. Kay, and J. N. Pearce, "The Origin of Gumbotil," Jour. Geol., Vol. XXVIII (1920), pp. 89-125.

part of gumbotil, resulting from weathering *under conditions of good drainage.*[3]

STAGES OF PROFILE DEVELOPMENT

Dependent upon time, climate, nature of the materials, and other factors, there are several stages of profile development to be recognized.

> Stage of Infancy
> Stage of Youth
> Stage of Maturity
> Stage of Old Age

The following description of these stages, with the exception of the last, is based on observations made in the glaciated area of the upper Mississippi Valley, and, therefore, is applicable only to areas having similar climatic and topographic conditions.

Stage of Infancy. A profile of weathering which is in its initial stage of change, but showing only incipient subdivisions of the weathered zone, may be said to be in *infancy.* Deposits on the so-called "second-flats" of some stream valleys, or some ridge-loess deposits adjacent to our major Midwest valleys show such a profile of weathering. Some flood-plain deposits are too recent to show any weathering and, therefore, are not even classed in this stage. The majority of the Indian Mounds of the upper Mississippi Valley do not possess weathered zones, except for the introduction of some humus material. This is the *initial part* of the infancy stage.

Stage of Youth. A profile of weathering may be said to be in a stage of youth when it possesses those subdivisions shown by the Wisconsin drift-sheets of North America (Fig. 23). In this case there are four clearly recognizable subdivisions: (1) a

[3] M. M. Leighton and Paul MacClintock, "Weathered Zones of the Drift-Sheets of Illinois," Jour. Geol., Vol. XXXVIII, No. 1, (1930), pp. 28-53; reprinted in Illinois State Geological Survey Report of Investigations No. 20, (1930).

top soil which has been more or less eluviated and in which most of the coarse-grained arkosic rocks and the limestones have been weathered out; (2) a brownish, more or less illuviated, compact and plastic subzone, into which clay particles from (1) have

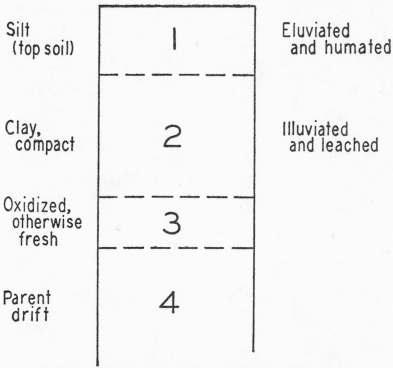

Silt (top soil)   1   Eluviated and humated

Clay, compact   2   Illuviated and leached

Oxidized, otherwise fresh   3

Parent drift   4

FIG. 23—Idealized diagram of a youthful profile of weathering.

been introduced, from which limestone pebbles have been dissolved, but in which arkosic rocks are still present; (3) a yellowish, oxidized zone, unleached of its calcareous material, and less compact than (2); this grades down into the unweathered parent material (4).

Only rarely do we find an Indian Mound in the upper Mississippi Valley which, when incised, shows some of these characteristics. One near Utica, Illinois, was examined by Dr. A. R. Kelly and the writer in 1931 and briefly described.[4]

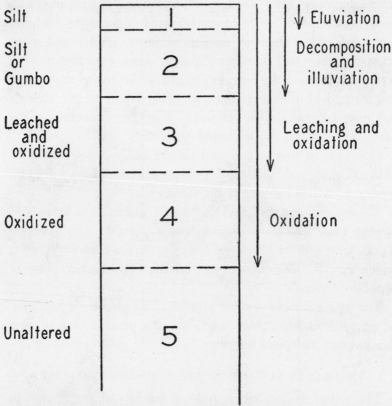

FIG. 24—Generalized profile of mature weathering. Mature weathering under conditions of good drainage produces a silty material in the No. 2 horizon whereas mature weathering under poor drainage produces gumbo.

Stage of Maturity. A profile of weathering may be said to be in a stage of maturity when it possesses the following subdivisions (Fig. 24): (1) a top soil not readily distinguishable from the youthful stage, but probably more siliceous in chemi-

[4] M. M. Leighton, "Some observations on the antiquity of man in Illinois," Trans. Ill. Acad. Science, Vol. 25, No. 4, p. 83, (1934).

cal composition and less fertile; (2) a very definite gumbo (compact, very plastic when wet, hard and jointed when dry) where the topography is flat and poorly drained, a silty material where the topography is rolling and well drained, with all gradations between for intermediate types of topography, pebbles few, small and of the most resistant varieties, granites and other arkosic rocks rare, limestones absent, some concentration of ferric iron oxide at the base; (3) material oxidized to rusty color and leached of calcareous material, otherwise but little altered; (4) material oxidized to yellowish color, but unleached of its calcium carbonate; (5) unaltered material.

This kind of profile is found on the older drift-sheets—Illinoian, Kansan, and Nebraskan, each successively older and more weathered where exposed at the surface.

No deposits of these ages in North America are known to contain evidences of early man, except possibly near Abilene, Texas, where in the Durst old soil beneath the Elm Creek Silts, which may be Sangamon in age, charcoal and flint chips were found by Sayles.[5]

The writer has not studied profiles of weathering which may be referred to the old age stage, but it is possible that lateritic deposits may represent this stage.

PROFILES IN SUB-HUMID AND SEMI-ARID CLIMATES

The writer made a brief study of profiles of weathering in west central Texas in connection with his examination of the geology of the silts containing evidences of primitive man near Abilene. This region is part of the open plains country, having an average rainfall of about twenty-five inches, a mean July temperature of 82°, a mean January temperature of 44°, and strong evaporative winds. It is distinctly sub-humid, bordering on

[5] Referred to in article by M. M. Leighton, "Geological Aspects of the Findings of Primitive Man, near Abilene, Texas," Medallion Papers No. XXIV, The Medallion, Gila Pueblo, Globe, Arizona, (1936), p. 25.

the semi-arid. It is a region of calcareous subsoils, or dark choco-
late-brown soils. Caliche is of widespread occurrence on deposits
of proper character, sufficient geologic age, and favorable topographic position. This unique material distinguishes the profiles
of weathering of this region from those of the more humid
upper Mississippi Valley.

The stages of profile development represented in this region
range from *infancy* to *maturity*. The silts on the second flats of
the streams commonly show a profile of weathering in the stage
of infancy. There is little or no leaching but the top soil is fairly
uniformly charged with humus matter. The somewhat higher
levels of the Elm Creek silts show profiles of weathering in early
youth—a humus-charged soil layer, a compact zone with columnar structure, twelve to eighteen inches thick, and leaching
down to a depth of eighteen inches. In these silts many artifacts
of primitive man have been found by Sayles and others. It is
believed that the early youthful profiles on these silts may possibly correspond in time to the youthful profiles on the Wisconsin drift of the upper Mississippi Valley. At several horizons
in these silts are dark layers which, at a distance, have the appearance of old soil layers, but a close examination reveals that
they possess no profiles of weathering, they are calcareous
throughout, and contain a fauna of small gastropod and pele-
cypod shells of both water and land forms. The dark layers
appear to mark intervals between the slack-water floods which
laid down the silts, during which humate salts were introduced—
intervals too short geologically for weathering processes to leave
their record. It is on the surfaces of these dark layers that the
stone hearths occur.

Reference has already been made to the Durst Silts below the
Elm Creek Silts (Plate X), which show mature profiles of
weathering with a well developed soil layer in the No. 1 horizon,
gumbo in the No. 2 horizon, a rusty zone at the base of No. 2,

PLATE X—View of Durst silts with old soil (Sangamon?) overlain by Elm Creek silts, near Abilene, Texas. The pick is directed to a flint chip embedded in the old soil. (Leighton, M. M., "Geological Aspects of the Findings of Primitive Man, Near Abilene, Texas," Medallion Papers No. XXIV, Gila Pueblo, Globe, Ariz. 1936.)

and caliche and much less weathered stony silt in the No. 3 horizon. The gumbo just below the soil, in another exposure a short distance down stream, has columnar structure and contains scattered small siliceous pebbles and iron-manganese pellets up to three-eighths of an inch in diameter. A brief petrographic examination of samples of the old soil was made by Dr. R. E. Grim of the Illinois Geological Survey, and this examination showed that the soil has all of the aspects of prolonged weathering, being composed of rounded grains of quartz, 1 mm. or less in diameter, bonded together with iron hydroxide, some amorphous silica grains, some larger grains of quartz, and a few pellets of iron, alumina, and manganese. Clay mineral matter is very scant, evidently having been largely eluviated. No feldspars were found. The gumbo is composed of a clay-mineral of the beidellite-montmorillonite family—a product of weathering, rounded grains of quartz, amorphous silica, iron hydroxide, and of the feldspars only orthoclase was found. In contrast with this composition, the rusty zone below shows much less clay mineral, no amorphous silica, a greater abundance of orthoclase feldspar, and some grains of plagioclase feldspar. Thus, the evidence for a mature profile of weathering seems complete.

A mature profile was also noted on Tertiary or Early Pleistocene gravel at a relatively low physiographic level, yet somewhat higher than the Elm Creek Silts. This exposure is described in The Medallion Papers No. XXIV of Gila Pueblo, already referred to in a footnote of this paper. The divisions of this profile are readily distinguishable: Horizon 1 is a dark topsoil, non-calcareous, Horizon 2 is a compact zone, with columnar structure, non-calcareous except for secondary calcium carbonate, and the pebbles are relatively few and small and show much weathering in contrast with those of Horizon 4. Horizon 3 shows a concentration of caliche, and Horizon 4 shows oxidized gravel, otherwise little changed.

CONCLUSION

It is evident from the foregoing that critical attention should be paid to profiles of weathering as an aid to the correlation of physiographic levels and the unravelling of the stratigraphy of surficial deposits. Some of these deposits are proving to be rich caches, especially in the southwest and the western plains, for archaeologists. They reveal that man in America does date back into geologic time to some extent. It is also apparent that much more work on the geology of the surficial formations with an eye to physiographic levels and profiles of weathering from one region to another, and especially from one climatic environment to another, is sorely needed. When this is accomplished, the last chapter of the Earth's history, which has been so commonly neglected in areas beyond the glacial border, will be clarified, and man's place in that history will in all probability be revealed.

THE PLEISTOCENE MAMMALS OF
NORTH AMERICA AND THEIR RELATIONS
TO EURASIAN FORMS

BY

EDWIN H. COLBERT

*Assistant Curator of Vertebrate Paleontology of the American
Museum of Natural History, and Associate Curator of
Geology and Paleontology of The Academy .of Natural
Sciences of Philadelphia*

I. INTRODUCTION

THE study of early man in the Old and New Worlds is necessarily closely connected with a study of the animals with which
he was associated. In order to understand primitive man and the
cultures that he evolved, it is essential to know as much as possible about the world in which he lived—about the climatic conditions that governed the course of his daily life, about the
nature of the country he inhabited, about the plants around him
and particularly about the animals with which he had to com-
pete for existence and which were so closely interwoven through
the pattern of his cultural development. To primitive man the
mammals that lived around him, particularly the larger mammals, were the chief source of his supply of food and clothing—
they were in effect the prime motivating factor in the establishment and the perfection of his early flint, stone and bone
industries. Therefore the mammals contemporaneous with early
man are especially important to the student of human evolution.

II. THE ESTABLISHMENT OF THE HOLARCTIC FAUNA

The study of the distribution of modern animals has shown
that the several continents may be grouped or separated according to the relationships of their faunas. Thus it has become evident from a study of continental animals, and of mammals in

particular, that the north temperate portion of the world, including North America, Asia north of the Himalaya Mountains, Europe and the northern tip of Africa, north of the Atlas Mountains, constitutes a single zoogeographic area, the Holarctic region, in which the animal life, especially the mammalian life, is essentially uniform. Other portions of the earth lie outside of this great Holarctic region, and are distinguished from it by their different mammalian faunas. Of course, differences exist within the Holarctic region too, especially between that portion contained in the eastern hemisphere, the Palaearctic division, and that contained in the western hemisphere, the Nearctic division. But these differences, numerous as they may be, do not obscure the general unity of the Holarctic fauna as viewed in its broader aspects.

Now there must be a very basic and deep-seated origin for this unified Holarctic fauna. An examination of the fossil faunas shows that such is the case.

Tracing the history of mammalian assemblages back through time, we find that during the Pleistocene period, the age of wide-spread glaciation, the broad consanguinity of the mammalian faunas of the north temperate zone was just as typical then as it is now. And carrying our studies back further in geologic time, through the Pliocene period and back to the upper part of the Miocene period, it may be seen that similar relationships of faunas held true even in those relatively distant days.

The reason for these similarities of fossil faunas in North America and Eurasia is not difficult to find. For it would seem evident that since upper Miocene times the two continents have been connected by a land bridge, joining Alaska and Siberia. This trans-Bering land connection undoubtedly has varied in extent through upper Tertiary and Quaternary times, being broad during the periods of general continental uplift, and narrow or even non-existent during the periods of general continental depressions. But for the most part it has undoubtedly been

PLATE XI—Pleistocene mammals contemporaneous with man in North America and Eurasia. From top to bottom: Mastodon—North America; Royal bison and horse—North America; Reindeer—Eurasia; Woolly mammoth—Eurasia and North America. Copyrighted by The American Museum of Natural History, painted by Charles R. Knight under the direction of Henry Fairfield Osborn.

a positive, uplifted element since about the closing phases of the Miocene period, and as such it has served as a broad corridor for intercontinental migrations and consequent intermingling of the Palaearctic and Nearctic mammalian faunas. Thus there was established, during late Tertiary times, a common basis of heritage for the mammals of North America and Eurasia.

III. SIMILARITIES AND DIFFERENCES BETWEEN THE PLEISTO-
CENE FAUNAS OF NORTH AMERICA AND EURASIA

Now it is evident that the common heritage of the Holarctic fauna will be indicated to a certain extent by the similarities between the Pleistocene mammals of North America and those of Eurasia. The similar elements in the faunas of these two regions may be attributed to two sources, namely, the upper Tertiary ancestral forms shared in common by North America and Eurasia, and the Pleistocene species that migrated back and forth across the Bering land bridge.

An examination of the Pleistocene faunas of the two divisions of the Holarctic region will show that in the broadest aspects, similarities between them greatly outweigh differences. Thus out of eleven orders of Pleistocene continental mammals of Holarctic distribution, eight were common to both hemispheres, while three were restricted either to the Palaearctic or to the Nearctic sub-regions.

DISTRIBUTION OF MAMMALIAN ORDERS IN THE
PLEISTOCENE PERIOD

	Eurasia	North America
Marsupialia (pouched mammals—opossum)........		x
Insectivora (shrews, moles, etc.)..................	x———x	
Chiroptera (bats)................................	x———x	
Primates (monkeys, apes, man)...................	x	[x][1]
Edentata (sloths, armadillos, glyptodonts).........		x
Rodentia (rodents).............................	x———x	
Lagomorpha (rabbits, hares)....................	x———x	
Carnivora (dogs, bears, cats, etc.)...............	x———x	
Proboscidea (mastodonts, elephants)..............	x———x	
Perissodactyla (horses, rhinoceroses, tapirs)........	x———x	
Artiodactyla (pigs, peccaries, hippos, camels, deer, giraffes, antelope, cattle).....................	x———x	

[1] Man migrated to North America at the close of the Pleistocene period.

The two orders restricted to North America, namely, the opossums and the edentates, migrated into this region from South America at the close of Tertiary times. The one order restricted to Eurasia, namely, the Primates, never reached North America until late Pleistocene or post-Pleistocene times, when man crossed from Siberia to Alaska.

This brief glance at the larger groups of mammals demonstrates the essential unity of the Pleistocene fauna of the Holarctic region. Now when the smaller taxonomic divisions, the families, genera and species, are considered, the differences between the mammals of North America and Eurasia become increasingly apparent. They may be presented in the following tabular form:

Pleistocene Mammals of the Holarctic Region	Of Universal Extent	Percentage
11 orders............	8 orders	73%
52 families..........	18 families	40
About 300 genera...........	About 30 genera	10

Of several hundred species of Holarctic Pleistocene mammals, only a very few were of universal extent throughout the region.

It is only natural that these differences in the Pleistocene mammals of North America and Eurasia should appear and increase, as we progress in our consideration from the larger to the smaller taxonomic units. The differences are due to various causes. In certain instances, families were restricted throughout their history either to one continent or to the other, even though the orders to which they belonged were of universal extent. Thus, in the lesser aspects of the problem there were differences in the Tertiary heritage of the Pleistocene mammals of the Holarctic Region. Then again, many groups failed to migrate from one region to another. This restriction to the Old World or to the New World might have been due to various causes, such as restriction in size and a dependence on a restricted environment, restriction based on tropical or semitropical adaptations, or restriction as the result of specialized adaptations to a forest en-

THE DISTRIBUTION OF PLEISTOCENE HOLARCTIC MAMMALS

Order	Family	Eurasia	North America
Marsupialia	Didelphiidae—opossum.............		x
Insectivora	Erinaceidae—hedgehogs.............	x	
	Soricidae—shrews..................	x ——————→ x	
	Talpidae—moles....................	x	x
Chiroptera	Hipposideridae—leaf nosed bats......	x	
	Vespertilionidae—common bats......	x ——————→ x	
Lagomorpha	Leporidae—hares, rabbits............	x —————— x	
	Ochotonidae—pikas.................	x ——————→ x	
Rodentia	Sciuromorpha:		
	Aplodontidae—sewellel..............		x
	Sciuridae—squirrels.................	x —————— x	
	Heteromyidae—kangaroo rats		x
	Geomyidae—gophers................		x
	Castoridae—beavers................	x —————— x	
	Myomorpha:		
	Spalacidae—bamboo rats............	x	
	Muridae—Old World mice..........	x	
	Cricetidae—New World mice........		x
	Dipodidae—jerboas, etc.............	x	
	Zapodidae—jumping mice...........		x
	Myoxidae—dormice.................	x	
	Hystricomorpha:		
	Hystricidae—Old World porcupines...	x	
	Erethizontidae—New World porcupines		x
	Caviidae—capybara, etc.............		x
Edentata	Megatheriidae—ground sloths........		x
	Megalonychidae—ground sloths......		x
	Mylodontidae—ground sloths........		x
	Dasypodidae—armadillos............		x
	Glyptodontidae—glyptodonts........		x
Carnivora	Canidae—dogs, wolves, foxes, etc.....	x —————— x	
	Procyonidae—raccoons, pandas.......	x —————— x	
	Ursidae—bears.....................	x ——————→ x	
	Mustelidae—weasels, badgers, etc.....	x ——————→ x	
	Viverridae—civets..................	x	
	Hyaenidae—hyaenas................	x	
	Felidae—cats......................	x —————— x	
Primates	Cercopithecidae—monkeys...........	x	
	Pongidae—apes....................	x	
	Hominidae—men..................	x ——————→ [x]	
Proboscidea	Trilophodontidae—primitive masto-donts........................		x
	Mastodontidae—mastodonts.........		x
	Elephantidae—elephants, mammoths	x ——————→ x	

Order	Family	Eurasia	North America
Perissodactyla {	Equidae—horses...................	x ←———— x	
	Chalicotheriidae—chalicotheres.......	x	
	Rhinocerotidae—rhinoceroses........	x	
	Tapiridae—tapirs...................	x ————— x	
Artiodactyla {	Tayassuidae—peccaries..............		x
	Suidae—pigs........................	x	
	Hippopotamidae—hippos............	x	
	Camelidae—camels.................	x ←———— x	
	Cervidae—deer.....................	x ————→ x	
	Giraffidae—giraffes.................	x	
	Antilocapridae—pronghorns.........		x
	Bovidae—antelopes, cattle, etc........	x ————→ x	

Arrows indicate direction of migration, when such migration took place during the Pleistocene period.

Horizontal lines indicate the universal Holarctic distribution of a family, established prior to the beginning of the Pleistocene period.

vironment. In other cases, the differences between the Pleistocene mammals of North America and Eurasia were due to the fact that in one region or the other certain groups of universal Tertiary extent became extinct at the close of Tertiary times. And in the smaller taxonomic units, particularly the species, the effects of evolutionary change even during the relatively short duration of the Pleistocene period were sufficient to cause differences between related or identical genera in the two regions.

Finally, some differences in the Pleistocene faunas of North America and Eurasia are not to be explained on the basis of our present knowledge. Why, for instance, did not the woolly rhinoceros of Eurasia, an animal admittedly capable of migrating over great expanses of arctic wastelands, accompany the woolly mammoth into North America?

IV. THE DEVELOPMENT OF MAMMALIAN LIFE IN THE PLEISTOCENE OF THE HOLARCTIC REGION

Generally speaking, it may be said that the transition from the Pliocene into the Pleistocene was a continuous process, marked by the unbroken sequence of the mammalian faunas in their larger aspects. But at the same time, this transition was characterized by the widespread and rather complete "turnover"

PLATE XII—Late Pleistocene mammals of North America and Eurasia. From top to bottom: Woolly rhinoceros and saiga antelope—Eurasia; Extinct moose (*Cervalces*), tapir and giant beaver—North America; Sabre-tooth cat, giant ground sloth (*Mylodon*), imperial mammoth and dire wolf—North America. Copyrighted by The American Museum of Natural History, painted by Charles R. Knight under the direction of Henry Fairfield Osborn.

of the lesser elements of the faunas. That is, most of the orders and families of mammals continued from the Pliocene into the Pleistocene, but there was an almost complete change in the genera and species between the two periods.

Now this change in the detailed composition of the faunas, particularly with regard to certain wide-spread types, affords a convenient and a reliable guide to the beginning of the Pleistocene period. Of course, the Pleistocene period is usually defined as beginning with the first continental glaciation, but over a greater portion of the earth's surface evidences of this glaciation, either direct or indirect, are lacking. Consequently it becomes necessary to rely on other criteria as definitive of the advent of the Pleistocene, and of these criteria, the spread of certain mammals would seem to be the most accurate. On this basis it would seem that the Pleistocene period, through a greater portion of the northern hemisphere, was initiated by the sudden appearance and the wide-spread migrations of four types of large mammals, namely the monodactyl horse, *Equus*, the true elephants such as *Archidiskodon*, the true camels, *Camelops* and *Camelus*, and cattle of the *Bos* group (*Bos*, *Bison* and *Bubalus*). This is not a new idea, having been set forth (in a slightly different way) as long ago as 1911 by Haug, and more recently, in 1935, by Hopwood.

Of these mammals, the horse is the most diagnostic of the opening of the Pleistocene, because we know almost unequivocally its direct ancestry, and because it spread almost to the four corners of the earth. Thus, the *topmost* Pliocene horse, *Plesippus*, gave rise directly to the lowermost Pleistocene horse, *Equus*, in North America. From North America, *Equus* spread almost simultaneously to Asia, Europe and Africa. Consequently it may be said that the sudden appearance of *Equus* in North America, Eurasia and Africa marks the beginning of the Pleistocene in those continents.

Similarly, the camel evolved in North America, appearing at the beginning of the Pleistocene on this continent as *Camelops*, and migrating to Eurasia, where it appeared as *Camelus*. Therefore the camel may be said to have accompanied the horse in its basal Pleistocene migration from the New World to the Old World.

The elephant, *Archidiskodon*, on the other hand, evolved in the Old World at the beginning of the Pleistocene, perhaps at the end of the Pliocene, and appeared in the New World with or shortly after the advent of the glacial period. And likewise, the cattle, of early Pleistocene origin in the Palaearctic region, migrated eastwardly across the trans-Bering land bridge to the Nearctic region.

Although the first appearance of these large, rapidly migrating mammals conveniently defines the opening of the Pleistocene period in the Holarctic region, we unfortunately have no such clear cut evidence to mark its end. The Pleistocene faunas, once established, continued in a rather uniform and uninterrupted manner until the close of the period, at which time the bulk of the mammals persisted on into recent times, and only a small percentage of them became extinct. Thus the end of the Pleistocene period gradually merged into the Recent period and no distinct line of demarcation can be drawn between them.

This merging of the Pleistocene with the recent is due to two causes, first that no new types of mammals appeared with the opening of recent times, so that any differences between the mammalian faunas of the two periods must be based solely on the extinction of Pleistocene forms, and second that certain "typical" Pleistocene mammals, now extinct, persisted on into the beginnings of the Recent period. To put it in another way, it may be said that we are so close to the Pleistocene period that there has been no time for really valid differences to become established.

It is an interesting fact that the persistence of Pleistocene mammals, now extinct, into the Recent period was much more marked in North America than in Eurasia. In the Old World

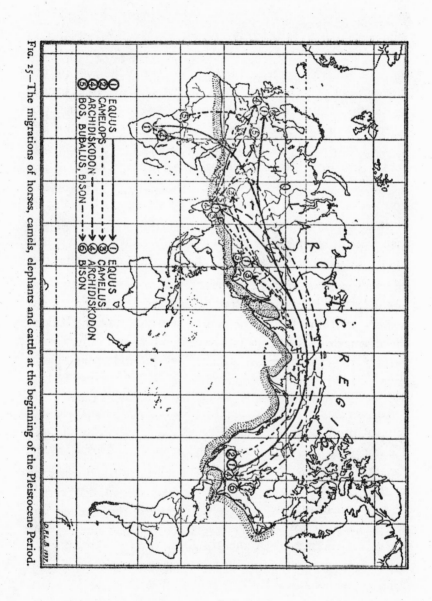

FIG. 25—The migrations of horses, camels, elephants and cattle at the beginning of the Pleistocene Period.

only a relatively small number of such mammals held over beyond the closing of the last glacial period. These are exemplified particularly by the woolly mammoth, the woolly rhinoceros and the Irish deer, all of which must have been living only a few thousands of years ago. In North America, on the other hand, a considerable number of Pleistocene mammals, now extinct, persisted on to a date that may be set within the last few thousand years. These were various ground sloths, the dire wolf, the California lion, the mastodon and the mammoth, the horse, certain peccaries now extinct, the camel, various types of musk-oxen now extinct, extinct forms of pronghorns, extinct species of bison and the giant beaver, *Castoroides*. Almost all of these animals were still living in North America when the first mongoloid immigrants reached this continent, and they did not become extinct until man was well established in the New World.

Why should there be this difference in extinction between North America and Eurasia? Why should many Pleistocene mammals linger in the New World into post-Pleistocene times, suddenly to become extinct, whereas in the Old World those mammals that survived the end of the Pleistocene period continued on to the present day?

One explanation that might be offered—although its validity is open to considerable doubt—is the late Pleistocene or post-Pleistocene arrival of man in North America. Curiously enough, the extinction of the North American Pleistocene mammals would seem to coincide remarkably well with the establishment of man on this continent. Is it not possible, therefore, that man was an instrumental force in causing the extinction of the horse, the camel, the mammoth, the ground sloth and the Pleistocene bison? Is it not possible that the mammals of North America, not being in an ecological balance with man as were the Eurasiatic mammals, were to some extent unable to adapt themselves to new conditions imposed by the arrival of man on this continent, with the result that certain forms died out?

Yet it is difficult to see how the infiltration of relatively small bands of primitive men, even though they were savage and aggressive, could result in the extinction of mammals so numerous as the Pleistocene horses and mammoths. Thus it would seem likely that the sudden extinction of these mammals in North America was the result of a complicated series of events.

Of course the differences in extinction discussed above are in a way more apparent than real. That is, when entire faunas are considered, it will be found that there was a close resemblance between North America and Eurasia, not only in the composition of their animal assemblages of Pleistocene times, but also in the persistence of a great bulk of the Pleistocene genera into modern times.

We have given some attention to the beginning of the Pleistocene period as defined by the appearance of certain new, rapidly migrating mammals. And brief mention has been made of the difficult problem of the close of the Pleistocene and the persistence of many Pleistocene types into what might be thought of as post-Pleistocene times. What is to be said with regard to the sequence of the mammalian faunas within the Pleistocene?

This is one of the most difficult and controversial aspects of the whole problem of Pleistocene mammals. Life during the Pleistocene period was essentially continuous, and there was seemingly but little evolutionary development, beyond specific changes, between the opening of the period and its close. The faunal assemblages found at various levels in the Pleistocene are different from each other mainly because of their geographic positions and their former ecological relationships, and to some extent by reason of the extinction of certain forms, and these facts must be kept in mind when distinctions are drawn between them.

Of course these statements do not apply to the species of Pleistocene mammals, because in these finer taxonomic divisions certain differences are to be seen in the mammals of various ages within the period. Thus, almost all of the early Pleistocene species are now extinct, whereas most of the late Pleistocene species are still living. But species, and particularly fossil species, are peculiarly dependent on the personal factor for their being; therefore they are of limited value in the broad, general comparisons of major divisions within the Pleistocene period.

V. THE ASSOCIATION OF MAN WITH PLEISTOCENE MAMMALS IN THE HOLARCTIC REGION

Man has been associated with Pleistocene mammals virtually throughout the extent of the period in Eurasia. Thus the important question connected with the association of man with Pleistocene mammals in the Old World is that dealing with the geological succession of mammalian faunas and their relationships to the several types of Pleistocene men.

In North America the question is of quite a different sort, as has been mentioned above. Here it is the less definite problem of whether or not man ever did exist on this continent in Pleistocene times. Naturally this whole problem is inextricably linked with the very difficult question of the upper limits of the Pleistocene period—a question that has been discussed briefly in preceding pages of this paper. At the present time we know quite definitely that man in North America was associated with many types of Pleistocene mammals, now extinct. Was this association *within* the Pleistocene period, or did it take place in post-Pleistocene times? As the problem now stands this is a matter of individual interpretation. We can be sure of one thing, however, and that is that many typical Pleistocene mammals in North America, such as the horse, camel, sloth and mammoth persisted until a few thousands of years ago. And the early mongoloid immigrants to a New World encountered a rich and varied fauna, in which many animals seem to our modern eyes strangely out of place in North America.

PLEISTOCENE AND POST-GLACIAL MAMMALS OF NEBRASKA

BY

ERWIN H. BARBOUR AND C. BERTRAND SCHULTZ

Nebraska State Museum, University of Nebraska

INTRODUCTION

NEBRASKA is approximately the geographic center of the United States and of North America, and may be considered to represent an average Great Plains area in so far as climate and fauna are concerned. Both northern and southern faunistic elements are to be expected in the extensive Pleistocene deposits of Nebraska.

The widespread occurrence of many of the Pleistocene formations in this State has made correlation possible. A fairly reliable mammalian faunal sequence has been established due to the abundant vertebrate fossils preserved in the deposits which range in age from lowest to uppermost Pleistocene.

Until recently it has been the consensus that little could be done in establishing any order of succession of the mammals of the Pleistocene. This was largely due to the fact that scarcely any systematic work had actually been attempted. Another reason for apparent lack of progress was that too often deposits were incorrectly referred to the "Aftonian" (lower Pleistocene) while in reality they were of much later age. This resulted in the "conclusion" that early Pleistocene fossils were not distinct from those of the middle or late Pleistocene.

A report was published by the Nebraska State Museum in

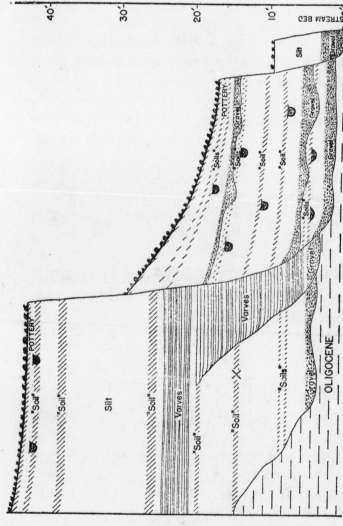

Fig. 26—Ideal section showing the geologic and physiographic history of the late Pleistocene and Recent in the valleys of the White and Cheyenne rivers in northwestern Nebraska. Artifacts were found near the base of the forty-foot terrace in the soil zone marked "X". Later events included the formation of a low (twenty-foot) terrace and a flood-plain. Hearths, or fire pits, are found in abundance at various levels in the low or twenty-foot terrace. The uppermost portion of the forty-foot terrace also contains hearths similar to those found in the twenty-foot terrace.

1934[1] listing over eighty species of mammals from the Pleistocene of Nebraska. An attempt was made at that time to determine the stratigraphic range of the various genera and species. Since then more extensive investigations by field parties of the Nebraska State Museum have revealed new fossil localities as well as many new specimens from already known deposits. Better geological evidence has also been obtained.

Material now at hand shows that, between the time of the earliest Pleistocene and the Recent, considerable evolution has taken place in many species and in a few cases there are suggestions of generic changes.

Unusual interest is attached to the first appearance and the extinction of many mammalian forms in central North America. It is the purpose of this chapter to consider and evaluate the importance of the Pleistocene mammalian remains as time indicators. The subject is presented here under three headings: early Pleistocene, middle Pleistocene, and late Pleistocene to Recent.

EARLY PLEISTOCENE

A lower Pleistocene fauna has recently been found in western Nebraska in the vicinity of Broadwater, in Morrill County. This discovery, in deposits representing the "high terrace" of the North Platte River Valley, has been the subject of a few preliminary remarks by the writers.[2] At the present time some thirty species of mammals are known from this early Pleistocene deposit, which is provisionally dated as late Nebraskan or Aftonian in age. The fauna as a whole is considerably older than the Hay Springs assemblage.

[1] Lugn, A. L. "Outline of the Pleistocene Geology of Nebraska." Bull. Nebr. State Museum, Vol. I, No. 41, Part 1, pp. 319-356, 1934. Schultz, C. Bertrand. "The Pleistocene Mammals of Nebraska." Bull. Nebr. State Museum, Vol. I, No. 41, Part 2, pp. 357-392, Table A, 1934.

[2] Barbour, Erwin H. and C. Bertrand Schultz. "Notice of a New Bone Bed in the Early Pleistocene of Morrill County, Nebraska." Bull. Nebr. State Museum, Vol. I, No. 45, p. 450, 1936.

The new early Pleistocene fauna from western Nebraska has revealed several interesting facts. *Stegomastodon mirificus* is apparently an important species in these deposits, but mammoths and long-horned bison, which are so abundant in deposits of Kansan age, are surprisingly absent. It is believed, and confirmed by present evidence from other parts of the state, that the mammoths and bison migrated into this region after the time represented by these earliest Pleistocene deposits. Muskoxen have not yet been found in deposits earlier than the Kansan, in which their remains are relatively common.

The fauna of the early Pleistocene (Nebraskan ? or Aftonian) includes the following mammals:

Sorex sp., shrew
Mylodon sp., large ground sloth
Lepus sp., jack rabbit
Sylvilagus sp., cottontail rabbit
Sciurid, squirrel
Geomys sp., pocket gopher
Thomomys ?, pocket gopher
Castoroides-like form, ancestral giant beaver
Dipoides ?, small beaver-like form
Peromyscus sp. (near *P. maniculatus*), field mouse
Ondatra sp., ancestral muskrat
Mimomys ? sp., ancestral field vole
Microtinid, vole
Neotoma ?, woodrat
Zapus sp. (near *Z. hudsonius*), jumping mouse
Canis sp. (near *C. latrans*), coyote
Canis sp. (near *Canis* [*Aenocyon*] *dirus*), large wolf
Satherium piscinaria, extinct otter
Felis ?, large cat
Stegomastodon mirificus, mastodont
Stegomastodon mirificus primitivus, mastodont
Equus sp. (near *E. excelsus*), extinct horse
Equus sp. (more primitive species), extinct horse
Equid (very light-limbed form), extinct horse
Camelops sp., large camel

PLATE XIII—Terraces exposed in the White River Valley, Man., standing in center, is examining hearth in the low or twenty-foot terrace.

> *Tanupolama* sp., small camel or llama-like form
> Camelid (possibly *Titanotylopus*), giant camel
> *Capromeryx* sp., small antelope
> Antilocaprid, probably *Tetrameryx*, antelope

MIDDLE PLEISTOCENE

Fossils of both Kansan and Yarmouth age are here considered as middle Pleistocene but are listed separately. The following mammals are now known from deposits of Kansan age:

> *Megatherium* sp., large ground sloth
> *Castoroides ohioensis nebrascensis*, giant beaver
> *Stegomastodon* sp., mastodont
> *Mastodon americanus*, mastodont
> *Mastodon moodiei*, mastodont
> *Tetralophodon (Morrillia) barbouri*, primitive mastodont
> *Archidiskodon hayi*, primitive mammoth
> *Archidiskodon imperator*, mammoth
> *Archidiskodon imperator scotti*, mammoth
> *Parelephas columbi*, mammoth
> *Parelephas jeffersonii*, mammoth
> *Mammonteus primigenius*, hairy mammoth
> *Equus excelsus*, extinct horse
> *Camelops* sp., camel
> *Titanotylopus nebrascensis*, giant camel
> *Cervalces roosevelti*, giant elk
> *Symbos cavifrons*, extinct muskox
> *Superbison regius*, long-horned bison
> *Superbison latifrons angularis*, long-horned bison
> *Superbison latifrons rotundus*, long-horned bison

The well-known Hay Springs fauna from Nebraska appears to be of middle Pleistocene (Yarmouth) age and may be somewhat older than the faunas from the California asphalt pits and the Conard Fissure of Arkansas. A list of the forms from the Yarmouth of Nebraska follows:

> *Scalops* sp., mole
> *Mylodon garmani*, large ground sloth
> *Mylodon nebrascensis*, large ground sloth
> *Megalonyx leidyi*, large ground sloth

Lepus giganteus, jack rabbit
Sylvilagus floridanus, cottontail rabbit
Citellus sp., ground squirrel
Cynomys niobrarius, prairie-dog
Geomys sp., pocket gopher
Thomomys sp., pocket gopher
Castoroides ohioensis nebrascensis, giant beaver
Castor sp., beaver
Ondatra nebrascensis, muskrat
Microtus ?, mouse or field vole
Canis latrans ?, coyote
Canis (Aenocyon) dirus nebrascensis, large wolf
Arctodus simus nebrascensis, giant bear
Mustela vison ?, mink
Smilodon nebrascensis, sabre-toothed tiger
Stegomastodon aftoniae, mastodont
Mastodon americanus, mastodont
Archidiskodon imperator, mammoth
Archidiskodon meridionalis nebrascensis, mammoth
Parelephas columbi, mammoth
Parelephas jeffersonii, mammoth
Equus excelsus, extinct horse
Equus excelsus niobrarensis, extinct horse
Equus colabatus nebrascensis, stilt-legged horse
Platygonus vetus, peccary
Mylohyus browni, peccary
Camelops kansanus, camel
Camelops vitakerianus ?, camel
Tanupolama americanus, small camel or llama-like form
Odocoileus sheridanus, deer
Capromeryx furcifer, small antelope
Symbos convexifrons, extinct muskox
Tetrameryx (Hayoceras) falkenbachi, four-horned antelope
Superbison ferox, long-horned bison

LATE PLEISTOCENE TO RECENT

The late Pleistocene has presented many complex problems with regard to the time of extinction of certain of the mammals.

PLATE XIV—The forty-foot terrace in White River Valley. Men, at lower left and lower right, are collecting invertebrates from the artifact and fossil mammal horizon.

The appearance of artifacts associated with extinct animals has made this even more involved and much more interesting.

The *Citellus* faunal zone has become a very important stratigraphic level over a large part of Nebraska. This zone is post-Sangamon and pre-Peorian or early Peorian in age, and has yielded abundant mammalian remains. The known fauna of the *Citellus* zone is as follows:

> *Citellus* sp., ground squirrel
> *Thomomys talpoides*, pocket gopher
> *Mustela vison*, mink
> *Archidiskodon imperator*, large mammoth
> *Archidiskodon imperator maibeni*, large mammoth
> *Parelephas columbi*, mammoth
> *Platygonus* sp., peccary
> *Camelops* sp., camel
> *Bison antiquus*, extinct bison

No artifacts or human remains have been found in the *Citellus* zone. However, evidence is constantly accumulating to show that man actually had reached North America soon after *Citellus* zone time, and probably before the last glacial advance. The classification of the Pleistocene is still in dispute, and the last American glacial epoch, the Eldoran, is complex and may include both the Iowan and Wisconsin advances, as well as several substages.

Recent work on river terraces in Nebraska is furnishing much needed data in the dating of late Pleistocene and Recent mammalian remains. Artifacts have now been found by the Nebraska State Museum field parties in two distinct terraces; one a twenty to twenty-five-foot terrace and the other a thirty-five to forty-five-foot terrace. A late Pleistocene dating for the latter terrace is not improbable.

Much new evidence strongly suggests that the early men who were associated with so many of the now-extinct animals of the

Pleistocene disappeared from the central North American region at the same time as these mammals. The reasons for the extinction of the mammals and the disappearance of man from the region at that time are unknown. Many entire families of mammals such as the Equidae, Camelidae, Megatheriidae, and Elephantidae were wiped out as well as many genera and species of other families. Among the now-extinct forms which were definitely associated with early man in central North America are: the horse (*Equus*), sloth (*Nothrotherium*), giant beaver (*Castoroides*), giant bear (*Arctodus*), mammoth (*Parelephas*), four-horned antelope (*Tetrameryx*), bovids (*Bison antiquus, Preptoceras,* and *Euceratherium*), and camelids (*Camelops* and *Tanupolama*).

Inasmuch as artifacts are so often found with certain of the now-extinct mammals, it is possible, but not probable, that man was a contributing factor in the extermination of these animals. Disease is often suggested as a cause. Arid conditions and dust storms are recognized as very important agencies, since twice in the Pleistocene (early Sangamon and early Peorian) great dust storms apparently caused the extinction of some of the mammals and drove others for a time to more livable climates, perhaps to the southwest or east.

So far no bones of extinct animals have been found associated with the earliest basket-maker remains of the Southwest or with the earliest Indian artifacts of the central North American region. The Indians of the plains may have belonged to an entirely distinct and later migration from Asia. Geological evidence points to the fact that considerable time had elapsed between the departure of the "mammoth and bison hunters" and the appearance of the early American Indians. Much more research is necessary for a better understanding of the Recent faunas, especially faunas associated with historical and prehistorical Indian remains.

PLATE XV—Hearth pit and charcoal layer (at level of two men) under twenty-five feet of overburden in the low terrace. Man above is examining a higher artifact horizon.

THE VERO FINDS IN THE LIGHT OF PRESENT KNOWLEDGE

BY

E. H. SELLARDS

*Director of the Bureau of Economic Geology,
University of Texas*

INTRODUCTORY STATEMENT

A very important locality for vertebrate, invertebrate, and plant fossils, found in 1913 at Vero on the Atlantic Coast in central-eastern Florida, was developed by the writer and others during the next succeeding three or four years. Human remains were first found in 1915 and the principal collections made in 1916.

The place of occurrence of these fossils is in a stream valley representing a partially filled inlet from Indian River sound. The excavations as well as the timber growth show that the old stream-bed or valley near Vero had a width of three hundred and fifty to five hundred feet for a distance of about three-fourths of a mile from the Indian River, which is itself an inlet from the ocean. The stream valley, however, is very shallow, the material which fills it having at the present time a thickness of not more than from four to six feet. A sluggish stream, known as Van Valkenburg's Creek, following an ill-defined channel, flowed through the valley which had been aggraded to within three or four feet of the surrounding land level. From the sketch map (Fig. 27) it will be seen that the broad valley is formed, near the place where the fossils are found, by two tributaries which enter, one from the north and one from the south. These streams originate only a few miles inland and their course is controlled by the Pleistocene beaches and dunes which here parallel the coast.

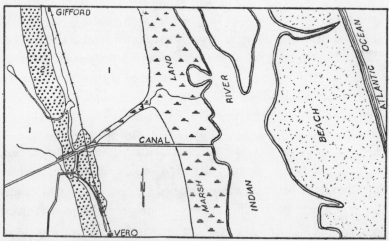

FIG. 27—Sketch map showing the locality near Vero from which fossil human remains have been obtained. Scale, 1 inch = 4,000 feet. No. 1, pine land; No. 2, sand dune; No. 3, stream valley. The human remains were found in the canal bank in this valley, west of the railroad.

A canal, constructed by the Indian River Farms Company, designed to afford drainage for lands lying some miles inland comes into and follows this old valley for a distance of about one thousand feet. The fossils are found in the stream valley in the banks of this canal.

GEOLOGIC CONDITIONS

The bed rock of the immediate locality is a marine shell stratum which is present underlying a large region adjacent to the Atlantic Coast and is known as the Anastasia formation.[1] Next overlying this shell bed is a sand deposit which at the time the fossils were found was supposed to be local in extent. Subse-

[1] Sellards, E. H., Florida Geol. Survey 4th Ann. Rept., p. 18, 1912.

quent observations, however, have shown that this stratum occurs widely in Florida, being present on both the east and west
coasts. To this sand deposit Cooke and Mossom have applied the
term Melbourne bone bed.[2]

This sand stratum, as found in the stream bed at Vero, has a
thickness of from one to five feet. It is in places strongly cross-
bedded. Cross-bedding is most pronounced near its base, and it
is near the base, also, that decayed wood and muck are found
lying in channels cut into the underlying shell marl. Numerous
vertebrate fossils are found in this sand stratum, some being exceptionally well preserved. Human remains are found here also.
Resting upon this sand and marl bed and in places cutting into
it is an alluvial deposit consisting chiefly of vegetable material
intermixed with sand, grading at the top in places into a fresh-
water marl. The average thickness in the stream valley of this
alluvial material is about two feet, although locally where the
stream cuts deeply into the underlying bed this deposit reaches
a maximum thickness of five or six feet. This alluvial deposit
contains vertebrate and plant fossils and, in the fresh-water marl,
occasional invertebrates. Human remains are found in this deposit also. In the original description of this locality and in many
subsequent papers by the author and others, these three units of
the section are referred to as follows: No. 1, the shell marl,
Anastasia formation; No. 2, the sand stream, Melbourne bone
bed; and No. 3, the alluvial material. The accompanying generalized sketch illustrates the relations of these three stratigraphic units, numbered 1, 2, and 3.

Parts of several human skeletons and many artifacts have been
found at Vero. In this paper reference will be made only to
human remains and other fossils which the writer has himself

[2] Cooke, C. Wythe, and Mossom, Stuart, Florida Geol. Survey 12th Ann.
Rept., pp. 218-226, 1929.

taken from the deposits, or which have been taken in his presence and under his direction.

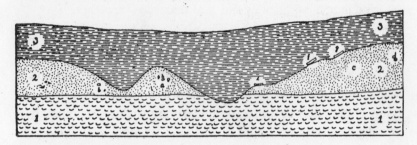

FIG. 28—Sketch showing the strata exposed in the south bank of the canal from 452 to 580 feet west of the bridge. (Horizontal and vertical scale, 1 inch equals 7 feet). Nos. 1, 2, and 3 in the sketch represent beds 1, 2, and 3 respectively of the general section. At one place near the middle of the exposure, bed No. 2 is cut out by bed No. 3. The dividing line between 2 and 3 here as elsewhere is well marked and is unmistakable. Human bones are found in bed No. 2 at *a*, this being the place from which the writer obtained a human astragalus, an external cuneiform, and parts of the pelvis in place, as well as some other bones and flints from siftings. At *b* in this stratum was found the flint spawl illustrated by fig. 11, page 138, 8th Annual Report, Florida Geological Survey. The type specimen of the fossil turtle, *Terrapene innoxis* Hay, was found in this stratum at *c*. A foot bone of a horse was found at *d*. Other fossils obtained in this stratum are listed later. Bone implements were obtained from the sand near *a* and near *d*.

Bed No. 3 consists of alternating beds of sand and muck which conform to the irregularities of the underlying deposits. Human bones were found at the contact line between 2 and 3, at *e*, *f*, and *g*. A number of other bones were also found in this deposit lying at or near the contact line. This bed contains also numerous bone implements, pottery, and a few arrowheads and ornaments. (From Florida State Geological Survey, 8th Annual Report, fig. 6, 1916.)

HUMAN REMAINS FOUND IN THE OLDER STREAM DEPOSIT, BED NO. 2

While excavating in the south bank of the canal four hundred and sixty-five feet west of the railroad bridge, the writer in June 1916, found human bones in place in the older stream deposit, stratum No. 2 of the section. The section at this place is as follows:

Thickness
Feet

Alluvial deposit consisting of alternating strata of sand
and muck, representing No. 3 of the general section. .   2½
Dark colored sand, representing No. 2 of the general
section 1½
Shell marl, representing No. 1 of the general section to
water level, about............................. 4

Details of the exposure in the canal bank at the place where
these bones were found is shown in the accompanying sketch
(Fig. 29). The top surface of stratum No. 2 here as elsewhere is
irregular, the irregularities being filled by the overlying deposits.
At the spot where the human bones were found, owing to stream-
wash previous to the deposition of the overlying deposit, bed
No. 2 of the section is only eighteen inches thick. The human
bones were found in this sand, about ten inches above the base.
The overlying alluvial beds are stratified and as usual conform
to the irregularities of the underlying formation. The human
bones at this place were found and removed by the writer, in
the presence and with the assistance of Isaac M. Weills and
Frank Ayers. The first bone found was a right astragalus; the
second bone taken in place was the right external cuneiform
which lay at the same level and about ten inches from the
astragalus. About twelve inches farther back in the bank was
found a piece from the right pubes and a part of the left ilium
including that part of the bone which articulates with the
sacrum. Upon sifting the sand in which these bones were embedded there were obtained in addition two phalanges, a section
from a limb bone and some other human bone fragments.

The dividing line between beds 2 and 3 of the general section
here as elsewhere is well marked and unmistakable and the human bones lay in bed No. 2. The overlying laminated deposit is
undisturbed and hence the bones cannot represent a recent

burial. The vertebrates associated with these bones are listed in a subsequent paragraph.

In bed No. 2 on the south bank of the canal, four hundred and sixty feet west of the bridge, Frank Ayers while working with

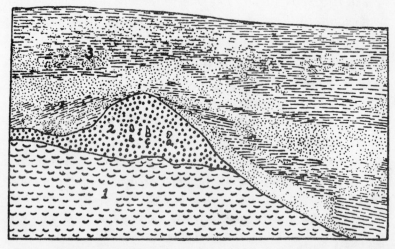

FIG. 29—Detail of section of the bank on the south side of the canal from about 458 to 468 feet west of the bridge. Scale vertical and horizontal, 1 inch equals 2½ feet. 1, 2, and 3 represent beds 1, 2, and 3 of the general section. Human bones are found in bed No. 2 at *a* and *b*. The scapula of a deer was found at *c*. The overlying material consists of alternating layers of sand and muck which had not been disturbed. These conform to the irregularities of the underlying formation. For a photograph of this section see Plate XVI.

(From Florida State Geological Survey, 8th Annual Report, fig. 5, 1916.)

the writer and under his direction found in place a thin sharp-edged flint which undoubtedly is a spawl from the manufacture of some kind of a flint implement. The place of this flint in the deposit is about a foot farther in the bank than the human bones referred to above and three or four feet farther east (Fig. 28). This flint is illustrated in the accompanying Fig. 28, locality *b*. Upon sifting the sand from this stratum at this locality five additional small flints were obtained.

With the small flints obtained from sifting the sands in which the human bones were embedded, was found a piece of a bone implement. Subsequently while sifting the sand from this stratum about ten feet farther to the west (four hundred and seventy-five feet west of the bridge) a second small implement, and also a small flint were found. The bone implements are polished and nicely finished. The second implement found, which is practically complete, is sharp pointed at one end and beveled at the other, probably for insertion into a shaft. The sand was carefully handled in sifting and there was no chance of these artifacts coming from any source other than bed No. 2 of the section.

OTHER FOSSILS FROM BED NO. 2

The fossils obtained from bed No. 2 have been described in several publications.[3]

The mammals that the writer obtained in place in this horizon at this locality are as follows: (Extinct species are indicated by asterisk.)

Didelphis virginiana	Mammut americanum*
Megalonyx jeffersonii*	Elephas columbi*
Chlamytherium septentrionalis*	Sigmodon sp.
Dasypus sp.*	Neofiber alleni
Equus leidyi*	Sylvilagus sp.
Equus complicatus*	Blarina sp.
Tapirus veroensis*	Procyon lotor
Camelops ? sp.*	Vulpes sp.
Odocoileus sp.	Aenocyon ayersi*

Trucifelis floridanus*

In addition to mammals, this deposit has afforded fish, batrachian, reptile, and bird fossils. In 1923, Dr. O. P. Hay pre-

[3] Sellards, E. H., Florida Geol. Survey 8th Ann. Rept., pp. 121-160, 1916. Hay, O. P., Carnegie Inst. Washington, Pub. 322, 1923. Shufeldt, R. W., Florida Geol. Survey 9th Ann. Rept., p. 36, 1917.

pared a list from all available material and found that he was able to list from bed No. 2 at that time twenty-eight species of mammals, four species of birds, one alligator and three turtles.[4] The fossils will not be further described here since, so far as the writer is aware, no one now questions the presence of this fauna in bed No. 2.

HUMAN REMAINS FOUND IN THE LATER STREAM DEPOSITS, BED NO. 3

Bed No. 3, the alluvial material of the stream valley, overlying bed No. 2, is made up of strata of nearly pure sand alternating with strata of sand mixed with vegetable debris. In February, 1916, Mr. Frank Ayers obtained a human right ulna which, although not found in place, was recognized as having been derived from the bank, since the degree of mineralization was similar to that of the associated vertebrate fossils. The skeleton from which this bone came, however, was not located at that time. Again in April, 1916, Mr. Ayers found the distal end of a humerus, which, although not in place, had recently fallen from the bank. The discovery of this bone led to the location in the bank of other bones belonging to the same skeleton to which belongs also the ulna found three months earlier. The place of these bones in the section may be seen in Fig. 28. All of these bones were at the base of bed No. 3, lying at the contact line between this and the next older deposit. By reference to Fig. 28 it will be seen that at this place the later stream deposits, bed No. 3 of the section, cuts sharply into the older formation, and for a short space cuts entirely through bed No. 2 and into the shell marl beneath.

The bones from this skeleton were taken from the bank by Ayers, Weills, and the writer. In addition to the ulna and humerus, there were obtained from cavings from the bank a part

[4] Hay, O. P., *Op. cit.*

of a sphenoid bone, scapula, and a left upper incisor; and in place in the bank the left ulna, a femur, radius, base of a jaw, parts of the skull, and two metatarsals. The first bone found in place was the left ulna, of which the proximal part only was present, although the distal part lacking the extremities was later obtained a few inches farther back in the bank. The bone next found, the left femur, of which only a part of the shaft is preserved, was lying near the ulna and at about the same level. Another piece from the shaft of this bone was obtained the following June, having been found several feet farther back in the bank. The radius, of which the proximal part only was obtained, was found five feet north of east of the ulna, and at the same place in the section, that is, at the bottom of the bed of sand and alluvial material. Owing to the slope of the bed at this place, however, this bone lay at level fully two feet lower than the ulna. The jaw and the parts of the skull were found chiefly between the ulna and the radius and from a few inches to two feet farther back in the bank. One of the foot bones, a fifth metatarsal, was taken about eight feet east of the ulna and at a level above that of the radius and approximately the same as that of the ulna. Above the human skeleton four feet of alluvial material are found at this place, consisting of alternating layers of sand and muck, which in places grade into soft fresh-water marl having a thickness of as much as two feet. Fossil plants including leaves, stems, and seeds are found in the muck bed. The plants, apparently, are but little changed from their original condition. While excavating in this bank in June 1916, additional pieces of the skull were found as well as a part of the shaft of the right femur and an additional incisor tooth.

A considerable amount of broken pottery is found in this horizon particularly at the locality on the south bank four hundred and fifty to four hundred and seventy-five feet west of the bridge. Bone implements are also numerous and were made evidently to serve a diversity of purposes. Well-worked flint artifacts are found also as well as occasional spawls from the manufacture of flints.

OTHER FOSSILS FROM BED NO. 3

The fossils obtained from the alluvial deposits of Bed No. 3 include plants, insects, fish, batrachians, reptiles, birds, and mammals. Plants are abundant. Berry, who has studied this flora, recognizes twenty-seven species. Of these, nineteen are known only as recent species; eight had previously been found in Pliocene or Pleistocene deposits. With regard to geographic distribution, seventeen of the species are now found growing either at Vero or within ten or twelve miles of that place; three species are now found within about fifty miles of Vero; and six species are not now known in Peninsular Florida. One species of this flora is extinct.[5]

The fossil insects in bed No. 3, all of which are beetles, include, according to Wickham, seven species, all of which are regarded by him as identical with existing species.[6]

A considerable vertebrate fauna is found in bed No. 3. Of mammals, the writer in 1916 was able to list the following: (Extinct species are indicated by asterisk.)

Didelphis virginiana	*Neotoma* sp.
Chlamytherium septentrionalis	*Scalopus* sp.
Dasypus sp. ?	*Vulpes pennsylvanicus* ?
Odocoileus osceola	*Canis* sp. cf. *C. latrans*
Neofiber alleni	*Procyon lotor* ?
Sylvilagus sp.	*Lutra canadensis*
Sigmodon sp.	*Lynx* sp.

Ursus indt.

[5] Berry, E. W., the fossil plants from Vero, Florida: Florida Geol. Survey 9th Ann. Rept., pp. 19-33, 1917.
[6] Wickham, H. F., Fossil beetles from Vero, Florida: Florida Geol. Survey 12th Ann. Rept., pp. 5-7, 1919.

Shufeldt has listed nine birds from this stratum of which two species are new.[7] A list of the fishes, amphibians, reptiles, and mammals found in this stratum has been given by Hay.[8]

THEORIES PROPOSED TO ACCOUNT FOR THE ASSOCIATION OF HUMAN REMAINS AND EXTINCT ANIMALS IN THESE DEPOSITS

To account for the association at this locality of human remains and artifacts with extinct animals on a basis other than that of contemporaneity, three theories, each unrelated to the other, have been proposed. Of these a theory so obviously incorrect as to have no merit is that of assumed relatively recent burial of the human remains by human agency.[9] The position in the earth of the human remains is shown in figures 28 and 29, and the immediately associated stratigraphic conditions are seen in the photograph of Plate XVI. From the photograph certain definite conditions as to the inclusion of the human remains may be determined. The sands of bed No. 2 are cross-bedded, and the cross-bedding has been in no way interfered with or disarranged as would necessarily have been the case if a grave had been dug and a body buried in the sand. From the photograph it may be seen that the overlying strata are bedded, and that strata of sand (light colored in the photograph) alternate with strata containing vegetable debris. It is likewise apparent from the photograph that the strata are thinner over the high points of the irregular floor of deposition. The obvious meaning of these conditions is that the floor on which the strata of bed No. 3 were being accumulated was irregular. The result is that the strata are thick in the depressions and thin over the high points. The assertion that the human bones at this locality were placed in the sand by burial is contrary to the plainly revealed record at this place.

That the human bones and the numerous artifacts of bed No. 3

[7] Shufeldt, R. W., Fossil birds found at Vero, Florida: Florida Geol. Survey 9th Ann. Rept., pp. 35-41, 1917.
[8] Hay, O. P., Florida Geol. Survey 9th Ann. Rept., pp. 43-68, 1917.
[9] Hrdlička, Aleš, Jour. Geol., vol. 25, pp. 43-51, 1917.

do not represent burials is equally clear. Of the bones of the skeleton found in the south bank of the canal west of the lateral inlet, the right ulna, part of a humerus, part of a scapula, one incisor, and parts of the skull had fallen from the bank. All of the other bones that have been obtained at this locality were found in place in the bank. The bones which apparently belong to this individual include, in addition to those mentioned, the left ulna, the shaft of the right femur (in two pieces), the proximal part of the left radius, the ascending ramus of the right lower jaw, two metatarsals, and numerous fragments of the skull and some pieces of ribs.

All of the bones are more or less broken and incomplete. The first bone found in place was the proximal part of the left ulna. An additional part of the shaft of this bone was subsequently found a few inches farther back in the bank. The second bone found in place was the proximal part of the shaft of the left femur. Two and a half months later, after the excavating had been carried farther back into the bank, an additional part of the shaft of this femur was obtained, the two pieces of bone being separated in the bank by a distance of eight feet. This bone, the two pieces having been put together, is illustrated in figure 3 of Plate 19 of the Eighth Annual Report of the Florida Geological Survey. The third bone found in place was the proximal part of the left radius. A photograph showing these three bones in place in the bank was reproduced in the American Journal of Science, July 1916, and in the Eighth Annual Report of the Florida Geological Survey, Plate 17, figure 1. The two bones, left ulna and left radius, it may be noted, are separated by a space of five feet. Vertically above the radius are twelve or fourteen inches of light colored, coarse, clean sand, which is intimately mixed with a quantity of broken marine shells, this part of the deposit representing material washed from the underlying deposits (Bed No. 1 of the section). This is followed by about ten or twelve inches of vegetable material and sand, including pieces of driftwood. Above this layer is a lens of coarse, clean sand, including some pieces of broken marine shells. This sand lens, as seen in the photograph, has a thickness of about six inches. Above this sand lens to the soil line are found fourteen or fifteen inches of material consisting chiefly of muck, including some sand, the depth of this bone beneath the surface being about forty-two inches. In passing to the right the deposit of sand immediately above the radius "pinches out" so that the piece of femur which lies approximately four feet farther west is immediately beneath the muck, as is also the ulna.

The record as to the conditions under which these bones were found is conclusive. Flat objects, such as shells and shell fragments, lie prevailingly in a single plane of deposition in these strata, and the deposits are cross-bedded, both of which features are common to deposition by water. A study of the section shows conclusively that these bones were washed to the place where now found by the waters of this stream and that they become entombed at the same time and in the same way as the sand, shell fragments, pieces of wood, and other materials of this deposit. These bones are therefore unquestionably fossils of this formation and were not subsequently introduced into the deposit by human agency, or in any other way.

Human bones were collected from bed No. 3 over the area indicated in the accompanying sketch (Fig. 30). The manner of occurrence of the human skull is instructive. Scarcely one-half of the skull was obtained, and the pieces that were secured were distributed over an area of not less than seven by three feet. The broken skull fragments fit together securely. Most of the skull pieces were found in the sand containing the broken pieces of marine shells, and it is evident that they were washed to their present resting place in the same way and at the same time as the other bones of the deposits. The absence of bones and parts of bones is as instructive as is the condition of the bones themselves. Of the jaws, for instance, there has been obtained only the right ascending ramus. This piece of bone is well preserved, and the break shows a sharp fracture. There is no reason, therefore, to

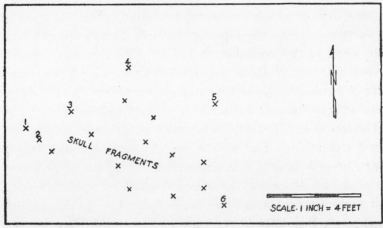

FIG. 30—Ground plan showing the location of human bones found in the canal bank at Vero in April and in June, 1916. Index to bones: 1, left ulna; 2, a part of the shaft of the same bone; 3, left femur; 4, radius; 5, metatarsal; 6, astragalus; 7, external cuneiform; 8, part of ilium; 9, a part of the shaft of the same bone.

doubt but that the part of the jaw that is missing, if included within this formation at all, is also well mineralized. The same is true of the radius of the left femur and of the skull bones, as well as of the skeleton as a whole. From the time of the location of these bones in April 1916, to the conference in October of the same year the bank at this place was worked only by hand trowels, and the material after being worked by the trowels was passed through screens, much of it being double screened through coarse and fine mesh. At no time were laborers allowed to work the bank with shovels or other implements. If the remainder of the jaw had been preserved within the area covered by this sketch, or in fact within a somewhat greater area, it would certainly have been recovered. The same is true of the missing and imperfect bones of the skeleton. These bones and parts of bones were either not washed into this formation, and for that reason failed of preservation, or if preserved in this deposit were lying some place outside of the area covered by this sketch.

It is evident that the bones of this skeleton had become thoroughly dried before they were moved and broken, this fact being indicated by the sharp fracture of the bones. It is certain that the breaks in these bones that were in place in the bank, such as the left ulna, the left radius, the right femur and the left femur, and the bones of the skull, occurred at the time the bones were washed to the place where they were found. Some of the bones may have been carried much farther by the stream at that time, while others possibly never found their way into this stream bed, thus accounting for the imperfection of the skeleton.

To assume that these bones represent a burial by human agency affords no adequate explanation of the separation of the radius and the ulna, of the displacement of the two parts of the right femur, nor of the broken and scattered condition of the skull as well as the scattering of the skeleton. On the other hand, recognition of the fact that the bones were washed by the stream to their present resting place affords an explanation of every phenomenon that is presented, including the broken condition of the bones, the separation of the radius and ulna a distance of five feet, the separation of the two pieces of the right femur a distance of eight feet, the position of the radius beneath fourteen inches of coarse sand and broken marine shells, the scattering of the parts of the skull, the presence of driftwood in the deposit, and the undisturbed bedding above the bones, as well as the imperfect representation of the skeleton as a whole.

The manner of occurrence of the bone implements and fragments of pottery affords equally plain evidence of stream wash indicating that under alternating conditions of quiet waters and flood waters there were accumulated the successive layers of muck and sand, with occasional inclusions of driftwood forming the stratified deposit which permanently sealed the bones and preserved them until the present time.

Another theory offered, in direct opposition to this one of burial, accepts the human bones and artifacts as primary inclusions in place in the deposit but maintains that the associated Pleistocene fossils are secondary, having been moved to their present position from some other locality. When this theory was first proposed, it was assumed that the source from which the associated fossils came was from a Pleistocene bog or bone bed farther up stream. Careful search having failed to locate such a bone bed, this theory was modified, and it was then assumed that the fossils found with the human remains were reworked from immediately subjacent beds.[10] It was also assumed that the human remains and artifacts were confined to the later, and the extinct vertebrates to the earlier, beds.

The evidence that the vertebrate fossils in the stream bed are primary and not secondary is very positive. Of the extinct wolf, *Aenocyon ayersi*, thirty or more bones of a single individual have been found at one place, while nearby were obtained the skull and femur probably of the same individual. The skeleton of this extinct animal is more fully represented, therefore, than is that of any one of the human skeletons. The extinct armadillo-like genus, *Chlamytherium*, is represented by a lower jaw, a bone from the skull, and many dermal plates, all found at one place and probably all belonging to a single individual. The extinct stork, *Jabiru weillsi*, is represented by a humerus, part of a coracoid, part of two ulnas, and two metacarpals, all found at one place and probably from one individual. The tapir is represented by a practically complete skull. There is in fact, as the writer has heretofore stated, no essential difference either in the com-

[10] Chamberlin, Rollin T., Further studies at Vero, Florida. Jour. Geol., vol. 25, pp. 667-683, 1917.

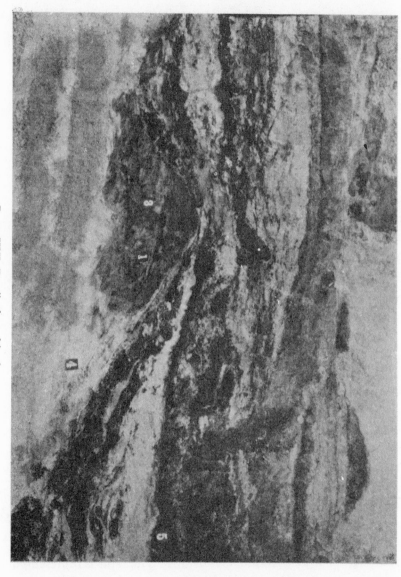

PLATE XVI–Detail of canal bank.

pleteness of the skeleton or in the manner of preservation between the human bones and those of the associated animals.

The suggestion is offered by Chamberlin, in connection with this theory in its revised form, that the writer was mistaken as to the human bones being actually present in bed No. 2, and the opinion offered that all of the human remains pertain to bed No. 3. The writer's reference of the human bones described above to bed No. 2 is based on very careful collecting by which he assured himself of the dividing line between beds 2 and 3 and of the place of the human bones in bed No. 2.

A third theory seeks to harmonize the observations at Vero by assuming that some of the extinct forms found in the bed No. 2 are perhaps derived from an older deposit, that others lived on in the southern clime longer than has hitherto been supposed, and that the presence of the Indian hunter had much to do with the final ringing down of the curtain on the drama of their ultimate extinction.[11]

CONCLUDING STATEMENT

With the view that the Indian hunter had much to do with the extinction of some of the large mammals the writer is in hearty accord. Under close scrutiny, the theory that others lived on in Florida longer than elsewhere in the United States loses much of its charm. A fauna that occupied Florida would quite certainly migrate northward, effective barriers being absent, across the interior of the United States as grazing and climatic conditions permitted.

On the other hand, much information has accumulated in recent years, indicating that the mammalian fauna, or a part of it, heretofore considered distinctive of the Pleistocene, may have continued in existence longer than heretofore supposed. The result is that for the non-glaciated regions we are losing our ac-

[11] MacCurdy, George Grant, Jour. Geol., vol. 25, p. 62, 1917.

cepted definition of the Pleistocene, based on the presence of extinct mammals. Such redefinition, however, would in no way affect the essentials of the problem. The conclusion that is in accord with the observations at Vero, and at many other localities in the western hemisphere, is that man reached this continent before the close of the Pleistocene as heretofore defined, and participated in the great drama of the extinction of the magnificent mammalian fauna of that period.

BIBLIOGRAPHY

A list of papers relating to the Vero locality was given by Leverett in 1931.[12] The list given by Leverett is apparently complete for the locality except one paper which has been issued since that date.[13]

[12] The Pensacola Terrace and Associated Beaches and Bars in Florida, by Frank Leverett, Fla. State Geol. Surv. Bull. No. 7. (Bibliography of fossil man and Pleistocene Vertebrates on the Pensacola Terrace, pp. 33-35.)

[13] A review of Evidence relating to the status of the problem of antiquity of man in Florida, by John C. Merriam. Science (N. S.), vol. 82, p. 103, 1935.

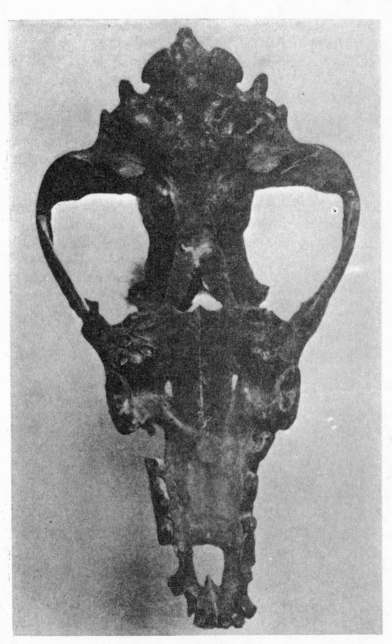

PLATE XVII–Skull of extinct wolf (*Aenocyon ayersi*).

THE PLEISTOCENE OF CHINA
STRATIGRAPHY AND CORRELATIONS

BY

PÈRE P. TEILHARD DE CHARDIN

*Consulting Palaeontologist of the National Geological Survey
of China*

As a result of stratigraphical and palaeontological work of the Geological Survey of China, and in consequence of investigations carried out recently by Dr. de Terra, Dr. von Koenigswald, and others, in India and Java, new light has been thrown on the Pleistocene history of eastern and southeastern Asia. It is the aim of the present paper to describe, as briefly and clearly as possible, the present stage of our conceptions concerning: (1) the Pleistocene stratigraphy of China; and (2) its correlations with the Pleistocene of the adjoining parts of the world. This will reveal a series of major and unsettled problems which we recommend for urgent investigation. We shall express them explicitly and suggest in conclusion a line of approach for their ultimate solution.

I. THE PLEISTOCENE SEQUENCE IN CHINA

A. NORTH CHINA

For various reasons (thicker and more fossiliferous deposits, better exposures, easier investigation) the Pleistocene sequence was recognized earlier and is better known in North than in South China. As shown in the columnar section, Fig. 31, the main characteristics of the late Cenozoic between the Tsinling range and the Mongolian plateau, are as follows:

1) A long Miocene peneplanation.

2) A protracted Pliocene and Villafranchian[1] period of lake deposition. Thick red clays occur along the margin of the basins occupied by the lakes.

3) A sharp post-Villafranchian, continental uplift, succeeded by the cutting of deep gorges and by an accumulation of gravels and red loam deposits along the slopes of basins. Fissure-deposits of the Choukoutien type.

4) A Late Pleistocene epoch with dominantly eolian sedimentation resulting in loess and sand-dunes, these latter interfingering with the deposits of the Lop Nor basin.

Faunistically, the Early Pliocene is characterized by typical Pontian forms: small Hipparions, *Aceratheridae, Giraffidae, Ictitherium*, etc. The Late Pliocene (pre-Villafranchian) fauna, still distinctly subtropical, is remarkable for a sudden appearance of Cervulidae (Munjack-like deer) and twisted-horned antelopes.

A marked disconformity (and a partial displacement of the lakes) occurs at the base of the Villafranchian, coinciding with an impoverishment of the Cervulidae-Antelope fauna, and with the arrival of new forms: horse and camel (from America), *Eucladoceros* deer (from the north-west?), bison (from the south?). Yet, this break is not so sharp as the one which separates the Villafranchian from the Middle Pleistocene. At the beginning of the Middle Pleistocene, the lakes had not only largely disappeared and been replaced by loamy fans, but the fauna had lost its archaic and sub-tropical elements (*Hipparion, Chalicotherium, Cervulus, Eucladoceros*) and several newcomers appeared, such as various euryceroid deer (from the north-west?), water-buffalo and *Sinanthropus* (from the south?).

Lithologically, physiographically, faunistically, and probably climatically, the "loess" differs strongly from the Middle Pleis-

---

[1] Conventionally, the Villafranchian is regarded in this paper as representing the Lower Pleistocene.

tocene "reddish clays," and represents a clearly independent stage. *Rhinoceros mercki, Machairodus*, most of the euryceroid deer, and a number of rodents have disappeared and been replaced by modern types (including the *Elaphus* deer and *Homo sapiens*). The sediments of loessic age form a complex assemblage: a true eolian loess, distributed along an external southeastern crescentic zone, is succeeded, northwestward, by wide extensions of sandy deposits, passing laterally into freshwater sediments which evidently were deposited in shallow temporary lakes (Sjara-osso-gol or Mongolian facies). The whole complex possibly covers several different stages, as will be suggested in due course.

B. SOUTH CHINA

A) SUCCESSION OF THE DEPOSITS

South of the Tsinling range the Pliocene is represented by tilted lacustrine deposits containing a rich tropical mollusk fauna (ornamented *Paludina, Ampullaria*). Unconformably above these freshwater sediments, extensive fans of gravel and loam[2] (subjected almost immediately after their formation to intense lateritization) mark an important period of epeirogenic movements. Then, probably succeeding this lateritization, a number of fissure-deposits were formed, containing a rich fauna characterized by *Ailuropus* and by typical Malayan types: *Stegodon, tapir, Rhinoceros*, orang, etc. Rewashed laterites in South China proper, and brown loams in the lower Yangtze basin mark the end of the Pleistocene.

B) CORRELATION WITH NORTH CHINA

In view of the fact that on the southern slope of the Tsinling range, lateritic soil is capped by Middle Pleistocene reddish clays of North China, I have so far been inclined to regard

[2] Some of these fans are regarded as of "glacial" age by Prof. J. S. Lee.

the lateritized fans of South China as earlier than Middle Pleistocene, that is, as Villafranchian. But, as explained below, we
begin to realize that these fans might better be referred to the
Middle Pleistocene, so as to become an exact equivalent of the
post-Villafranchian loams and gravels of North China.

In any case, so far as the *Stegodon*-bearing fissure-deposits
of Szechuan, Yunnan, Kwangsi are concerned, a Middle Pleistocene age is fairly well established. In spite of the fact that
there we only know so far of a single form (a water buffalo)
on which we can base a correlation, it would appear that the
Stegodon fauna of the South is equally old as the Sinanthropus
fauna of the North.

2. CORRELATIONS WITH FOREIGN REGIONS

At several levels of the columnar section (Fig. 31) correlations can be traced between the late Cenozoic of North China
and that of other countries.

a) The uppermost, *Equus*-bearing, lake deposits of North
China are safely comparable with the *Equus*-beds of India (Upper
Siwaliks: Tatrot, Pinjor) and of Europe (Villafranchian).
For the three areas definite faunal analogies become obvious:
the appearance of horse and camel, both in China and in India;
appearance of horse, Bovinae, *Nyctereutes* (a characteristic dog),
Eucladoceros deer, etc., both in China and in Western Europe.
And, furthermore, deposition of the lacustrine or fluviatile beds
in these areas is succeeded by strong continental uplifts.

b) To the Middle Pleistocene gravels and reddish loams
of North China corresponds most obviously the post-Villafranchian "Boulder Conglomerate" of North India; and also, probably, the Trinil beds of Java; and perhaps the Cromer Forest-
beds of Western Europe.[3] In the Forest-bed euryceroid deer

[3] This correlation coincides with Dr. Hopwood's views who synchronized the
Cromer beds with the Middle Pleistocene of Asia "Fossil elephants and man,"
Proc. Geol. Assoc., Vol. XLVI, pt. I, 1935. It is therefore significant that a

appear akin to Chinese types. As for the Trinil beds, they are almost actually linked with the *Sinanthropus*-beds by a chain of *Stegodon*-bearing fissures extending from Java to the Yangtze basin through Indochina. Curiously enough, (as pointed out recently by de Terra)[4] in the four considered areas (China, Java, India, Europe) the here synchronized beds contain the first sure traces of Man.

c) In a general way, the loess of China is closely connected with the Late Pleistocene loess of Europe and with the Potwar silts of North India. The problem of a closer synchronism, however, is still unsettled. My earlier assumption that the whole of the Chinese loess is of Würmian age must possibly be corrected, as will be pointed out below.

3. CONCLUSIONS AND REFLECTIONS ON PENDING PROBLEMS IN PLEISTOCENE CORRELATIONS

At the present stage of our stratigraphic work on the Late Cenozoic of China, the following problems require an immediate consideration:

A. AGE OF THE POST-PLIOCENE LATERITIZED FANS OF SOUTH CHINA

As mentioned above, it would be more satisfactory to consider the lateritized fans of South China as Middle Pleistocene (just as the "boulder clays" and clay deposits of North China and India) instead of as Villafranchian, as I had previously believed. The question can probably be settled by new researches carried on, either in West Yunnan where the lateritized fans come in contact with the *Equus*-beds discovered in 1926 by Dr. W. Granger, or in Burma, where they merge perhaps directly with the Siwalik

---

Cromerian type of industry was discovered in the Boulder Conglomerate of northern India (see footnote 4).

[4] "Cenozoic cycles in Asia and their bearing on human prehistory." Proc. Am. Philo. Soc., Vol. 77, No. 3, 1937.

Boulder Conglomerate. If, by chance, the lateritized fans of South China would turn out to be of Middle Pleistocene age (and therefore contemporaneous with the *Stegodon*-bearing fis-

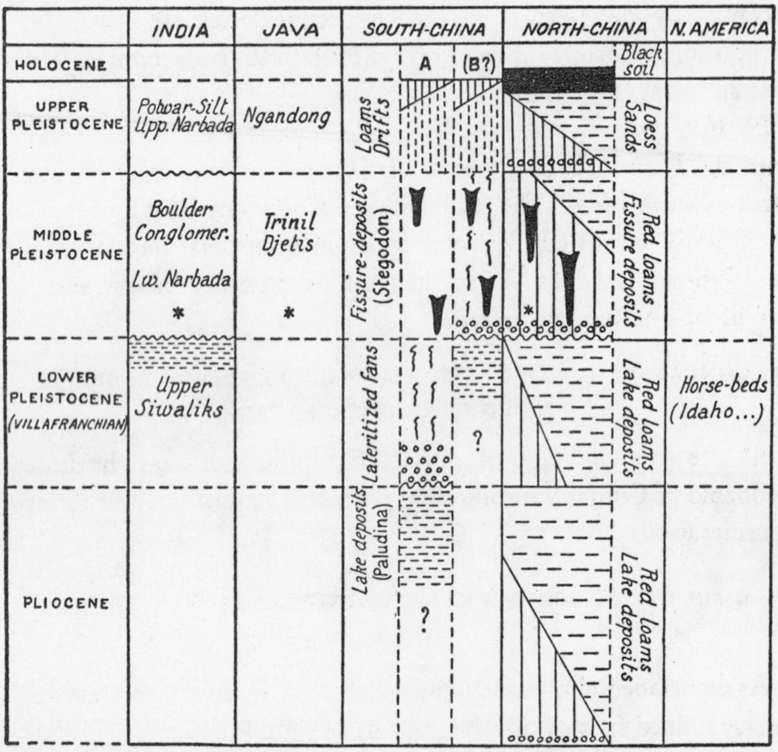

	INDIA	JAVA	SOUTH-CHINA		NORTH-CHINA	N. AMERICA
HOLOCENE			A	(B?)	*Black soil*	
UPPER PLEISTOCENE	*Potwar-Silt* *Upp. Narbada*	*Ngandong*	*Loams Drifts*		*Loess Sands*	
MIDDLE PLEISTOCENE	*Boulder Conglomer.* *Lw. Narbada* *	*Trinil Djetis* *	*Fissure-deposits (Stegodon)* *Lateritized fans*		*Red loams Fissure deposits* *	
LOWER PLEISTOCENE (VILLAFRANCHIAN)	*Upper Siwaliks*		*Lake deposits (Paludina)*	?	*Red loams Lake deposits*	*Horse-beds (Idaho...)*
PLIOCENE				?	*Red loams Lake deposits*	

FIG. 31—Tentative correlation of the late Cenozoic formations in China, Java, India and North America (according to Teilhard, de Terra and von Koenigswald).

For South China, an alternative interpretation B is suggested, modifying the proposed interpretation A (see text). Horizontal lines: fresh-water deposits. Vertical lines: fan deposits. An undulating line between two successive formations means an angular unconformity. A star marks the first sure traces of Man.

sures of the same area) their parallelism would be striking both with the Boulder Conglomerate of the Siwaliks and with the "reddish fans" of North China, the three formations appearing simultaneously above tilted Pliocene deposits (see Fig. 31, alternative B).

B. AGE OF THE CHINESE MALAN LOESS AND ASSOCIATED BEDS

If, by analogy with the Boulder Conglomerate of India, the Middle Pleistocene "reddish fans" of North China are correlated

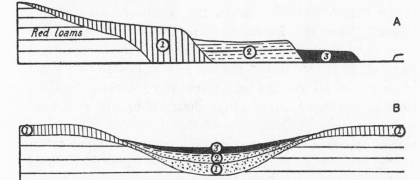

FIG. 32—A. a schematic relation of the terraces along the Loho river (Jehol, North China); 1. Malan loess terrace; 2. torrential sandy terrace (Loho formation); 3. lower terrace capped with black soil. B. suggested structure of a basin in Manchuria; 1. Malan loess and corresponding lower sands; 2. middle sands ("Loho sands"); 3. black soils, with Late Paleolithic or Neolithic industry, and perhaps with a residual Pleistocene fauna.

(see de Terra) with the *second* Himalayan glaciation ("Mindel"), it follows that the succeeding Malan loess, and associated sediments should represent both the third and fourth glaciations, and not only the last or Würmian loess of Europe. Hence, we should recognize instead of a single cycle, two cycles, and therefore, *two* loess formations in the Late Pleistocene of China. How and where can we hope to solve the age problem of the Chinese loess?

1) A first line of attack would be a closer study of the stratigraphical relationships between the true eolian Malan loess and its associated sandy-lacustrine formations. Following my own inter-

pretation, it was assumed that the Late Pleistocene "Sjara-osso-gol sands" for instance are, as a whole, a lateral facies of the Malan loess. But the relations between eolian loess and basin-sediments may prove to be more complex.

In the Sjara-osso-gol basin itself, of course, I still believe that the *Rhinoceros tichorhinus* sands and clays are mostly contemporary with the thick loess capping the adjoining Shensi hills. But, in the Manchuria-Hailar basins, the conditions are probably different. Years ago, I observed along the Loho river in Jehol (Fig. 32A) that the loessic Malan terrace I is followed by a lower sandy terrace II, and this one in turn dissected by a still lower terrace III, covered with black soils containing neolithic cultures. In a depression of a type illustrated by Fig. 32B, commonly met with in Changchun, Harbin, Djalainor, etc., it may well be that the basin-sediments represent three different stages: a series of lower sands corresponding to the loamy Malan loess of the slopes; a series of middle sands corresponding to the terrace II or the Loho; and a series of younger black soils. If so, the loess and the lower sands might be synchronized with the third glaciation (just as the Potwar loessic silt of India); the middle sands with the fourth glaciation; and the black soil with a postglacial epoch.

2) In such a case, the missing equivalents of the third or "Riss" might be found by subdividing the "Malan stage." But another possibility presents itself. The "third glacial stage" might be recognized in some pre-Malan loam, above the Middle Pleistocene reddish clays (such as e.g. the fossiliferous red loam, containing an apparently younger fauna, recently described by Mr. W. C. Pei from the locality 3 of Choukoutien). In this case, the Malan loess would remain "Würmian," except for the younger black soils, a stratigraphic position which is more satisfactory, in view of the Upper Pleistocene fauna and human industry found in the loess.

3) As a final and direct way of solving the problem, I would suggest that a careful analysis be made of the wonderful system of fans and terraces bordering the northern foot of the Tienshan[5] in the Urumchi region (Sinkiang). Since these terraces are connected with both glacial formations in the Tienshan, and with typical Malan loess along the Dzungary basin, it would seem that the conditions here are just as favorable for Pleistocene stratigraphic studies as in Northwest India. Very promising also is the terrace formation in western Ordos, but the absence of glacial deposits will not permit of correlations with glacial stages.

C. CONNECTIONS WITH EUROPE

As outlined above, a successful trial is in development just now for bridging (with the help of fossiliferous fissure-deposits) the Middle Pleistocene of North China with the Middle Pleistocene of Java. A similar effort should be made for linking China with Western Europe on a palaeontological basis. An increasing number of fossils has come to light in Hungary through the work of Dr. Kormos, in southern Germany near Steinheim, and at Norfolk, England, which show striking similarities with the Lower and Middle Pleistocene faunas of China such as the euryceroid deer, the water-buffalo, *Mimomys*, etc. I believe that a thorough comparative study of these forms will enable us to correlate the Pleistocene formations of the glaciated and non-glaciated areas of the palaearctic world.

D. CONNECTIONS WITH NORTH AMERICA

So far the apparent continental connections between Eastern Asia and North America during the late Cenozoic are insuffi-

---

[5] Along the southern border of the Tienshan (Turfan) the earlier Pleistocene fans are tilted.

ciently known. In my opinion two problems are outstanding in importance:

1. THE CORRELATION OF THE VILLAFRANCHIAN FAUNA OF CHINA WITH THAT OF NORTH AMERICA

If we base our stratigraphic correlations on such forms as the horse, the camel, the Lagomorpha and various Carnivora, it is possible to correlate right now the Villafranchian beds of China (and consequently the Upper Siwaliks of India) with such American formations as the horse-beds of Idaho, described by Dr. Gazin and others. Supposing that such a synchronism was firmly established, and that a correlation was worked out between the horse-beds and glacial stages in North America, it should be possible to correlate the glaciations of Asia with those of North America.

2. THE CORRELATION BETWEEN LATER PLEISTOCENE FORMATIONS IN CHINA AND NORTH AMERICA

This correlation which has such a vital bearing on human pre-history in America, might be established by investigating more closely the late Pleistocene sands and black soils of Manchuria. Here, a late Palaeolithic culture occurs in apparent association with a residual Pleistocene fauna (*R. tichorhinus*), exhibiting a stratigraphic pattern which closely resembles that of the culture-bearing late Pleistocene formations of Nebraska, Colorado and New Mexico.[6]

[6] This possibility was mentioned by Dr. de Terra at the occasion of the round table conference on Asiatic chronology held on March 20th, 1937, in Philadelphia.

PALAEOLITHIC INDUSTRIES IN CHINA

BY

PEI WEN-CHUNG

Research Fellow of the China Foundation for the Promotion of Education and Culture, and Geologist, Cenozoic Research Laboratory, Geological Survey of China

I. INTRODUCTION AND SUMMARY

UNTIL about forty years ago, it was thought by archaeologists that China was not occupied by Palaeolithic people. However, recent discoveries tend to show that throughout all the main epochs of the Old Stone Age, China was inhabited successively by primitive men. We now have record of a series of the lithic industries which were left by them.

This paper will be devoted to giving a brief summary of four industries as represented mainly by various sites at Choukoutien and in Ordos. Anyone wishing a detailed description of the implements from these various industries is referred to the original works.

The question of the extent to which Chinese and European Palaeolithic industries may be correlated in detail, is especially interesting to this Symposium. However, its solution is at present impossible owing to at least two insurmountable difficulties:

1) The complicated sub-division of the European Palaeolithic industries. So far, without counting those not yet generally accepted, there are ten main and thirty-seven sub-divisions of Palaeolithic industries. Unfortunately, the characteristic types of tools upon which European prehistorians base their claims for such a great number of sub-divisions, are not yet known in China.

2) An industrial development is often only local. In different regions there may be different human races which may have quite different industries, regardless of the fact that they lived at the same time.

Because of these two difficulties, I suggest submitting a correlation of the Palaeolithic industries of Europe and China based chiefly upon the geological age of the industries (Fig. 33). A comparison by means of the types and workmanship of the implements will also be considered, but we shall see of what little aid this will be.

II. THE OLDEST INDICATION OF HUMAN HAND WORK

1. NIHOWAN

On his return from China, Professor Breuil communicated to the French Institute of Anthropology his belief that the oldest indication of human hand work in China is neither the quartz implements worked by *Sinanthropus* at Choukoutien, nor the chert implement from Locality 13, but is a faceted stone, collected by Père Teilhard de Chardin from Hsiashakou of the Nihowan lacustrine deposit. Breuil describes this piece as being artificially worked by many blows on different faces. In addition to this simple implement, he believes, there are many worked and utilized bones which are the same as those known in the *Sinanthropus* Industry. There are also some pieces of bones which seem to be burned.

The accompanying fauna, (*Hipparion, Equus,* and *Chalicotherium*) has been, in the Chinese geological sequence, relegated to Sanmenian I, or Upper Pliocene. However, human activity of such an ancient date can hardly be affirmed by a single evidence. Further research by Chinese geologists and prehistorians at this locality is imperative for the near future.

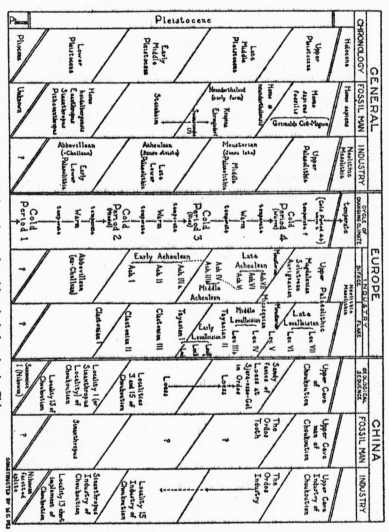

FIG. 33—Correlation chart of prehistoric industries in China.

2. LOCALITY 13 OF CHOUKOUTIEN

From the viewpoint of palaeontology, the fossiliferous Locality 13 of the Choukoutien region seems to be somewhat older than the *Sinanthropus* locality, judging from the presence of the archaic fossils of *Siphneus tingi*, *Hystrix lagrelii*, and a special form of *Euryceros* (*Sinomegaceros*) in the former deposit. The geological age of this locality has been relegated to Sanmenian II or an early phase of Lower Pleistocene rather than to Upper Pliocene, because of the absence of such typical Pliocene forms as *Hipparion* and *Chalicotherium*. In 1934, an implement made of chert was discovered *in situ*. It was worked alternately on two faces and is somewhat similar to a coup de poing known in the Abbevillean Industry in France. In addition to this single implement, we found also some isolated burnt bones and some broken foreign stones on which the artificial working is not evident. Until possible further discovery at Locality 13, we still hesitate to admit the presence of a true human industry of the earliest Lower Pleistocene time in China, even though it is indicated by one single implement of undoubted human origin.

III. THE EARLY LOWER PALAEOLITHIC OR CHOUKOUTIEN SINANTHROPUS INDUSTRY

The Lower Palaeolithic Industry in China is represented by the Choukoutien *Sinanthropus* Industry. So far, it is known only at Locality 1 of the Choukoutien region. We may consider the culture attained by the *Sinanthropus* in three categories: the use of fire, the lithic industry, and the osseous industry.

The use of artificial fire employed by prehistoric man is established by the finding of charcoal, ashes, and burnt bones in the different cultural layers of the Choukoutien cave.

The lithic industry is indeed very rudimentary. It is a flake industry, and the implements are made generally of quartz, occasionally of chert and other hard sandstones. The well-retouched implements are rare, among thousands of flakes without secondary work. The implements are crude, including scrapers, points, chisels, choppers, and a certain number of gravers. Among thousands of broken bones and antlers, we have

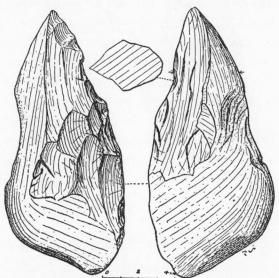

FIG 34—Chopper in green sandstone from Loc. 15 of Choukoutien, x ½.

observed a number of worked, utilized, and worked and utilized specimens. Professor Breuil and I are now carrying on a detailed study of these specimens.

IV. THE LATE LOWER PALAEOLITHIC

At Locality 15 of the Choukoutien region, we collected many hundreds of chert and quartz implements. The geological age of this locality seems to be contemporary with that of Locality 3, or Lower Middle Pleistocene, and younger than that of Locality

1, where we found *Sinanthropus*. Consequently, the industry found in such an age would represent the Late Lower Palaeolithic in China.

The Choukoutien Locality 15 Industry has not yet been studied in detail. The tools of Locality 15 are more or less the same as those of *Sinanthropus*, and are always the uncharacteris-

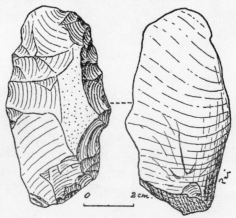

FIG. 35—Double side-scrapers in chert from Loc. 15 of Choukoutien, x 2/3.

tic ones such as choppers, side scrapers, chisels, and points (Fig. 35).

V. THE MIDDLE PALAEOLITHIC—THE ORDOS INDUSTRY

The Middle Palaeolithic in China is represented by the Ordos Industry from Shuitunkkou and Sjara-Osso-Gol in Ordos, discovered by PP. Licent and Teilhard and described by Professor H. Breuil. The accompanying fossils are *Elephas namadicus*, *Rhinoceros tichorhinus*, *Bos primigenius*, etc. Their geological age is attributed to the Late Middle Pleistocene and is recognized as contemporary with the upper part of the loess.

The Ordos Industry consists of many types: points, scrapers,

FIG. 36—Different implements from Sjara-osso-gol in Ordos, natural size, (after Breuil).

borers, gravers, etc., (Fig. 36) made chiefly of quartzite. Although a little better retouched, they are comparable with those collected from the *Sinanthropus* deposit. In addition to these types, there are examples of micro-gravers (*micro-burin*), and micro-point, which indicate that they are more advanced than those of the *Sinanthropus* Industry.

VI. THE UPPER PALAEOLITHIC—THE CHOUKOUTIEN UPPER CAVE INDUSTRY

The Upper Palaeolithic in China is represented by the industry known as the Upper Cave Industry of Choukoutien. This industry is quite poor in lithic implements, being represented only by a few pieces, such as scrapers and points made of quartz, which are not much better in workmanship than those from the *Sinanthropus* deposits. This industry shows a much advanced stage by the presence of worked bones and ornamental objects, such as bone pendants, bone needles, perforated pebbles, perforated teeth, etc. The accompanying fauna includes certain extinct forms such as *Hyaena spelaea* and *Ursus spelaeus* and some southern Asiatic species now not existing in the region, such as *Cynailurus jubatus*. Its geological age should be attributed to the Upper Pleistocene.

VII. THE PROBLEM OF CORRELATION WITH THE EUROPEAN PALAEOLITHIC INDUSTRIES

As I have mentioned, there are at least two great difficulties in making a correlation between the Palaeolithic industries in Europe and in China, if we consider only the technique of tool-making and the types of implements. However, we may overcome these difficulties by a correlation based upon geological and palaeontological studies.

In considering the geological age of the European Palaeolithic industries, we may divide them into four main sub-divisions: Early Lower Palaeolithic (Abbevillean and Early Clactonian); Late Lower Palaeolithic (Acheulean I-V, Late Clactonian, and Early Tayacian, Mousterian, and Micoquean); and Upper Palaeolithic (Levalloisian VI and VII, Aurignacian, Solutrean, and Magdalenian). Their geological ages are respectively: Lower, Early Middle, Late Middle, and Upper Pleistocene.

Coming to the Palaeolithic industries in China, we know definitely their geological ages. Thus they may be correlated with those of Europe by means of a fixed geological age.

Judging by geological and palaeontological studies, the *Sinanthropus* Industry in China corresponds chronologically to the Abbevillean (Ex-Chellean) and earliest Clactonian in France and England. But the contemporary implements are quite divergent in type and technique.

In respect to the lithic industry of *Sinanthropus*, a comparison by technique with the Abbevillean of Europe is impossible. *Sinanthropus* worked the stone implement chiefly by means of the simple "bipolar" flaking technique, which is practically unknown to the prehistoric times of Europe. On the other hand, the Abbevillean bifaces were made by alternating flaking with hammerstone; no analogy of workmanship whatsoever between these two industries can be found. Experiments have shown that the Clactonian, also a flake industry, is composed of flakes made on an anvil; but such a technique is so far not established in the *Sinanthropus* Industry.

The most common type of tool employed by *Sinanthropus* is the side-scraper, which may be found in any Palaeolithic epoch of Europe, from Clactonian up to Magdalenian. Other types, such as small bifaces or point, pitted stones, gravers, end-scrapers, etc., are chiefly known in the European Upper Palaeolithic. However, they are not the characteristic types upon which pre-historians base their sub-divisions. Personally, I doubt the possibility of establishing a correlation which admits that the *Sinanthropus* Industry corresponds to the Aurignacian, Solutrean, or Magdalenian of France.

The trace of the use of fire is hardly known earlier than Mousterian in Europe, but in China we have noticed definite evidence of artificial fire as early as the *Sinanthropus* time. This is due possibly to the fact that the favorable conditions have preserved the evidence in the Chinese cave.

In Europe, the bone artifacts are practically unknown earlier than in the Tayacian, Mousterian, and Upper Palaeolithic levels. However, the European Abbevillean, Clactonian, and Acheulean Industries are found mostly in the open air stations where bones are rarely preserved; consequently, the bone implements dated as Lower Palaeolithic are scarcely known in Europe.

In comparsion with the European Upper Palaeolithic discoveries, the so-called bone implements from Choukoutien *Sinanthropus* site are not those such as bone points with cleft base, (*la pointe à base fendue*) of Aurignacian, nor the points with forked or cut base (*la pointe à base fourchue ou à base biseautée*) of Magdalenian in French caves, but are only those which are the simple bone splitters and chips. Also, the antlers worked by *Sinanthropus* are not perforated staves (*batons percés*) but are only those which were simply cut and utilized. Can we, then, suppose that the osseous industries of Choukoutien are comparable to those of Upper Palaeolithic in Europe?

In summary, it seems to me that, until we find some characteristic types, a correlation between the *Sinanthropus* Industry and the Palaeolithic industries in Europe cannot be made merely by the study of the implements themselves.

CONCLUSION

In conclusion, we may say that according to the studies of geology and palaeontology, the succession of Palaeolithic industries in China is very evident, and that these industries represent the main sub-divisions of the Pleistocene recorded in prehistorical Europe. But because of the differences in raw materials adapted for tool-making, and because of the various humanities known to Europe and Asia, a more detailed correlation by means of the implements themselves cannot at present possibly be made between the Palaeolithic industries in Europe and those in China. We must await further discoveries.

REFERENCES

Anderson, J. G. Essays on the Cenozoic of North China. Mem. Geol. Surv. China, Ser. A. No. 3, 1923.

Black, Davidson. Evidences of the Use of Fire. Bull. Geol. Soc. China, Vol. XI, 1931.

Black, Davidson, Teilhard de Chardin, P., Young, C. C., & Pei, W. C. Fossil Man in China. Mem. Geol. Surv. China, Ser. A, No. 11, 1933.

Boule, M., Breuil, H., Licent, E., & Teilhard de Chardin, P. Le Paléolitique de la Chine. Archives de l'Institut de Paléontologie Humaine, Mem. 4, 1928.

Breuil, H. Le Feu et l'Industrie Lithique et Osseuse à Choukoutien. Bull. Geol. Soc. China, Vol. XI, 1931.

—— Industries de pierre et d'os à Choukoutien. L'Anthropologie, XLV, Nos. 5 & 6, 1935.

Pei, W. C. Notice of the discovery of quartz and other stone artifacts in the Lower Pleistocene hominid-bearing sediments of the Choukoutien Caves deposit. Bull. Geol. Soc. China, Vol. XI, 1931.

—— Report of the excavation of the Locality 13 in Choukoutien. Bull. Geol. Soc. China, Vol. XIII, No. 3, 1934.

—— The Age of Sinanthropus—An Attempted Correlation of

Quaternary Geology, Palaeontology, and Prehistory in Europe and China. (In press.)

Teilhard de Chardin, P. Les récents progrès de la Préhistoire en Chine. L'Anthropologie, XLV, Nos. 5 & 6, 1935.

Teilhard de Chardin, P., & Pei, W. C. The Lithic Industry of the Sinanthropus deposits in Choukoutien. Bull. Geol. Soc. China, Vol. XI, 1931.

—— New Discoveries in Choukoutien. Bull. Geol. Soc. China, Vol. XIII, 1934.

ADAPTATION TO THE POSTGLACIAL FOREST ON THE NORTH EURASIATIC PLAIN

BY

V. GORDON CHILDE

Professor of Prehistoric Archaeology, University of Edinburgh

By 7000 B. C. a forested plain, stretching across northern Europe continuously from England to the Urals, presented to its first colonists problems similar to those facing the aboriginal inhabitants of comparable zones in North America. Geology and the botanical study of peat bogs reveal changes in the environment to which men had to adapt themselves and at the same time afford a handy chronological framework for the prehistorian. In the central area round Denmark and the southwestern Baltic the following sequences have been dated by geochronological methods as explained in Clark's recent book.[1]

Date B.C.	Baltic phase	Forest	Climate
	Yoldia Sea	birch first pines	Pre-Boreal (cold, dry)
7500	regression Ancylus Lake	pines first mixed oak-woods hazel	Boreal (warm, dry)
5000	transgression Littorina Sea	Mixed oak-woods	Atlantic (warm, moist)
2500	gradual regression		Sub-Boreal (warm, drier)
800			Sub-Atlantic (cold, moist)

It must be insisted that this table is applicable only in the central

[1] J. G. D. Clark, "The Mesolithic Settlements of Northern Europe." Cambridge, 1936.

zone and even there with reservations. The character of a forest is conditioned by climatic and edaphic factors, and climate in turn is a function both of latitude and of distance from the sea. Pollen diagrams show significant variations even in Boreal times as between England, Zealand and Esthonia; in Atlantic times the effect of the marine transgression must have been far less potent east of the Baltic than round the North Sea; the curves of isotherms and isohyets would have been displaced eastward but not flattened out. And so, even as far west as Great Poland, the pollen diagram from the peat moss at Biskupin exhibits only fractional fluctuations in the composition of the local forest. In a general way the woodlands of Central Russia today give a fair impression of the landscape of the whole plain in Boreal times; it has undergone no radical change despite variations such as the immigration of the spruce and a temporary advance of sporadic oaks as far as Olonetz. Similarly the decalcified old moraines of Holland and Northwest Germany can never have supported such luxuriant oak woods as flourished on the newer moraines of Schleswig and Denmark in Atlantic times: there was then no impenetrable belt of forest separating the northern coasts from the Central European löss lands.

By late Boreal times the whole forested plain from Yorkshire to Esthonia was occupied by hunters and fishers living in small groups and camping on the banks of sluggish streams, meres and lakes. The unity of their culture is best demonstrated by the distribution of specialized types of hunting and fishing implements—"harpoons," fish-spears, and dart-heads of bone—that have been mapped by Clark. The homogeneous culture defined by these types may be termed Maglemosean. But the Maglemoseans differed from the older palaeolithic hunters of the steppes and tundras and from other contemporary mesolithic groups in an adaptation to forest life. This adjustment is symbolized by the

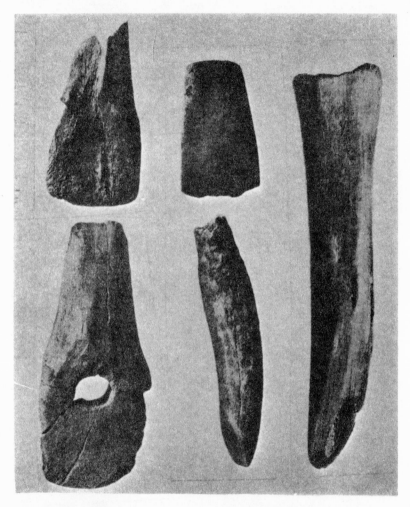

PLATE XVIII—Heavy tools from Kunda, Esthonia Archaeological Cabinet, University of Tartu.

possession of adzes and chisels of antler, bone and stone as Schwantes first insisted.

But while in the central area the specialized bone hunting tools are restricted to Boreal times, the heavy tools persisted unchanged even into the Bronze and Iron Ages so that isolated specimens cannot at once be labelled Maglemosean. Hence in 1931 I was not yet able to prove that the distribution of the "heavy industry" coincided with that of the Boreal Maglemosean. A macrolithic flint industry associated with microliths of Maglemosean type was subsequently identified by Clark in southeastern England and eventually proved to go back to Boreal times. East of the Baltic, sites like Kunda at first seemed to reveal a bone culture bereft of heavy industry. But the old Kunda-finds were made up of fishing and fowling implements, lost in a shallow mere. In 1934-5 the fishers' actual camping places were located and yielded, on excavation,[2] antler adzes, antler chisels, socketed bone chisels, perforated antler mounts and stone adze-blades with ground edges (see plate XVIII). The distribution of "heavy industry" is thus shown to coincide with that of the other type-fossils already in Boreal times (Fig. 37).

The uniformity of Maglemosean culture is further emphasized by other significant traits—notably knives made from boars' tusks, the possession of tame dogs and of a boat (of skins?) propelled by paddles, and the drill technique in decoration. Nevertheless, as might be expected in such a vast and diversified area, local differences occur and are reflected even in the distribution of the bone points that Clark has mapped. But in particular conical arrow-heads, single barbed lanceolate points (of Clark's Lohusu form) and ice-picks are confined to the East Baltic lands and extend thence to the Urals.

There is thus a very real distinction even in Boreal times be-

[2] R. Indreko, "Vorlaufige Bemerkungen über die Kunda-Funde," Sitzungs-berichte gelehrten esthnischen Gesellschaft, 1934, 1936.

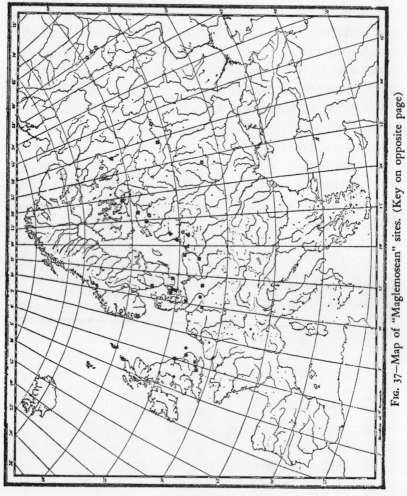

FIG. 37—Map of "Maglemosean" sites. (Key on opposite page)

tween a west Ancylus facies, represented classically at Mullerup (Zealand), and an east Ancylus facies, best seen at Kunda. The differences are due partly to divergent cultural contacts. The geometric microliths found in the western stations are technically indistinguishable from the Tardenoisian and were presumably taken over by the Western Maglemoseans from Tardenoisian immigrants, coming from the southwest. Kunda lacks these geometric forms but has yielded a few Swiderian points, presumably derived from the South Russian palaeolithic cultures. Other differences are conditioned by divergent environment. Pebbles replace flint for adze blades because flint was less accessible east of the Baltic than in England or Denmark. (The technique of polishing, used for sharpening their edges, has presumably been taken over from bone work.)

Then, even at the climatic optimum of the Boreal phase, the winters east of the Baltic must have been much severer than in Denmark or England, just as they are today. Ice-picks and conical arrow-heads are an adjustment to this more rigorous climate. The conical arrow-heads were presumably used, like their mod-

---

Key to Fig. 37.

☐   Heavy industry associated with Maglemosean types

◪   Stone adze-heads (Boreal)

◪   Antler adzes (Boreal)

◪   Antler chisels (Boreal)

◣   Socketed bone chisels (Boreal)

◺   Socketed bone chisels (post-Boreal or undated)

●   Important Maglemosean assemblages (Boreal)

○   Important Maglemosean assemblages (post-Boreal)

ern descendants, for killing fur-bearing animals without damaging their pelts unnecessarily.[3]

A particularly significant adjustment to the east Ancylus environment was the dog-sleigh. Wooden sledge-shoes have been found in a late Boreal peat at Heinola and in an early Atlantic layer at Ylastaro in Finland.[4] These runners provide the earliest evidence for the use of a sledge and indeed for the application of non-human motive power to transport, substantially antedating (if the geochronologists' figures are correct) the oldest dated Oriental vehicles. The sledge would facilitate that intercourse between the scattered bands of fishers and hunters that must be postulated to explain the uniformity of Maglemosean equipment. And in fact the Ylastaro runner was made from the wood of *Pinus cembra* that does not grow west of the Urals. And a derivative of the Heinola runner, found in a late Atlantic bed at Kuortine, Finland, is identical with one from Gorbuno in the Urals.

In peripheral regions where geological or botanical datings are inapplicable, an eventual extension of the Maglemosean complex beyond the limits of Clark's may be deduced from the distribution of type-fossils, though their age may be in doubt. In western Norway, Viste near Stavanger and Skipshelleren on Bolstad Fjord near Bergen[5] have yielded typically Maglemosean assemblages. But geologically Viste at least is equated with the *Tapes* strand, the Norwegian equivalent of the Littorina transgression.

Eastward Maglemosean types extend right across central Russia to the Urals and as far south as the Ukrainian border. Veretye

[3] P. A. Dmitriev, "Ochota i rybolovstvo v vostochno-uralskom rodovom obshchestve.". Izvestia Gaimk, 106, 1934, p. 193.

[4] T. I. Itkonen in Suomen Museo, XXXVIII-IX (1931-2), 60; XLI, (1934), 1-21; XLII (1935), 22; U. T. Sirelius, in Festschrift P. W. Schmidt, 1928, 949-958.

[5] A. W. Brøgger, Vistefundet (Stavanger, 1908); J. Bøe, "Boplassen i Skipshelleren," Bergen, 1934.

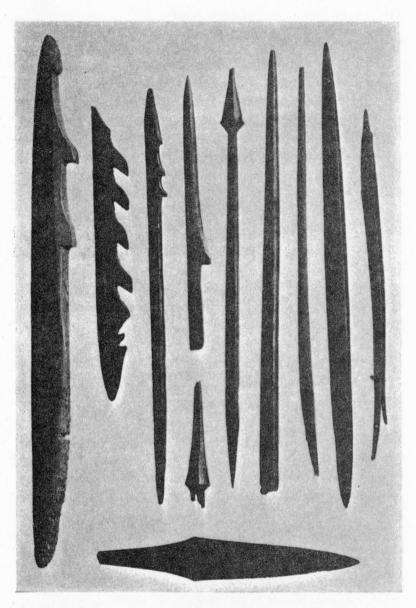

PLATE XIX–"Harpoons" and conical arrow-heads from Ural Mosses. Finnish National Museum.

on L. Lacha in Olonetz yielded a shaft-hold adze, an ice-pick, conical arrow-heads, harpoons, like Clark's forms 8 and 9, and a Pernau fish-hook. Among the finds from Ls. Ayatskoe and Shigir in the central Urals are other Maglemose types (Plate XIX) while stray specimens can be cited from intermediate regions. Bone chisels and harpoons and a boar's tusk knife come from Lialovo near Moscow, antler adzes, bone "harpoons," points and a Pernau fish-hook from Pohorilova near Korop in Chernigov,[6] but all these sites are post-Boreal; at Lialovo, and apparently at Pohorilova, the Maglemosean forms are even associated with neolithic pottery; in the Ural mosses perhaps with Bronze Age wares! The late Maglemosean types of Russia *may* be due to a survival into Sub-Boreal times of a complex already spread there in the Boreal. But the existing data are definitely incompatible with Menghin's thesis, claiming the Ural relics as pure representatives of an Upper pleistocene "bone culture cycle" of which Maglemose would be only a late and hybrid offshot.

Still they do not suffice to prove the contrary thesis of a gradual spread of the Maglemosean from the southwest. Clark has indeed detected Magdalenian motives in Maglemose art; Indreko has found possible prototypes for Maglemosean "chisels," conical arrow-heads, and ice-picks in French and South German palaeolithic stations; and Rust has uncovered near Hamburg the summer camps of reindeer-hunters in Pre-Boreal times some items of whose equipment might be intermediate between Magdalenian and Maglemosean. But till more be known of the subsequent history of the South Russian mammoth-hunters, a derivation of the Maglemosean from the southeast cannot be excluded. Finally the Finnmarkian of the Arctic coasts of Russia and Norway with flake- and core-axes that point on to the Maglemosean but "moustiriform" flakes and cores suggesting connections with

[6] *Russ. Antrop.* Zhurna, Moskva, 1925, XIV, 37-82; Antropologiya, Kiiv, 1930, IV, 175.

Siberian and Chinese palaeolithic cultures may open up the possibility of an Asiatic ancestry for our complex.

It is premature to pronounce on the origin of the Maglemosean; its subsequent history is better known. The Littorina transgression isolated Britain which was soon occupied by a genuine neolithic culture. In the central region the ensuing climatic changes produced a more favorable environment. The Ertebølle culture of Denmark may be regarded as an adjustment of the Maglemosean to the new conditions, with large oyster banks and sealing and deep sea-fishing giving an opportunity for more sedentary life. But pottery, appearing already at the time of the maximum of the Littorina sinking, may have been borrowed from neolithic immigrants moving in from the Danube valley or from Western Europe. Certainly before the Atlantic phase ended the introduction of cereals and sheep from outside the plain made possible the rise of a food-producing economy and the neolithic cultures termed "Nordic" in Denmark, Southwest Sweden and North Germany.

In the Baltic basin proper the effects of the transgression had been less catastrophic; in Sweden, Esthonia and Finland dwelling-places without pottery but with ground stone axes of the Limnhamn, Lihult, Voisek and Suomusjärvi types represent adjustments parallel to Ertebølle. And on these coasts the gradual regression of the Littorina Sea provides a time-scale for correlating subsequent stages of development since the fishers' settlements tend always to come down close to the shore.

As the environment had changed but little and the old economy of ice-fishing, hunting and fowling persisted, the old equipment survived well into Sub-Boreal times. The old bone "harpoons," slotted points, fish-hooks and arrow-heads continue to be made. Stone increasingly replaces bone for heavy tools, but the "celts" are used as adzes or gouges and still betray their ancestry in bone forms; in Central Russia the antler tools and roughly flaked flint adze heads tend to survive. Innovations first attested in this period are resin chewing,[7] a haphazard traffic in amber, skis (from Sub-Boreal peats in Finland) and regular burials, generally extended as with the "Nordic" "funnel-necked beaker" culture.

Pottery, however, appears, but in extraordinarily uniform shape from the Baltic to the Kama. The vases are throughout built up in rings, ovoid in shape with almost pointed bases; a universal element in the decoration is one or more horizontal rows of pits, sometimes made with a belemnite. (These features recur in a quite different economic milieu in the domestic pottery of Swedish megalith builders and in English Peterborough ware.) In Finland[8] the earliest pottery appears when the Littorina Sea had contracted to eighty-seven per cent of its maximum extent, and three stylistic phases can be recognized before agriculture and stock-breeding were introduced by the battle-axe folk from further South, when the shore was between sixty and fifty per cent of its maximum height. In Central Russia pit-and-comb ornamented pottery (resembling Finnish styles II and III rather than I) is found in dwelling-places throughout the forest zone, and there too agriculture and pastoralism were probably introduced by battle-axe folk. Most of the Maglemosean types cited above are associated with this pit-and-comb ware. But still it lasted very long. At Federovskoe in Kostroma[9] bits of copper ornaments were associated with typical ovoid pots. And beyond the Urals at Borbuno near Nijni-Tagilsk pit-and-comb sherds, a sledge-shoe, conical arrow-heads and other archaic forms seem to be contemporary with pottery of the Late Bronze Age Andronovo culture. Similarly, though pit-and-comb ware occurs on the Jenessei and Angora, such vases may be found in Bronze Age graves. Hence, as with Maglemosean types, so with

[7] S. Pälsi in Suomen Museo, XXXVIII-IX (1931-2), 64.
[8] A. Europaeus in Acta Archaeologica, 1 (1930), 165-190; 205-220.
[9] A. Ya. Bryusov in Trudy sektsiy' archeologiy, Ranion, II (1928), 26-32.

pit-and-comb pottery the further east we go, the later it seems to be. But one must beware of mistaking the spread of archaeological exploration for the spread of culture. In any case the old adjustments persisted a long time in eastern and Asiatic Russia.

This permanence is a convenience to the prehistorian. It enables us with some confidence to link up with the Finno-Ugrian peoples the makers of pit-and-comb pottery and so their Maglemosean ancestors.

THE EVIDENCE OF THE DENTITION ON THE ORIGIN OF MAN

BY

WILLIAM K. GREGORY

Curator of the Department of Comparative Anatomy
The American Museum of Natural History

AND

MILO HELLMAN

Research Associate, Physical Anthropology
The American Museum of Natural History, New York

In their several expeditions to the Siwalik Hills of India, Dr. Barnum Brown of the American Museum of Natural History, in 1921, Mr. G. E. Lewis of the Yale North India Expedition, in 1932, and Dr. H. de Terra of the Yale-Cambridge Expedition of 1935, have all collected fragmentary jaws and isolated teeth of extinct anthropoid apes. We have had the privilege of studying these rare and valuable fossils and technical descriptions of them have already been published or will be published in the near future.[1]

The special interest of this Siwalik anthropoid material in the present connection is that it represents some of the numerous species and genera of the anthropoid stock, in which stock, as all authorities now agree, are to be found our nearest known subhuman relations.

We shall center attention in this paper only on the crowns of the lower molar teeth. It will be noticed (Plate XX-A) that

[1] Cf. Brown, Gregory and Hellman, 1924; Gregory and Hellman, 1926; G. E. Lewis, 1934; and two forthcoming papers by Gregory, Hellman and Lewis and by G. E. Lewis.

in the lower molars of fossil anthropoids on the outer or labial side there are three cusps, on the inner or lingual side, two, and that between these two series there is a definite and characteristic system of ridges, grooves and valleys.

This system of cusps and grooves makes up a pattern which in 1916 one of us called the *"Dryopithecus* pattern." For convenience we have given odd numbers, 1, 3, 5, to the cusps which are on the outer or labial border, and even numbers, 2, 4, to those on or near the lingual border. The base of cusp 3 is enclosed by two grooves forming a V and the apex of this V meets a lingual transverse groove between 2 and 4, thus forming a Y. The inner apex of cusp 3 comes so far to the lingual side that it widely separates cusp 1 from cusp 4, whereas 2 and 3 are in contact. In 1916 and in subsequent papers we have held that the *Dryopithecus* pattern of the lower molars was the ancestral anthropoid pattern from which were evolved, on the one hand, the several lower molar patterns of the existing species of apes and, on the other, those of the lower molars of man.

The *Dryopithecus* pattern is subject to marked changes in general appearance caused by the wide range in the rates of antero-posterior and transverse growth of the crown. In the extremely long narrow molars named *Sugrivapithecus gregoryi* by Lewis the breadth index of m_2 falls to 78.6. In *Bramapithecus thorpei*, on the contrary, in the excessively wide crown of m_2 the breadth index rises to 106. But in both these cases, although the *Dryopithecus* pattern is somewhat distorted in appearance, it preserves the Y 5 arrangement, with cusp 4 widely removed from cusp 1.

All the modern anthropoids retain the *Dryopithecus* pattern in its essentials, although it is overlaid by divergent specializations. In the gorilla the molars are elongate anteroposteriorly, the cusps high, the ridges sharp, the surface of the enamel but little disturbed by secondary wrinkles. In the chimpanzee the molars are less elongate, there are small accessory cross ridges and the sur-

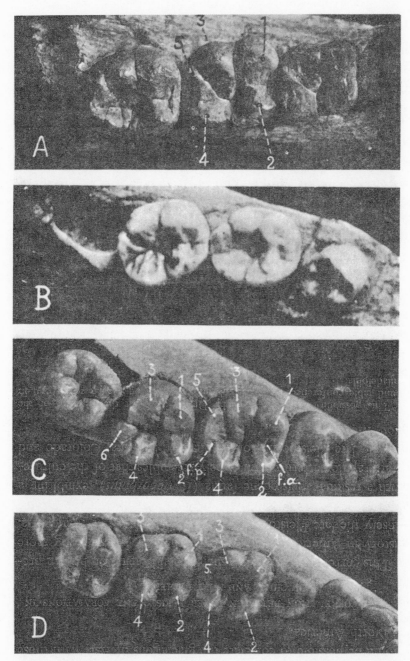

PLATE XX—The "Dryopithecus pattern" and its Derivatives in Man. A. *Dryopithecus frickae*. B. *Homo neanderthalensis* (Ehringsdorf child). C. *Homo sapiens* (Indian, Northern Mexico). D. *Homo sapiens* (Hindu, Eastern India).

face of the unworn crown is often rough with many wrinkles and bead-like outgrowths.

In the orang the cusps tend to be submerged in the deepening crown and there is an excessive development of the secondary

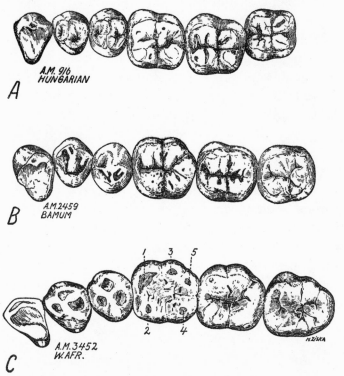

FIG. 38—Variants in the lower molar patterns in modern man. *Circa* 3/2.

wrinkles. These are especially well seen in new or little worn crowns, and in the end they obscure or obliterate the primary grooves and leave only the basic features of the *Dryopithecus* pattern.

In general it may be said that the primitive *Dryopithecus* pattern becomes modified according to two different but cooperating methods or principles: first, by polyisomerism, involving the subdivision or multiplication of parts, as of the ridges and wrinkles on the crown; and secondly by anisomerism or change of dimensions and proportions.

In wide contrast to the patterns of the lower molars of recent anthropoids are those of many modern men, especially of the white race. Let us look, for example, at the second lower molar in the mandible of a European (Fig. 38-A). We see that there are but four main cusps, two on the outer, two on the inner, sides of the crown and that these cusps are separated by two rectilinear grooves, the one running anteroposteriorly, or as the dentists say, mesio-distally, the other directly across it from the outer to the inner side (bucco-lingually). Cusps 1 and 4 seem to meet at the cross-roads.

Surely there is but little suggestion here of the *Dryopithecus* pattern of anthropoids. And yet molar 1 of many human dentitions has retained the 5th cusp, it has retained a central Y and cusp 2 is in contact with cusp 3, substantially as in the *Dryopithecus* pattern. Thus there is a marked difference between molar 1 and molar 2 in the total number of cusps, the pattern of the grooves and the contacts of the cusps at their bases.

In 1928 one of us (M. H.) made a fairly extended investigation of the racial distribution of the various crown patterns of the human lower molars. He classified them under four groups, named respectively Y_5, plus 5, half Y_4, plus 4. The racial distribution of these patterns is set forth in his article in the Proceedings of the American Philosophical Society for 1928. The exact percentages do not concern us here except to note that on m_1 the Y_5 pattern is usually retained even in the white race, while on m_2 the plus 4 is very abundant in whites, less so in Australians, Negroes and Amerinds, which often retain what seem to be more primitive conditions throughout the dentition.

In a goodly number of African Negroes (Fig. 38-B & C) the

Y_5 or *Dryopithecus* pattern is retained on all three lower molars, but transitional and even plus 4 patterns are not rare on m_2.

But is there no explanation for these changes in the contacts of the molar cusps? If we view these patterns as merely static entities, we have no clue to the varying positions of the grooves. But D'Arcy W. Thompson, in his brilliant work on "Growth and Form," has called attention to the fact that wherever there are several adjacent growth centers, which are growing at unequal rates, the boundaries or sutures between them will vary as one or another growth rate increases or decreases. Such a shifting pattern is seen at the pterion of the skull in man and the higher primates; and the extensive researches of Professor Ashley-Montagu and his predecessors have shown what an inconstant pattern this is. To make the application of this principle to the pattern of the lower molars, the grooves between the cusps are analogous with the sutures between skull bones, and these grooves will be pushed about into various patterns according to the varying rates of growth of the cusps which they border. Therefore in passing from a Y_5 or *Dryopithecus* pattern of m_1 to a plus 4, it is necessary only to change the rates of the several cusps in various ways which one of us has followed in considerable detail but which it is not necessary to describe further at this time.

In certain human molars (Plate XX-C) cusp 6 appears on the distal margin of the crown between cusps 5 and 4. Cusp 6 is not rare on the molars of Amerinds and is abundant in Australians. Cusp 6 is either the direct derivative of the cusp 6 which appears as a variant in *Dryopithecus*, or it is a closely parallel development in anthropoids and man.

In the palaeanthropic division of humanity (Plate XX-B) the *Dryopithecus* pattern is more or less obscured by fairly abundant and coarse secondary wrinkles, which approach but do not equal those of the orang. These wrinkles, however, lie near the surface and are soon worn off. Nevertheless the Y_5 or *Dryopithecus* pattern may be clearly seen in m_1 of *Sinanthropus*, Heidelberg, Ehringsdorf and Le Moustier. In these forms, although an approach to the cruciate pattern is being made through the enlargement of cusp 4, yet the old contact of cusps 2 and 3 is still present though reduced to a narrow isthmus.

Transitional conditions from the palaeanthropic to the neanthropic, or *Homo sapiens* patterns are observable especially among Negroes (Fig. 38-B & C), Australians and Amerinds (Plate XX-C).

Now among all the known species of fossil anthropoids, which one or ones most closely approach the human Y_5 pattern of the lower molars? Two claimants to this honor, if honor it be, may be seriously considered. The first is the mandibular fragment described under the name of *Bramapithecus thorpei* by Lewis in 1934. This approaches and even surpasses many human molars in the breadth indices of the first and second lower molars. It still retains, however, the unmodified *Dryopithecus* pattern of m_1, m_2 and has not yet risen above the *Dryopithecus* level to the transitional conditions seen in the palaeanthropic hominids.

The second claimant for close relationship with man is the genus *Australopithecus* (Fig. 39, 6) described by Dart in 1925 and by Broom in 1936-37. This genus, from the Pleistocene of South Africa, is obviously too late in time to be a direct ancestor to man but it was nevertheless a survivor of the general *Dryopithecus* stock, and as Dr. Broom has shown, it tends to connect man with the ancestors of the gorilla and chimpanzee. The first permanent lower molar of *Australopithecus* exhibits an almost human variation of the *Dryopithecus* pattern, in which cusp 4 is enlarged and the lingual transverse groove is nearly in line with the buccal transverse groove. The tooth as a whole, however, had probably overshot the human mark in its high breadth index.

Now if we are willing to admit that the plus 4 pattern in modern man came from the Y5 pattern by changes in the rate of growth of the several cusps, and that the Y5 pattern was derived in its turn from the *Dryopithecus* pattern of primitive anthro-

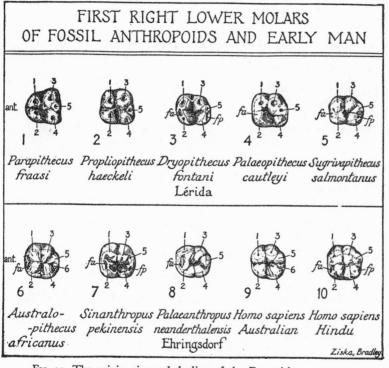

FIRST RIGHT LOWER MOLARS
OF FOSSIL ANTHROPOIDS AND EARLY MAN

FIG. 39—The origin, rise and decline of the *Dryopithecus* pattern.

poids, we have to ask next, whence came the *Dryopithecus* pattern itself?

The answer to this question has been found, we hold, among the patterns of the molar teeth of the numerous fossil primates which existed, if we may trust the record as it stands, long before the *Dryopithecus* pattern was evolved. The *Dryopithecus* pattern reached the climax of its development in the Pliocene but

the earliest examples of it may date back to the Middle or Lower
Miocene. For the greater part of the Oligocene there is unfor-

FIG. 40—Structural stages in evolution of upper and lower molar teeth of man.
Scales various.

A-H, upper molars, left side.
  A. Upper Jurassic, triangular stage (pantotherian). After G. G. Simpson.
  B. Cretaceous, triangular stage (*Deltatheridium*). After Gregory and Simp-
     son.
  C. Lower Eocene, "tritubercular" stage (*Didelphodus*). After Gregory.
  D. Middle Eocene, transitional stage (*Pronycticebus*). From Gregory, after
     Grandidier.
  E. Upper Eocene, tubercular stage (*Necrolemur*). From Gregory, after
     Stehlin.
  F. Upper Miocene, primitive anthropoid stage (*Dryopithecus*). From
     Gregory, after Pilgrim.
  G. Pleistocene, primitive man (Le Moustier) stage. After Gregory.
I-IX, lower molars, right side.
  I. Jurassic, tritubercular stage, with incipient heel (pantotherian). After
     G. G. Simpson.
  II. Cretaceous, primitive tuberculo-sectorial stage (*Deltatheridium*). After
     Gregory and Simpson.
  III. Lower Eocene, tuberculo-sectorial stage, with low heel (*Deltatherium*).
     After Gregory.
  IV. Middle Eocene, transitional stage (*Pronycticebus*). From Gregory after
     Grandidier.
  V. Upper Eocene, tubercular stage (*Necrolemur*). From Gregory after
     Stehlin.
  VI. Lower Oligocene, five-cusped proto-anthropoid stage (*Propliopithecus*).
     From stereoscopic photograph by Prof. J. H. McGregor.
  VII. Upper Miocene, five-cusped anthropoid stage (*Dryopithecus*). After
     Gregory.
  VIII. Pleistocene, primitive human stage (Le Moustier), retaining five
     cusps. After Gregory.
  IX. Recent, human stage, after disappearance of fifth cusp. After Gregory.

tunate hiatus in our records, but at the beginning of this epoch
we find two structural stages existing in two very small lower

jaws that were discovered in the Lower Oligocene deposits of the Fayum of Egypt and described with a full realization of their importance by a famous palaeontologist, the late Dr. Max Schlosser of Munich. Of these, the more advanced, which he named *Propliopithecus* (Fig. 39, 2) had the five main cusps of the *Dryopithecus* pattern but the system of grooves was incomplete and cusp 5 on m_1 was still small and in a median position. Moreover, cusps 1 and 2, 3 and 4, were arranged in nearly transverse pairs, whereas in later times the enlargement of cusp 5 and of cusp 4 pushed 3 and 4 out of directly transverse alignment.

In the more primitive of these two Lower Oligocene stages, which was named *Parapithecus* (Fig. 39, 1) by Schlosser, the four main cusps tend to be arranged in two transverse pairs and the fifth cusp is seen in an early stage of development. The anterior pair, constituting the anterior moiety of the crown, have a somewhat steep posterior wall, behind which is the central depression of the posterior moiety guarded posteriorly by cusps 3, 5, 4. To vertebrate palaeontologists this arrangement will inevitably suggest the so-called tuberculo-sectorial pattern of the lower molars of the numerous genera and species of primates found in the Eocene deposits of Europe and North America.

It should be noted that *Parapithecus*, although retaining traces of the older tuberculo-sectorial pattern of the lower molars, had already acquired the anthropoid dental formula of $\frac{2, 1, 2, 3}{2, 1, 2, 3}$.

To sum up so far as we have gone, the *Dryopithecus* pattern and its numerous variants and immediate predecessors are associated exclusively with the higher anthropoids and man, all of which have a dental formula in the adult dentition of $\frac{2, 1, 2, 3}{2, 1, 2, 3} \times 2 = 32$, and are confined to the Upper Tertiary.

On the other hand, the predecessors of the *Dryopithecus* pattern, which are all variants of the tuberculo-sectorial pattern, are found in the early Tertiary deposits and are associated with dental formulas ranging from 32 to 40.

Let us consider then the tuberculo-sectorial pattern which preceded and was ancestral to the *Dryopithecus* pattern.

In 1916 one of us (WKG) published a diagram showing a comparison of the patterns of the upper and lower molars of *Pelycodus trigonodus*, one of the oldest and most primitive known primates, from the Lower Eocene of Wyoming, with the corresponding teeth of man.[2] The cusps were named in accordance with the nomenclature proposed by the late Professor Osborn but we are not concerned for the moment with the names of the cusps. Even at that time it was well known to Osborn, Matthew and other vertebrate palaeontologists that in *Pelycodus trigonodus* the division of the crown into two moieties, called respectively the trigonid and the talonid, was particularly clear.

Now when such lower teeth are properly articulated with their upper teeth, it will be seen that the anterior moiety called the trigonid fits into what some odontologists have called the interdental embrasures of the upper molars, while the depressed basin of the posterior moiety or talonid receives the inner apex or so-called protocone of the upper molar.

If we make a series of occlusion diagrams showing the interlocking relations of the upper and lower molars of *Pelycodus*, Gibbon, Gorilla and Man[3] we must realize that in the gorilla all that enlarged posterior moiety of the tooth behind cusps 1 and 2 is strictly homologous with the talonid of *Pelycodus*, while the anterior moiety of the gorilla tooth, including cusps 1, 2 constitutes what is left of the trigonid, after the loss of the antero-internal cusps or paraconid. In man the relations are essentially

[2] Studies on the Evolution of the Primates, 1916, Bull. Amer. Mus. Nat. Hist., XXXV, art. 19, p. 254, fig. 11.

[3] Gregory, William K. 1922. "The origin and Evolution of the Human Dentition." Baltimore, Williams and Wilkins. (P. 120, fig. 315.)

the same but here the trigonid basin has been reduced to a small depression called the "fovea anterior" by Selenka and the "pre-cuspidal fossa" by Hrdlička, while the posterior moiety has expanded transversely and now constitutes much the greater part of the crown; this part was named "talonid" by Osborn (1907,

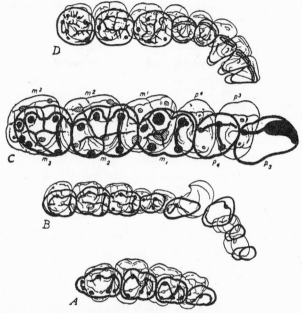

FIG. 41. Occlusion diagrams: *Pelycodus*, Gibbon, Gorilla, Man.

p. 53) and "postcuspidal fossa" by Hrdlička (1924). Even eminent authorities have sometimes failed to realize that in the human lower molar there are inescapable traces both of the trigonid and the talonid of the tuberculo-sectorial molar of the basal primates of the Lower Eocene.

Vertebrate palaeontologists have not been satisfied to stop even here in the digging down into earlier and earlier horizons in the past history of the molar patterns in the remote predecessors of man. In all primates the transverse diameter of the talonid nearly equals or more often exceeds that of the trigonid. But in some of the more primitive procarnivores and insectivores of Lower Eocene (Fig. 40, *III*) and Paleocene epochs, the transverse diameter of the talonid was less than that of the trigonid, the latter being at that time of a definitely triangular cutting type.

If now we follow this trend down into the upper Cretaceous we find that in the wonderfully primitive placental insectivores (Fig. 40, *II*) that were found by Dr. Walter Granger in the Gobi Desert as the contemporaries of the later dinosaurs, the transverse diameter of the talonid is much less than that of the trigonid.

In this Upper Cretaceous insectivore it will be seen that the trigonids fitted into the reversed V's of the interdental embrasures between the upper molars, while the narrow talonids articulated with the narrow internal spurs of the upper teeth; thus it is noteworthy that even at this extremely remote epoch the essential relationships of the trigonid and the talonid to the several parts of the upper molars were already foreshadowed.

Finally in the Upper and Middle Jurassic in the primitive members (Fig. 40, *I*) of the Pantotheria or Mesozoic insectivores, described by Owen, by Osborn and by Simpson, the talonid is only a very small spur or heel from the base of the high trigonid, and at that immensely remote epoch there is hardly the remotest suggestion of the human condition, but the upper and lower molar teeth now approach the condition of simple reversed triangles, which were postulated in the Theory of Trituberculy by Cope and Osborn.

The changes from the primitive triangular lower molar and thence to the tuberculo-sectorial primitive primate and ultimately the *Dryopithecus* pattern and its derivatives were all associated with a progressive reduction of the total number of teeth, from 64 in a primitive Mesozoic mammal (*Amphitherium*) to 32 in normal man.

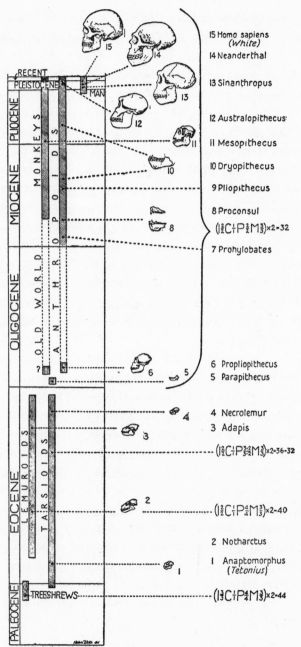

15 Homo sapiens
(White)

14 Neanderthal

13 Sinanthropus

12 Australopithecus

11 Mesopithecus

10 Dryopithecus

9 Pliopithecus

8 Proconsul

$(I\frac{2}{2}C\frac{1}{1}P\frac{2}{2}M\frac{3}{3})\times2\text{-}32$

7 Prohylobates

6 Propliopithecus
5 Parapithecus

4 Necrolemur
3 Adapis

$(I\frac{2}{2}C\frac{1}{1}P\frac{3\cdot2}{3\cdot2}M\frac{3}{3})\times2\text{-}36\text{-}32$

$(I\frac{2}{2}C\frac{1}{1}P\frac{4}{4}M\frac{3}{3})\times2\text{-}40$

2 Notharctus

1 Anaptomorphus
(Tetonius)

$(I\frac{3}{3}C\frac{1}{1}P\frac{4}{4}M\frac{3}{3})\times2\text{-}44$

FIG. 42—Early Man and his predecessors in geologic perspective, showing the later stages in the reduction of the "dental formula."

Our present conclusions, which may now be stated in the reverse order from that followed above, may be summarized thus:

(1) The "precuspidal" and "postcuspidal" fossae of Hrdlička are respectively the highly modified traces of the trigonid and talonid of more primitive mammals, and the tuberculo-sectorial lower molar pattern of Eocene primates gave rise eventually to the *Dryopithecus* pattern.

(2) Taking into consideration all known recent and fossil anthropoids, the *Dryopithecus* pattern (Plate XX-A) is subject to extreme variation in regard to proportions but is singularly constant in the fundamental arrangement of the five principal cusps and of the several grooves at their bases.

(3) Of all the known variations of the *Dryopithecus* pattern, that of the first lower molar of *Australopithecus africanus* (Fig. 39, *6*) is the closest to the human modification of the *Dryopithecus* pattern, although the tooth itself is perhaps far too broad to give rise to that of man.

(4) Of known human lower molars, those of the palaeanthropic division of mankind, especially m_1 of the Ehringsdorf child (Fig. 39, *8*) and of *Sinanthropus* (Fig. 39, 7), are the least modified away from the *Dryopithecus* pattern.

(5) Between the palaeanthropic variants of the *Dryopithecus* pattern and those of the neanthropic division (*Homo sapiens*) (Fig. 39, *9 & 10*) almost every conceivable intergradation and combination can be seen.

(6) Contrary to most authors (except Hrdlička), we feel that the evidence from the dentition strongly suggests that the older palaeanthropines were at least structurally ancestral on the one hand to *Homo neanderthalensis* and on the other to *Homo sapiens*.

Plate XXI—Family tree of the Primates. Wall-painting in the American Museum of Natural History, New York.

THE SIWALIKS OF INDIA AND EARLY MAN

BY

HELLMUT DE TERRA

*Research Associate of The Carnegie Institution of Washington and
Associate Curator of Geology and Paleontology of
The Academy of Natural Sciences of Philadelphia*

Explorations in the Siwalik Hills of India which were recently
carried out under the auspices of Yale University, The Carnegie
Institution of Washington and the American Philosophical Society have thrown new light on questions pertaining to human
origins and early cultural records. In particular the discovery of
artifact bearing formations above late Tertiary rocks containing
fossil anthropoid remains once more focuses attention upon the
buried evidence which the Siwalik Hills can furnish in regard
to human evolution.[1]

From the time when Falconer and Cautley[2] found here the
first fossil primate (1836) paleontologists and anthropologists
have speculated on the role which the uplift of the Himalayas
may have played in the evolution of the Siwalik anthropoids. Of
these no less than eight genera and twenty-two species have so
far been recorded and with the growing number of fossil human
remains found elsewhere, anatomists begin to re-examine the evidence which the study of primate dentition affords as to the
ancestry of man.[3] Mathew, Barrell and Black, to name only a
few scholars, thought that the hypothetical process of human

---

[1] H. de Terra, P. Teilhard, T. T. Paterson in "Science," *83*, 1936, also
"Nature."

[2] "On remains of a fossil monkey from the Tertiary strata of the Siwalik
Hills," Trans. Geol. Soc. London, vol. 5, 2nd series, p. 499, 1836.

[3] See Gregory and Hellman's report in this volume.

emergence from an ancestral Siwalik ape was determined by the growth of the Himalayas. This, they argued, so profoundly altered the habitat of the most advanced primates that under biological stress conditions a new proto-human form evolved, the type which Grabau[4] has recently portrayed as a wandering creature in search of an oasis.

In other words it was presupposed that at the time when the mountain uplift took place, a critical stage in the evolution of the Siwalik anthropoids had already been reached. But in the light of recent geologic studies in which the speaker has had a small share, it appears that these two events did not coincide. For it now becomes evident that the greatest abundance of anthropoids occurred at a time long after the mid-tertiary mountain-making and prior to the Pleistocene uplifts (Fig. 43). This course of events, which I have sketched elsewhere,[5] clearly indicates that the uplift of the Himalayas can certainly not be solely responsible, as has been supposed, for a stimulus powerful enough to have promoted a progressive specialization in the anthropoid group. Thus we are once more confronted with this elusive and controversial scientific problem.

The geological side of the problem clearly concerns itself with the causes for the extinction of the Siwalik fauna. There is abundant evidence at hand to show that climate played a decisive part in this event.

On geologic and paleontologic grounds we can surmise a retreat of the tropical belt from what is now the temperate zone, either by general displacement or by narrowing. It has been stated that the fauna of the Lower Siwaliks required a tropical habitat and that the medium in which the fossils were preserved indicates similar climatic conditions. In other words the tropical belt extended at that time to the Himalayan foothills (Fig. 43).

[4] "Tibet and the Origin of Man." Geogr. Annaler, Stockholm, 1935.
[5] "Cenozoic cycles in Asia and their bearing on human prehistory," Proc. Am. Phil. Soc., vol. 77, No. 3, pp. 289-308, 1937.

Age	Formation	Rock composition	Fossil record of anthropoids	Cultural records	Climate in foothills (monsoon with varying intensity)	Glacial cycle in Kashmir-Himalaya
Upper Pleistocene	Upper Siwaliks 5000–7000 feet	Redeposited Potwar silt, ±200 feet Terrace IV			Cool temperate	4th Glaciation Terrace IV
		Erosion Terrace III			?	3rd Interglacial Terrace III
		Potwar loessic silt, and basal gravel ±350 feet Terrace II			Cold Temperate	3rd Glaciation Terrace II
Middle Pleistocene		Erosion / High gravel terrace in Soan valley / Erosion Terrace I		Rolled Chelleo-Acheulean handaxes	?	2nd Interglacial Upper Karewas Terrace I
		Boulder Conglomerate zone—fans and terrace gravels with erratics, ±1800 feet		Worked flakes (pre-Soan industry)	Cold peri-glacial conditions	2nd Glaciation Karewa gravel fans
Lower Pleistocene		Pinjor zone—pink silt and sand, concretionary clays, ±2200 feet	Palaeopithecus (2) / Dryopithecus (1) / Ramapithecus (1)	Soan industries	Warm temperate	1st Interglacial Lower Karewas
		Tatrot zone—grey conglomerate-sandstones and buff silt, ±1000 feet			Cool temperate	1st Glaciation lowest moraines and fan deposits
Pliocene	Middle Siwaliks 6000 feet	Dhok Pathan zone—coarse, brownish grey sand and soft sandstone with polychrome clays and shales but no bright red coloring	Sivapithecus (3) / Sugrivapithecus (2) / Dryopithecus (4) / Hylopithecus (1) / Palaeopithecus (1)		Subtropical	
		Nagri zone—hard, resistant, coarse sandstone of grey or drab color and red silt, 2000 feet	Sivapithecus (2) / Bramapithecus (1) / Dryopithecus (3) / Palaeosimia (1) (ancestral Orang)		Tropical	
	Lower Siwaliks 8300 feet	Chinji zone—bright red or warm purplish, hard or nodular shales and light grey, soft, micaceous san'stone with conglomerate layers, 3500–6000 feet	Sivapithecus (1)			
Upper Miocene		Kamlial zone—hard brown and grey sandstone and variable shale with concretions, silicified coniferous wood, 2000–3300 feet				

FIG. 43—The geologic history of the Siwalik Hills in NW-India. (Note: the numerals in parenthesis refer to the number of species known so far. Horizontal double lines indicate major unconformities.)

Similarly, in North China the Pliocene fauna, especially the lower and middle Pliocene, consisted mainly of warmth loving types whose skeletal remains were entombed in formations which bear the stamp of a warm climate. The upper Pliocene of both regions, however, both as regards fauna and sedimentary medium, reflects more arid and colder temperatures.[6] We take this as an indication for a displacement of the tropical belt and certain considerations lead us to suspect that this climatic shift was directed southward. If such were the case, we would naturally expect evidence for a southward migration of warmth loving Siwalik animals as well as a progressive southward shifting of those weathering agencies which made for tropical soil formation. Unfortunately, in peninsular India, both fossiliferous upper Pliocene and early Pleistocene formations are unknown, but we do know of richly fossiliferous middle Pleistocene in central India and of Plio-Pleistocene faunas in Burma and Java. According to Pilgrim,[7] two out of three proboscideans in the middle Pleistocene Narbadda fauna of Central India are derived from the Siwaliks and so is *Hippopotamus* and *Equus namadicus*. The buffalo (*Bubalus palaeindicus*) is another Upper Siwalik type. Pilgrim does not attempt to trace the ancestry of the remaining forms, but there is no reason why a few of the other genera in the Narbadda fauna may not as well be of Siwalik derivation. The Siwalik elements in this middle Pleistocene fauna are the ones which are climatically specialized. All this is highly suggestive of a migrational trend from the Siwalik Hills southward across the Indian Peninsula.

More illuminating still is the age relationship of these fossilifer-

[6] See P. Teilhard de Chardin, "Notes on continental geology" (Bull. Geol. Soc. of China, vol. XVI, p. 211, 1937), who emphasized the absence of true fossil laterite formations in late Pliocene and Pleistocene formations of North China and their presence in South China.

[7] "On the occurrence of El. antiquus (namadicus) in the Godavari Alluvium etc." Rec. Geol. Survey Ind., vol. 32, 1905.

ous beds in the Narbadda to the underlying laterite. The fossil bones as well as the early Paleolithic tools found associated with them are free from any signs of lateritization which may mean that the climate in middle Pleistocene time was not tropical enough to form laterite. During the early Pleistocene, however, laterite was formed in central India, which would indicate that at that time the tropical belt extended at least as far north as the Narbadda and Godavari rivers. Now, if our contention is correct, that the tropical zone became progressively narrower, it must follow that in southern India the middle Pleistocene should contain laterite. Although the age of the south Indian laterite has not as yet been properly fixed, it is known through our recent and through previous studies that the Chellean handaxes entombed in the laterite gravels of Madras show distinct signs of lateritization formed *in situ*. On the west coast of India, near Bombay, I collected Chellean and other early Paleolithic tools in fluvial gravels which had undergone a certain amount of lateritization. From these observations we conclude that in middle Pleistocene time the climatic zoning in India had generally attained its present arrangement.

In order to appreciate fully these indications of migratory movements in India and their bearing on human prehistory, we must turn to Java and Burma. Von Koenigswald[8] has recently shown that the Trinil fauna with which the famous *Pithecanthropus* remains were found associated, is composed of sixteen mammal genera. By comparing this list with that given by Pilgrim from the Narbadda fauna we find that half of the genera are common to both of these widely separated regions. Of twenty-eight genera known so far from the early and middle Pleistocene beds of Java, comprising the Tji Djolang, Kali Glagah and Djetis faunas, sixteen genera occur in Indian forma-

[8] "Zur Stratigraphie des javanischen Pleistozän." Kon. Ak. Wet. Amsterdam, vol. 38, 1935.

tions of Upper Siwalik age. This means that in late Pliocene and early Pleistocene times the fauna of Java was composed of indigenous and Siwalik elements. Special significance is attached to the appearance of *Elephas namadicus* in the Trinil fauna, a form commonly found in the middle Pleistocene of India but also reported from Choukoutien in China.

The Pliocene "Irrawaddy Series" of Burma also recorded migrations of Siwalik mammals. According to Noetling[9] almost half of the fossil fauna is composed of India Siwalik forms. Quite a number of these occur in southern China.[10] In other words, if the Siwalik mammals followed the southward displacement of the tropical belt, they must have lingered for some time in southern Asia where eventually an exchange with faunistic elements from Malaya took place. The major migration route evidently led along the coast ranges of Burma towards the delta lowlands of Malaya and south China and the final stage of dispersal toward Java was reached at the very close of Pliocene time when this island had just fully emerged from the sea. On such a route the climatically specialized animals would have encountered genial habitats, and at the same time the varying nature of the countries they crossed would have stimulated their evolution.

Now, the anthropoids of the Siwalik fauna certainly were in a process of progressive evolution when climatic changes had set in and migrations had become necessary. Hence, at a critical stage in their history, they partook in the general fate of dispersal, and the shifting of climatic zones might well have provided those stimulating elements which previously had been linked to catastrophic mountain building events. In this light the dispersal would appear to have depended on regional migrations so that the ultimate emergence of certain proto-human types may be expected in various regions of tropical southern Asia.

[9] Rec. Geol. Surv. Ind., vol. 28, 1895.
[10] E. H. Pascoe, Mem. Geol. Survey Ind., vol. 40, 1912, p. 38.

In this connection it is interesting to point out the great gap in our records of prehistory in the Siwalik Hills which embraces the late Pliocene and early Pleistocene periods. No sure traces of anthropoids are known from the Tatrot and Pinjor zones (Fig. 43)[11] and the first records of early humans appear at the very close of Siwalik history, namely in the Boulder Conglomerate zone. The artifacts found by T. T. Paterson and myself in 1935 in this zone are large flakes of quartzite or of metamorphic rock, sometimes slightly trimmed by a few blows at one end, but never acquiring a definite shape of any sort. It can be shown that they are derived from a simply split pebble. Typologically these artifacts resemble somewhat the early Clacton industry in Europe. The gravel fans from which they were collected were spread out in front of the valley outlets of the NW-Himalayas and locally reach a thickness of over two thousand feet. Such heavy accumulations of alternating pink or gray sand, silt and gravel, are difficult to explain unless the special factors are known which lead to their formation. One of these was the second ice advance in the adjoining mountains which is clearly recorded in the foreland by faceted boulders and erratic blocks in the Boulder Conglomerate. The reason I correlate this fan formation with this particular glaciation becomes evident from the fact that it was only during the second ice advance that the valley glaciers managed to proceed as far as their valley outlets to the border of the Punjab plains. In this manner the groundmoraine filling of the glacial troughs, carved out by the second glaciers, merges with the Boulder Conglomerate of Upper Siwalik age. Now, this glaciation cannot have been the first one,

[11] Colbert (Trans. Am. Phil. Soc., N. S., XXVI, pp. 29-30) quoted *Simia* and *Ramapithecus* from the Upper Siwaliks. The former is based on a single canine of doubtful location; the latter was found by G. E. Lewis in beds which he considered either of Tatrot or Dhok Pathan age. To me the second choice appears to be more correct.

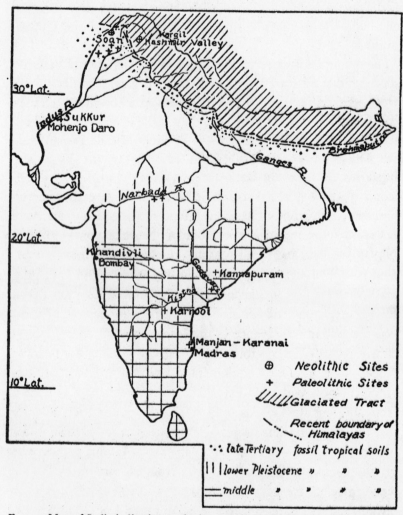

FIG. 44—Map of India indicating geologic records of climatic changes and location of some prehistoric sites.

as Dainelli[12] had previously stated, because the boulder fans overlie unconformably a thick series of fossiliferous early Pleistocene beds, the so-called Tatrot and Pinjor zones of the Upper Siwaliks.

These zones whose early Pleistocene age is irrevocably established by the Tatrot-Pinjor fauna, attain a thickness of almost three thousand feet, and therefore represent a considerable time period of the Pleistocene. In fact, they make it possible to prove that the second major glaciation is of early Middle Pleistocene age. The third and fourth glacial advances in the Kashmir-Himalayas, on the other hand, are progressively weaker than the second glaciation, their terminal moraines lying over twenty miles away from the boulder fans. Hence it is evident that Early Man entered this region at the closing stage of the second glaciation, for the flakes were found only in stratigraphic association, either with boulder fans (as at Jammu, and near Poonch) or with coarse outwash gravels of late Siwalik age. Their geologic position and their typologic aspect is such as to exclude any other interpretation. Of special interest to geologist and archeologist alike, is the crustal deformation which these fans suffered through continued Himalayan mountain uplifts. At one place the Boulder Conglomerate is tilted to 80° along a thrust-fault at the northeastern border of the plains; in other regions it is gently arched or warped. This early race that had manufactured the crude tools had indeed entered unstable ground, made doubly dynamic by the superimposing of glacial cycles upon a steadily rising belt of foothills.

A long interval followed the deformation of the great Upper Siwalik fans. The surface relief of the foothills and plains underwent dissection which is especially marked in those regions where the Siwalik formations had previously been planed. The

[12] "Studi sul glaciale," in Relazioni Scient. della Sped. De Filippi, Ser. II, vol. III, Bologna, 1922.

boulder fans and gravel trains which had buried this older, little dissected relief, were now trenched by the rivers that flowed out of the mountain front and thus was formed the first terrace in the plains region (Fig. 45). Relatively few remnants of this highest terrace came under observation but in the Soan valley their position is clear in relation to the Boulder Conglomerate and younger loess-like formations. On such a high terrace were found at Chauntra some hundred rolled tools mainly coups-

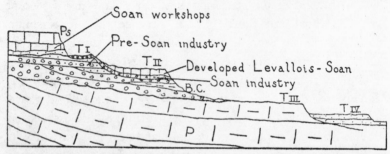

FIG. 45—Generalized cross section through right slope of Soan valley above Chauntra, Punjab. (Ps.=Potwar Silt. B.C.=Boulder Conglomerate. P.=Pinjor Zone.)

de-poing, also choppers and flakes of Chellean and Acheulean type. The handaxes were lying a few feet distant from an old terrace gravel from which apparently they had been washed out and been redeposited in a younger gravel underlying the loessic Potwar silt. These finds for the first time in Asia disclosed early Paleolithic handaxe industries in association with datable Ice Age gravels. Their stratigraphic position immediate between the loessic formation of the third glaciation and the Boulder Conglomerate, makes it possible to date the Chelleo-Acheulean in the cis-Himalayan regions as early second Interglacial. From where did these ancient hunters of the plains come?

To this we can only reply that the Chellean to late Acheulean handaxes of Chauntra typologically resemble the early handaxe technique of Madras in southern India. The Madrasian facies of the Chellean thus clearly extended all across peninsular India to the Himalayan Hills. In this distribution we recognize a great expansion of the earliest Stone Age cultures. Considering the wealth of Chellean and Acheulean tools found in southern India as compared to their scarcity in NW-India it seems as if these Old Stone peoples came from the south to expand from the tropical belt to the mountain barrier from which the glaciers had retreated. This migratory expansion is substantiated by finds of Chellean and Acheulean tools in the middle Pleistocene of the Narbadda valley in Central India which lies on the route to the northern plains. Here a middle Pleistocene fauna with *Elephas namidicus* and *Hippopotamus namadicus*[13] appears in direct association with Chelleo-Acheulean tools, thus corroborating the dating based in the Punjab on Ice Age stratigraphy. The regional extension of the Narbadda fauna to the northern plains (especially in the Ganges and Jumna valleys) makes it very probable that these hunters spread their cultures to NW-India while engaged in the pursuit of game.

This race also may have brought to the north a special tradition of stone tool manufacture to which I have given the name Soan culture, because it was first abundantly encountered along the Soan river in northwest India. This is a series of successive industries in whose manufacture Levallois and Clacton techniques were employed as also a primitive pebble tool technique. The flakes were struck from prepared cores of quartzite or trap rock, and then shaped to make scrapers, blades, knives, most of which show steep-angled working edges, made by strong step flaking. Very characteristic tools are the pebble chopper or handaxe and the utilized core. The latter is indistinguishable from ordinary Clacton and Levallois cores and is recognized as

[13] H. de Terra and P. Teilhard de Chardin, "Observations on the Upper Siwalik formation and later Pleistocene deposits in India." Proc. Am. Phil. Soc., vol. 76, No. 6, 1936.

a tool only by the marks of utilization. The handaxe shows in the earlier stages a scalloped edge due to alternate flaking on either side and in the more advanced types a pseudo-flake core or else a disc. Mr. Paterson, my expedition associate, has been able to distinguish in this Soan culture different stages of which the latest is characterized by steep-ended scrapers and long thin flake scars, reminiscent of upper Paleolithic technique. This would mean that the Soan culture had a very long stratigraphic range and geologic observations lend certain support to this contention.

The early Soan tools appear either on the highest terraces of the rivers or in the basal gravel of the Potwar loessic silt. Their age therefore is late second interglacial to third glacial. The later Soan tools which show a more developed Levallois technique were found embedded above the basal gravel in the lower silt layers in form of regular workshops. Hence their manufacture is later, yet still of third glacial age. The latest Soan tools with steep-ended, keeled push-plane scrapers were found over an outcrop of Pliocene conglomerate and in a gravel underlying redeposited Potwar clay which was probably formed during the fourth glacial period (Fig. 43). In this distribution it is noteworthy that no Chellean or Acheulean tools appear in deposits later than Potwar gravel, while Soan workshops of later Soan industries are numerous at the base of the overlying loessic silt. This also would indicate that the industries with Soan tradition survived long after the Chelleo-Acheulean cultures had become extinct.

Workshops as well as rewashed artifacts occur almost exclusively along drainage channels, a mode of distribution suggestive of temporary open camps occupied by nomadic hunters.

THE ANTIQUITY OF MAN IN THE PACIFIC AND THE QUESTION OF TRANS-PACIFIC MIGRATIONS

BY

DANIEL SUTHERLAND DAVIDSON

Assistant Professor of Anthropology, University of Pennsylvania

The islands of the Pacific east of southeastern Asia constitute a region of many strange contrasts in flora, fauna and physiographical conditions. In no instance, however, are the antitheses more marked than in respect to the antiquity of man, for Java has given us the oldest known precursors of the human family, whereas Polynesia is the most recently occupied extensive area of the world.

For the great period of time between these two extremes our knowledge is woefully meager. Not only is the entire area poorly known archaeologically but the little work done has not yet added much to the conclusions suggested by indirect evidence and theoretical considerations. The dense tropical vegetation makes the finding of sites exceedingly difficult, the humid conditions are not conducive to the preservation of perishable artifacts or of skeletal remains, the abundant precipitation washes away associated hearth and debris remains to leave the few heavy or non-perishable artifacts without a datable context, and the lack of glaciation and the more or less similarity in biota throughout the ages enhance the difficulties of dating those remains which may come to light.

Yet, in spite of these discouraging conditions, certain aspects of the prehistory of the Pacific seem fairly clear, at least in outline form. Many peoples have moved out of southeastern Asia and they must have passed along or through the East Indies before coming to New Guinea, and along or through New Guinea before reaching the lands beyond. Thus under the proper conditions we should expect to find their physical and cultural remains stratified in those regions through which two or more have passed. For the East Indies there can be no doubt that the Malays are of relatively recent arrival. They are found along the coasts of the more important islands whereas Indonesians occupy the inland and upland regions except for the few groups of Negritoes who now appear in only the very mountain fastnesses in the Philippines and the Malay Peninsula. In New Guinea similar Negritoes inhabit the mountain districts and are surrounded by Papuans who in turn have relinquished the northern, eastern and southeastern coasts to the Melanesians.

Thus we are led to the belief that the Negritoes once inhabited much more extensive areas in both the East Indies and New Guinea and that the ancestors of the Negroid Papuans and Melanesians passed through the East Indies at some time prior to the invasion of the preponderantly Mongoloid Indonesians and Malays in spite of the present lack of direct proof of such an occupation. We may suppose, therefore, that Negritoes, Papuans, Melanesians, Indonesians and Malays came to the East Indies in the order named. Since the Malays seem to have been well established in the East Indies long before the beginning of the Christian Era it seems not unreasonable to believe that a minimum of three millenia may have elapsed since the Mongoloid peoples assumed more or less complete control of the region by exterminating by war or by assimilation the earlier Negroid occupants. By inference their first arrival in the region must be considerably earlier.[1]

[1] Heine-Geldern, R., "Urheimat und früheste Wanderungen der Austronesien," Anthropos, 27, (1932), 600, conservatively sets 1,500 B.C.

Still earlier peoples must be fitted into the chronology. The geographical locations of the Australians and Tasmanians indicate that they preceded the Negritoes, Papuans and Melanesians. That Australoids, possibly the direct ancestors of the Australians, passed through Java is demonstrated by the Wadjak remains which unfortunately cannot be accurately dated although there are reasons for believing them late Pleistocene or early Recent. Such an antiquity would fit very well with evidence from Australia where there have been many claims of finds of remains of dingo, brought by the Australians, with extinct Pleistocene fauna.[2] However, the period in which these extinct animals ceased to exist has not been accurately determined, hence this evidence at present is of little help in our problem. Of the human skeletal remains in Australia none is of established Pleistocene antiquity although suspicions of such age have been advanced in respect to the Talgai skull. For the Tasmanians the available cultural data are fragmentary and unsatisfactory but suggestive of Pleistocene antiquity.

Theoretical cultural considerations also permit us to infer a late Pleistocene or early Recent migration of Australians. The lack of the bow and arrow, ceramic industry, horticulture and domesticated animals suggests that they departed from southeastern Asia before these important cultural traits were present, presumably at the latest early in the Recent period. The polished stone axe, the spearthrower and more recently the harpoon seem to have diffused to the Australians, hence we may suppose that these traits also were lacking in southeastern Asia at the time of the Australian exodus. On the other hand the possession of the dingo may indicate that the Australians did not leave Asia much before the end of the Pleistocene.

Tasmanian culture contains virtually nothing which we can

[2] For bibliography see Davidson, D. S., "The Relation of Tasmanian and Australian Cultures," Pub. Philadelphia Anthro. Soc., I, (1937).

expect to trace archaeologically other than simple stone artifacts, although the peculiarities of these may be found to be local to Tasmania. However, since Tasmanian culture as known ethnologically seems to be basic to Australian culture we have grounds for the belief that the minimum antiquity of their migration from Asia must be the maximum limit of the time of Australian migration.

Thus our direct and indirect data suggest that Australoid peoples moved out of Asia in relatively early times, that Negroids migrated in the early or middle Recent period, and that Mongoloid peoples followed them a few millenia ago. This conclusion is enlightening if we take into consideration the areas occupied for, in addition to the East Indies and the islands to the north, all of which are within easy reach of Asia, the Mongoloid peoples also colonized Micronesia and Polynesia, regions which could be reached only in ocean-going watercraft capable of extended sea journeys; whereas the Negroid and Australoid peoples confined their colonization to a chain of islands few of which are separated by straits more than fifty miles in width *at present sea level*, with the added exceptions of certain groups of islands in eastern Melanesia, such as Fiji, Santa Cruz and New Caledonia.

The confinement of the Australoid and Negroid peoples to areas within short distance of one another suggests that at the times of their respective migrations they were not equipped with craft capable of extended journeys on the open sea. Otherwise we should expect them to have settled eastern islands not known to have been visited until the Polynesian period.

All available facts indicate that the Australians or the Tasmanians were never equipped with seagoing craft at any time.[3] For Melanesia and the East Indies the chronology of watercraft has not yet been satisfactorily determined, but if we may judge

[3] Davidson, D. S., "Chronology of Australian Watercraft," J. Polynesian Soc., 44, (1935).

by certain similarities in type from the East Indies to Polynesia many forms of Melanesian watercraft are relatively recent acquisitions, either introduced by the migrating Polynesians or diffused from the west shortly before or possibly subsequent to the Polynesian migration. Thus, although direct evidence is lacking, it seems permissible to suspect that one reason why the Melanesians never penetrated farther east may have been the lack of suitable watercraft during the early period of their expansion.

We have no evidence as yet to demonstrate that the antiquity of occupation of the more distant islands of Melanesia, such as the Santa Cruz, New Hebrides, Loyalty and Fiji groups and New Caledonia, is other than relatively recent. The few data at our disposal indicate that the artifacts in the oldest archaeological deposits are the same as the typically "Neolithic" specimens in use today.[4] Indeed in New Caledonia, the farthest outpost of Melanesia, pottery is found in what seem to be the oldest deposits and by cross-reference to other areas it should be possible eventually to establish a maximum antiquity for these remains. Since the distant islands could hardly have been reached in very simple craft, although it is conceivable that they could have been discovered by accident in craft ordinarily not employed for long ocean journeys, it may be that they were settled not much before the period of Polynesian expansion.

Another reason for the suspicion that the early Melanesians and their predecessors did not possess sea-going craft is furnished by the little we know of the history of watercraft in general. The available evidence from Egypt and India indicates that ocean navigation was not prominent until sometime during the

[4] Speiser, F., "Ethnographische Materiallen aus den Neuen Hebrides und den Banks-Inseln," Berlin, 1929; Sarasin, F., "Ethnologie der Neu-Caledonier und Loyalty-Insulaner," Munich, 1929; Ivins, W. G., "Flints in the South-east Solomon Islands," J.R.A.I., 61, (1931); Furer-Haimendorf, C. von, "Zur Urgeschichte Australiens," Anthropos, 31, (1936).

first millenium B.C., although lengthy coastwise journeys and excursions to nearby islands apparently had been common at least in Egypt in earlier times.[5] The Chinese are not known to have done much more than follow the coast until about the beginning of the Christian Era.[6] Thus in view of the general inferiority of Melanesian culture it would seem that we have no right to assume that their watercraft and art of navigation were superior at any given time to the attainments of the peoples of all the high civilizations of the ancient world, especially since the modern Melanesians are not great navigators nor, with the exception of the historic Fijians, great boat builders. In addition, as already remarked, there seems to be some historical continuity between some historic Melanesian craft and those of the East Indies and the available evidence does not suggest that these traits have great antiquity.

The Polynesians (and Micronesians), the most recent invaders of the Pacific, are the only peoples known to have reached any of the islands east of Fiji. Geneological traditions and other evidence indicate that they invaded Polynesia about 400 A.D., and it thus seems permissible to believe that their expansion was centered in the East Indies during the first few centuries of the Christian Era, the very period when the art of navigation on the open sea seems to have been attaining prominence in the East Indies and China.

It is important to note that Polynesian traditions lack any mention of predecessors or of the subsequent arrival of strangers in islands they colonized nor has extensive archaeological search revealed any evidence of the presence of other peoples prior to or following the period of Polynesian expansion.

The manner of Polynesian migration seems to have been quite

[5] See Forde, D., "Ancient Mariners," London, 1927.
[6] See Donnelly, J. A., "Early Chinese Ships and Trade," China J. of A. and S., 3, (1935); Bishop, C.W., "The Rise of Civilization in China," Geog. Rev., 22, (1932).

different from that of the earlier peoples who migrated to the East Indies and New Guinea. Finding the latter regions fully occupied the Polynesians apparently did not make serious effort to dispel the inhabitants, but moved onward to have the good fortune to discover uninhabited regions, leaving only here and there small colonies or other evidences of their passage through the region. But it was only through possession of ocean-going watercraft and their ability as navigators that they could migrate along, through and around a well settled area.

There is no evidence to indicate that earlier invaders of the East Indies and New Guinea migrated in such fashion, although we may suppose that the occupants of invaded regions resisted encroachment with equal determination at all times. The distributions of the various peoples thus seem to indicate that the Malays, Indonesians, Melanesians, Papuans, Negritoes, and Australians migrated at the expense of their immediate predecessors only to relinquish ultimately their oldest possessions to those who followed them. If we interpret the distributions correctly, all of these movements seems to have been those of direct mass assault on contiguous territories, figuratively speaking. Such expansions in being continued to contiguous areas reflect a terrestial and coastwise movement rather than an offshore maritime migration.

Of these several migrations the late northward movement of the Malays and the apparently relatively recent eastward extention of the Melanesians seem to be the only ones which required ocean journeys of over one hundred miles. These journeys, we have many reasons to believe, may have taken place not long before the period of Polynesian migration. Indeed some of them may have been contemporary with the Polynesian expansion.

On the basis of these considerations support for theories of pre-Polynesian migrations across the Pacific is not forthcoming.

It seems not unlikely that claims for such voyages would not have been made were it not for the belief that certain appearances in American cultures could be explained only as derivations from the Old World via the Pacific. But advocates of such historical relationships have attempted to bolster their case in respect to the few traits for which a suspicion of unitary origin seems justified by placing in the same category numerous other traits which either show only the most distant resemblances or are cloaked under general or ambiguous terms.[7] Furthermore to bring all these traits to America it is necessary to suppose that Melanesians, Malays, Asiatics and other peoples each succeeded in reaching the New World not merely once, but repeatedly and at various points along eight thousand miles of American coasts. The supposition of such a mighty traffic seems most fantastic.

For the few traits in America concerning which suspicions of Old World derivation seem reasonable advocates of trans-Pacific influences either have ignored the possibilities of other explanations or have dismissed them without adequate cause. Some traits may represent independent American developments, some may have diffused from Asia to America overland via Bering Strait on the one hand and to Malaysia and Melanesia on the other, some may have been brought to the New World via the long coastwise route. These possibilities should be more thoroughly explored before conclusive opinions are offered, but first of all we need a stricter basis of definition for those traits for which claims of non-American origin have been advanced. However, since most traits in the trans-Pacific controversy are of such a nebulous character that their antiquity in any area can never be settled it cannot be doubted that satisfactory conclusions as to their origins never will be reached.

[7] For example, exogamy, totemism, matrilineal organization, body decoration, agriculture, pottery, irrigation, deification of kings, megalithic construction, mummification, etc. These traits as they stand can be valued at zero for comparative purposes.

DOMESTICATED PLANTS IN RELATION TO THE DIFFUSION OF CULTURE

BY

E. D. MERRILL

Administrator of Botanical Collections, Harvard University, and Director of the Arnold Arboretum

W HEN the Europeans came in contact with the primitive and advanced civilizations in North and South America at the close of the fifteenth century it was perhaps but natural that they should attempt to explain what they found here in the form of advanced cultures on the basis of man's achievements in the Old World. Not far removed from the scholasticism of the Middle Ages, naturally the writings of classical authors were invoked to find support for the idea of trans-Atlantic contacts at a much earlier date than 1492. Many apparently thought that the high civilizations found in Mexico, Yucatan, Central America, Bolivia and Peru could only be explained on the assumption of ancient contacts between the peoples of the Old and the New World.

Those who turned to the classics found their explanation in Plato's account of Atlantis, the beginning of the Atlantis cult that will not down and the precursor of the extreme wing among the modern diffusionists who predicate a single source of origin and a universal dissemination of culture.

Yet before the close of the seventeenth century serious doubts arose regarding the authenticity of the Atlantis account and any possible bearing that the Atlantis theory might have had on the development of culture in the New World. In 1670 Ogilby[1]

---

[1] Ogilby, J. "America: being an accurate description of the New World," [1-6], 1-629, illus., 1670; another edition, 1671.

voiced these objections and his logical conclusions are thoroughly in accord with the ideas of modern conservative ethnologists, but utterly opposed to the views of the extreme diffusionists.

But the Atlantis explanation of the similarities and assumed similarities between the Eurasian and American cultures was not the only one, for before 1670 the peoples of ancient Greece, Italy, Carthage, Phoenicia, Palestine, Wales, and China had been invoked to explain this enigma, and by that time or somewhat later the Irish, Egyptians, Japanese and others were involved. The idea persisted, and still persists, that somehow, sometime, there must have been contacts of advanced peoples across the Atlantic or the Pacific Oceans, or both, long antedating the voyage of Columbus.

Ogilby proceeds to discuss the various explanations that had been offered, other than the Atlantis theory that he had disposed of, and even on the comparatively little data that were then available concluded that these ancient contact theories were all untenable on the basis of philology, customs, and other factors. His final conclusion was the generally accepted modern concept that man reached America over a northern route from northeastern Asia.

As noted above, the Atlantis cult was the precursor of the extreme diffusionist group among modern anthropologists. Briefly, as expounded by what may be called the Manchesterian school of this group under the leadership of Smith[2] and Perry,[3]

[2] Smith, G. E. "The origin of pre-Columbian civilization in America." Science, n.s.44: 190-195, 1916: 45: 241-246, 1917 (with numerous references to other papers chiefly those of his own and his associates). "Human history." i-xviii, 1-472, f.1.67, 1929. The influence of ancient Egyptian civilization in the east and in America: The making of man. 393-420, 1931.

[3] Perry, W. J. "The children of the sun, a study in the early history of civilization." i-xv, 1-551, 16 maps, 1923.

all culture, including agriculture, originated in Egypt, and from this center, commencing in the ninth or eighth century B.C., this culture complex was diffused by migrations of culture-bearing peoples in all directions, after several hundred years ultimately reaching the pacific coast of the Americas and leavening the aboriginal population of North and South America with the ferment of ancient civilizations of the Old World.

The biologist can only look on these curious contributions to the science of ethnology as highly imaginative and sometimes entertaining fiction. The hypothetical highly cultured peoples of a hypothetical ancient Atlantis or an ancient Mu, the ancient "heliolithic" peoples of ancient Egypt, or the "children of the sun" of Perry, or even the ancient Druidical peoples of Cooper who centered about Salisbury Plain all fall in one category. These imaginary peoples as expanding and civilizing groups who extended their influence literally "to the ends of the earth" to the biologist are merely figments of the imagination.

The extreme diffusionists, having keen minds for similarities, see resemblances between Eurasian and American cultures rather than differences, and explain the resemblances or fancied resemblances, such as the famous elephant trunks,[4] on the basis of ancient contacts, overlooking or understressing the differences.

G. Elliott Smith's[5] categorical statement "It does not seem to occur to most modern ethnologists that the whole teaching of history is fatal to the idea of inventions being made independently" in support of his claims that all American higher cultures were derived from Egypt via India, Malaysia, and Polynesia, is merely begging the question. The biological evidence is absolutely and wholly in favor of an independent development

[4] Smith, G. E. "Elephants and ethnologists." i-viii, 1-135, f. 1-52, 1924.
[5] Smith, G. E. "The origin of the pre-Columbian civilization of America." Science, n.s., 44: 190-195, 1916.

of agriculture in America, and if such a complex art as this, involving the domestication of plants and animals, selection, breeding, the use of fertilizers, the construction of terraces, and the application of irrigation could thus be independently developed in America, there is every reason to believe that the higher cultures based on this agriculture could also be so developed.

I have several times quoted de Candolle's[6] logical conclusions of 1883 as expressed in the closing paragraph of his classical "Origin of cultivated plants": "Dans l'histoire des végétaux cultivés je n'ai aperçu aucun indice de communications entre les peuples de l'ancient et du nouveau monde avant la decourverte de l'Amérique par Colomb." The trained biologist at once recognizes the implications of this simple statement. It was so manifest that de Candolle did not consider it desirable or necessary to amplify it further, for in these few words he effectively answered the disciples of Atlantis, Mu, and the extreme diffusionists.

When we consider the beginnings of agriculture, and agriculture must have been a thoroughly established art very many centuries before advanced cultures based upon it were possible, we find that it originated in certain favored regions remote from each other, and in each center based on certain definite and distinct plants, or on plants and animals, actually occurring as feral species either in or in close proximity to the regions wherein the art itself originated. All basic cultivated food plants and all domesticated animals were derived from feral forms, and all of them were originally of relatively restricted distribution as wild species.

The centers of origin of both agriculture and culture were

[6] Candolle, A. de. "Origine des plantes cultivées." i-viii, 1-379, 1883; "Der Ursprung der Culturpflanzen." i-x, 1-590, 1844; "Origin of cultivated plants." i-viii, 1-468, 1885.

peculiarly restricted. Considering the world as a whole, these areas were the highlands of Mexico, Bolivia, and Peru in North and South America, parts of Asia Minor (a very important center), parts of Central Asia, limited areas in northern India, central and southern China, and perhaps Abyssinia. It is from these peculiarly restricted areas that all of our basic cultivated food plants and domesticated animals came, and it is in these same restricted areas that early advanced civilizations were developed.

But was there any such thing as an unlimited diffusion of this agriculture? The definite answer is no. Within the limits of North and South America, and within the limits of Eurasia including Africa, many cultivated plants and some domesticated animals were very widely distributed at an early time, in fact many of them attained an almost universal distribution, within one hemisphere or the other, before the dawn of recorded history. This was diffusion, but a diffusion limited by the boundaries of the one hemisphere or the other. It was the expanding and colonizing European nations that gave the impetus to universal dissemination of cultivated plants and domesticated animals, previous to that time there being absolute geographic limits to such distribution.

Both in America and in Eurasia, when the biologist surveys the scene, he is impressed with the fact that everywhere agriculture extended far from its limited places of origin long in advance of the higher cultures, originating in favored localities that were based upon it. The basic food plants and certain domesticated animals and the art of caring for them, were transmitted by diffusion from one people to another until agriculture affected the lives of large groups of less advanced peoples thousands of years before these same people were in any considerable degree affected by what we call culture. Everywhere the spread of culture failed to keep pace with the spread of agriculture.

If there was such a phenomenon as the universal diffusion of advanced cultures, then long antedating such diffusion there would have been a general dissemination of the plants and animals basic to agriculture. We have seen that the limits of distribution of cultivated plants and domesticated animals were the boundaries of the eastern and the western hemispheres; we may logically conclude that these same geographic limits were effective barriers to the dissemination of cultures based on agriculture.

Because of the striking demarcation of American as compared to Eurasian agriculture, not in methods, for the methods were the same—field and terrace culture, irrigation, adaptation of plants to varying conditions, the use of fertilizers, selection, and plant breeding—but in the domesticated plants and animals themselves, which, without exception, were native American species, the only logical conclusion that the biologist can draw is that agriculture in America was developed independently and was not influenced in the slightest by any agricultural development in the Old World. As agriculture in America was autochthonous, we may assume that so also were the cultures based upon it. There is no evidence of any contacts across either the Pacific or the Atlantic, disciples of Atlantis, of Mu, closet anthropologists, near anthropologists, popular writers, the extreme diffusionists, and other sensational writers to the contrary notwithstanding, that in any manner affected the development of agriculture or of culture in America until after the advent of the Europeans in the last decade of the fifteenth century.

Let us assume that by chance advanced peoples of Eurasia did reach America long in advance of Columbus. Unless they found here a distinctly developed agriculture it would have been utterly impossible for them to exist as civilized beings and thus affect in any way the advancement of culture in America, for they brought no food plants with them. With all the agricultural knowledge of their own particular culture area at their command they simply could not locate, and develop as cultivated species, the few potential food producing ones among the tens of thousands of native American plants that they might observe. An extensive and intensive empirical knowledge of wild plants and their economic uses acquired through many generations of close contact with them would be an absolute prerequisite to the selection of any species for domestication under existing conditions of several thousand years ago. The number of native species used for food by the American Indians north of Mexico is graphically indicated by Yanovski's[7] recent list of over eleven hundred in four hundred and forty-four genera and one hundred and twenty families of plants, but very few of which were ever cultivated.

Let us again quote G. Elliott Smith[8] who, in appealing to ethnologists to accept his extreme views on Egypt as the one and only source of origin of pre-Columbian American culture states: "All that I aim at achieving at present is to persuade ethnologists to do what is constantly being done in every *true* science, namely, impartially to examine the foundations upon which its theory rests. If they will consent to do this I have no doubt as to the outcome."

I commend to all ethnologists, including the conservative group as well as the extreme diffusionists, the critical consideration of this intriguing problem of man in his relationship to cultivated plants and domesticated animals, with particular reference to their places of origin, and when, by whom, and how they were disseminated. What he has done with them under domes-

[7] Yanovski, E. "Food plants of the North American Indians." U. S. Dept. Agr. Miscel. Publ., 237: 1-83, 1936.
[8] Smith, G. E. "The origin of pre-Columbian civilization in America." Science, n.s., 45: 246, 1917.

tication has a distinct bearing on problems appertaining to diffusion of culture. Whenever possible to do so I also recommend that preconceived theories be subjected to the acid test of biological facts that the author of the passage quoted above manifestly failed to do.

ON AUSTRALOPITHECUS AND ITS AFFINITIES

BY

R. BROOM

*Keeper of Vertebrate Paleontology and Anthropology
Transvaal Museum, Pretoria, So. Africa*

In 1924 an interesting Primate fossil skull was discovered in a limestone cave at Taungs in Bechuanaland. This was brought to Professor R. A. Dart of the Witwatersrand University, Johannesburg, who at once recognized that it belonged to an interesting new type of anthropoid. With great skill and care he removed all the matrix from the face and teeth, and he found that the face was preserved in almost perfect condition; and the greater part of the brain case was also found to be in a satisfactory state.

Dart briefly described the find under the name *Australopithecus africanus* in "Nature" and he considered it to represent a new type of anthropoid which in a number of respects came closer to man than to the chimpanzee or gorilla, and he suggested that it was probably near to the ape from which man had been descended. Scientists in England were at first inclined to think that Dart claimed too much for his ape and that it was probably only a variety of chimpanzee.

A few weeks after Dart's description had appeared I examined the type, and in the main confirmed Dart's conclusions. I also made a drawing representing the probable appearance of a median section. This I sent to Professor W. J. Sollas of Oxford, and he wrote a short paper on it, also in the main supporting Dart's opinion. Unfortunately the skull is that of a young animal with the milk teeth functional and the first upper and lower molars just coming into use, and thus probably an animal of five years of age; and many held that some at least of the human-like characters are due to the infantile condition, and that an adult would prove to be much more chimpanzee-like and less like man.

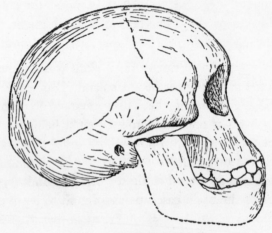

FIG. 46–Side view of skull of *Australopithecus africanus* Dart. One-half natural size.

A little later Dart removed the lower jaw and fully showed the crowns of both the upper and lower teeth. It then became at once manifest that in structure the milk molars closely resemble those of man and differ very greatly from those of any of the living anthropoids. In 1928, I wrote a short paper on this milk dentition, and argued that there must be some close affinity between this fossil ape and man, and that it could not be nearly allied to the chimpanzee. Gregory of New York also wrote a paper pointing out that in nearly every character in the dentition *Australopithecus* comes much nearer to man than to the living anthropoids, and Adloff of Königsberg has gone so far as to affirm that it is practically human.

Still there remained a doubt in the minds of many, and it seemed to be advisable, if possible, to secure an adult skull.

In August 1934 I was appointed to a post in the Transvaal Museum. For about two years I was mainly engaged in collecting and describing fossil reptiles, but about the middle of 1936 I thought it would be well to start on the study of the limestone caves of the Transvaal to see if I might find either traces of primitive man or a new specimen of *Australopithecus*, and in any case I was pretty sure to find some new fossil mammals. Mr. G. Von Son of the Transvaal Museum told me that he had seen in a cave at Gladysvale about sixteen miles north of Krugersdorp a jaw that looked like that of man. He had left it in the cave wall hoping to dig it out later, and when he returned he found someone had destroyed it. With Mr. Von Son I visited Gladysvale, and found among some pieces of the bone breccia remains of the horse *Equus capensis*, the fossil pig *Notochoerus meadowsi*, and a new species of *Procavia*, but I could find no trace of man or anthropoid apes.

Mr. Herbert Lang and Dr. A. Roberts told me of another cave at Schurveberg fourteen miles west of Pretoria where there was a good deal of bone breccia lying about near the old lime workings. Here I found much breccia with the jaws and bones of small mammals doubtless brought into a cave by owls. These on examination proved to belong mostly to extinct species of *Cryptomys*, *Mystromys*, and of a new subgenus allied to *Otomys*. With these rodents there was a new species of elephant shrew which had to be placed in a new genus *Elephantomys*, and a number of specimens of a small shrew which is probably identical with the living *Myosorex tenuis*. There were

also the remains of a moderately large cat which I have called
Felis whitei and parts of a giant baboon which has to be placed
in a new genus *Dinopithecus*.

At the beginning of August 1936 two of Professor Dart's
students—Mr. H. le Riche and Mr. G. Schepers—came over
from Johannesburg to see me. They told me that in a cave at
Sterkfontein six miles from Krugersdorp some skulls of a small
fossil baboon had been found, and that they had been at this
cave and had also been fortunate in finding some brain casts of
this little ape. I immediately arranged to go over to Krugersdorp
with them; and at the caves I met Mr. G. Barlow, who is man-
ager of the limeworks there and also caretaker of the caves. A
good many years before he had worked at Taungs, and had seen
the Taungs ape skull. He told me that many skulls and skeletons
of this ape had been thrown into the limekilns, no one apparently
taking any interest in the bones, but he added that he fancied a
somewhat similar large ape occurred in the caves at Sterkfontein;
and curiously enough Mr. Cooper, who owns the caves, in
writing a short account of the caves for a little guide book to
the places of interest round Johannesburg had written, "Come
to Sterkfontein and find the missing-link."

A short examination of one of the caves that has been worked
for lime showed portions of small ape skulls in the walls; and I
asked Mr. Barlow to keep a sharp lookout for any important
bones, and especially for anything that looked like the Taungs
ape. I was again at the caves a couple of days later and Mr. Barlow gave me three nice little fossil baboon skulls and much of
the skull of a large carnivore. A hunt in the debris in the
cave revealed a good deal more of this large carnivore. On
examination it proved to be the skull of a form apparently
allied to the sabre tooth tiger *Megantherson*, and I described

it as *M. barlowi.* When a better specimen is discovered it may prove not to belong to this genus, but it is certainly a larger felid.

The following week I again visited Sterkfontein when Mr. Barlow presented me with the brain cast of a large anthropoid

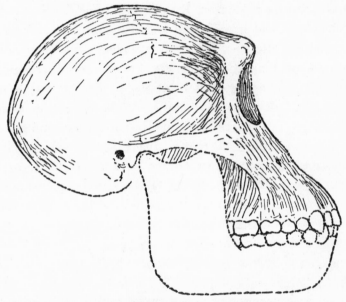

Fig. 47—Side view of skull of *Australopithecus transvaalensis* Broom. One-half natural size.

which had been blasted out a few days previously. I hunted for some hours but could find no other remains among the debris, but I got the cast of the top of the skull in the cave wall. I returned again the following day with Mr. Lang, Mr. Fitz Simons, and Mr. White, and three Kafir boys. A further search resulted in the discovery of the base of the skull, much of the parietals, and part of the occiput. In the matrix that lay on the right side of the brow I discovered, on cleaning it out, the displaced right maxilla with much of the malar and the 2nd premolar and 1st and 2nd molars. The right 3rd molar was also discovered, but quite detached. In the matrix on the left side there was later discovered much of the left maxilla with the beautifully preserved 1st and 2nd premolars and the 1st and 2nd molars. There are also preserved the sockets of the two incisors and of the canine.

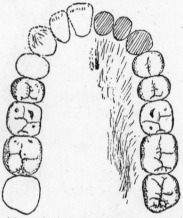

Fig. 48—Upper dentition of *Australopithecus transvaalensis* Broom. Three-fourths natural size. The right incisors and canine have been restored. As the middle line is missing from the back of the palate the palatal width is doubtful.

It will naturally take some months before a full description can be made of the skull, as much careful development must first be done; but something may be said at this stage.

The animal is clearly allied to the Taungs ape, but owing to the one being a child and the other adult, in only a few points can satisfactory comparisons be made. The brain in the Sterkfontein ape has a broader frontal region and is a little smaller than in the Taungs ape. The only teeth that can be compared are the 1st upper molars. They are nearly similar in size but the crown pattern differs in a number of details. As, however, none of the species of mammals associated with the Taungs ape have been found in any of the caves at Sterkfontein, while in at least two cases there are other species of the same or closely allied genera, we may safely assume that the geological ages of the two apes differ considerably and it seems well to place the Sterkfontein ape in a distinct species, and I have called it *Australopithecus transvaalensis*.

There is little doubt that *Australopithecus* must be regarded as an anthropoid ape somewhat allied to the chimpanzee and the gorilla, and only a little larger than the former. In structure the teeth, however, differ very considerably from those of either the chimpanzee or the gorilla, and resemble much more closely those of primitive man—especially those of Mousterian man. They resemble also in a number of characters the teeth of some of the species of dryopithecid apes recently discovered in the Pliocene of the Siwaliks of India.

When we obtain the much fuller evidence that will be afforded by the lower jaw teeth, I think it likely that *Australopithecus* will prove to lie somewhere near the common ancestor of the chimpanzee, the gorilla, and man, and a little higher than the dryopithecids. Not improbably it will be seen to be a little way along the line that branched off to grow up to man. And there seems no doubt that it is the fossil ape nearest to man's ancestor at present known.

There is one curious fact that may be noted. The teeth of *Australopithecus* resemble more closely in a number of respects those of modern man than do the teeth of the undoubted primitive man *Sinanthropus*. This would seem to indicate that in Pleistocene times there were a considerable number of types of primitive man which had evolved in different ways, and that it was from only one of these types, still unknown, that modern man arose.

Quite possibly before another year is past we will have other skulls and perhaps much of the skeleton of *Australopithecus*, and be able to add much more to our knowledge.

ESKIMO CULTURES AND THEIR BEARING UPON THE PREHISTORIC CULTURES OF NORTH AMERICA AND EURASIA

BY

KAJ BIRKET-SMITH

Nationalmuseet, Copenhagen, Denmark

THE assertion that the Eskimos are the descendants of the cave men of the Upper Paleolithic is an old one, and I am not going to give a full account of the history of the problem here. It will suffice to say that both cultural and somatical arguments have been advanced. At present, however, the racial and the cultural aspects of the question must be considered distinct. The problem is how far the unquestionable similarities are due to relation by blood and culture, and how far they should be ascribed to environment.

Leaving alone the somatical evidence we may well ask why the hypothesis has so often been considered a failure. I believe that to some degree at least the answer must be that Eskimo culture was treated as a whole, without proper regard to its geographical and especially to its chronological distinctions. And *if* the problem is to be solved at all we must, of course, in the first place go back as far as possible into the past of the Eskimos.

The systematical investigation of Eskimo archeology was initiated by Th. Mathiassen on the Fifth Thule Expedition under the leadership of Knud Rasmussen. He found there, in the old house sites west and north of Hudson Bay, the remains of a culture remarkably different from that of the present inhabitants of this region. Whereas the Central Eskimo tribes of to-day live

an inland life during much of the year, hunting caribou and
fishing trout in rivers and lakes, and only spend the winter and
spring hunting seal on the ice, the early culture was closely connected with the sea, and whaling which has now entirely disappeared in these parts, was evidently of paramount importance to
the ancient population. From the first place where it was found,
Thule in North Greenland, this culture was called the Thule
culture. Mathiassen also stated that while the Thule culture is
strongly divergent from the present-day culture in the Central
Eskimo regions, it vividly recalls the culture still to be found in
the outer parts of the Eskimo area, i.e. in North Alaska and
Greenland, so that there was once a complete chain of sea hunters extending from Bering Strait to the Atlantic; but in the
Central region it has succumbed before an advance of Eskimo
tribes from the interior, probably as a result of an uplift of the
land. There is also ample evidence that the Thule culture originated in Alaska and spread eastwards. The intensive research
work which was consequently carried on by Mathiassen and his
collaborators in Greenland has also given some hints as to the
age of the Thule culture. In West Greenland the Eskimo remains have been correlated with the finds from the mediaeval
settlements of the Norsemen. The earliest Eskimo finds there,
containing a pure Thule culture, can with tolerable accuracy be
dated to the 10th century A.D. If Alaska is to be considered the
cradle of the Thule culture, it must be of somewhat greater age
there, but hardly older than the beginning of our era.

So far the Thule culture is the best known of the early stages
of Eskimo culture, but evidence is rapidly accumulating concerning other phases also. Jenness has shown that the old culture
about Hudson Strait, called by him the Cape Dorset culture, had
a peculiar stamp which may, or may not, be ascribed to Indian
influence, e.g. from the Beothuk of Newfoundland. Very little,
however, is known of the Cape Dorset culture, and its relation,

both chronologically and otherwise, to the Thule culture is far from being clear.

In the region around Bering Strait we find, between Point Barrow on the Alaskan and Kolyma on the Siberian coast, evidence of another very remarkable form of Eskimo culture, characterized by some problematic implements and a highly developed art. This so-called Bering Sea culture was also recognized by Jenness as early as 1926, and since that time extensive excavations have been made on St. Lawrence Island. In some preliminary reports Collins has traced the development of art, showing that this rich and variegated style passes through an intermediary stage (Punuk) to the more degenerate art of the modern Eskimos. It also seems to be older than the Thule culture. The scroll-like patterns of the Bering Sea art are unique among the Eskimos, and perhaps their origin should be looked for somewhere in the late Stone Age of Eastern Asia. It is quite clear, however, that even if the Bering Sea culture is so far the oldest stage of Eskimo culture found, it is far from being primitive and cannot throw light on the origin of Eskimo culture as a whole.

The culture of the Aleutian Islands and southwestern Alaska occupies a very peculiar position within the Eskimo region. Both linguistically and culturally there is a greater difference between Prince William Sound and Point Barrow than between the latter place and Greenland. Just how this should be explained is not quite clear, but the difference is certainly very deep-going. The stratification which Dall many years ago believed to find in the remains on the Aleutian Islands has been proved by Jochelson to be based upon a misinterpretation of the conditions. In Cook Inlet, however, Dr. de Laguna was able to distinguish between three periods of cultural development. The last period was also found, in nearly identical form, in Prince William Sound, whereas in Prince William Sound most traces of earlier occupation seem to have been washed away by the sea on account of a recent sinking of the shore line. The difference between the stages is, however, very small.

The outcome of these reflections must be, unfortunately, that archeology so far leaves us in the dark, when we ask about the origin of Eskimo culture. Under these circumstances it seems justifiable to try other means and turn to ethnology. I mentioned before that in the Central Eskimo region the Thule culture had succumbed to an advance of Eskimo tribes from the inland. This very day we find on the Barren Grounds west of Hudson Bay a small group of Eskimos, the so-called Caribou Eskimos, who live without any connection with the sea, hunting caribou and fishing all the year round. A detailed analysis of their culture shows this to be of an extremely primitive character. Furthermore there is not the slightest evidence of their ever having lived by the sea. When we associate this with other considerations which will take us too long to discuss here, it is no far step to the assumption that these Caribou Eskimos are the last remnant of the primitive or Proto-Eskimo people, a remnant that has remained on the wide tundras with their enormous flocks of caribou, untouched for the most part by the development that took place on the coast.

As representatives of an ancient culture layer the Caribou Eskimos are of great importance to the history of arctic culture; but if we are to arrive at a real understanding of the Proto-Eskimo culture, it is necessary to regard it in relation to that of the surrounding peoples. If we turn to the great interior regions of Canada we find that the summer life of the Indians is practically the same as that of the Eskimos, whereas their winter occupation is entirely dependent upon the snowshoe. Hatt has shown that nothing less than a revolution has been caused in the life of the polar peoples by the invention of the snowshoe. Before this it was impossible to move about in the soft and deep

snow of the forests, and thus the natives had to keep to rivers
and lakes, where fishing could be pursued from the ice. In other
words they had to live exactly as the Caribou Eskimos do.
Thus it seems possible to distinguish between two periods in
the cultural development of northern North America: (1) a
period of basic culture, characterized by ice-fishing in rivers
and lakes during the winter and of which the Caribou Eskimos
are the only representatives to-day; (2) a specialized stage in
which the occupation of the winter took different paths, adapt-
ing itself either to sealing on the ice of the Polar Sea among the
Eskimos, or to the hunting on snowshoes among the Indians
of the woodlands.

It has been possible to follow these lines further and associate a considerable number of culture elements to one or the
other of these cultures, but it will take us too far to enter into
details. For our purpose the ice-fishing stage is, of course, of
greatest interest, and the next question of importance is how far
in North America it can be traced.

In the boreal woodlands of Canada and Alaska we find the
snowshoe culture fully developed, but on the northern plateaus
of British Columbia and in the Great Lakes area we have reached
the outskirts of its diffusion. It is true that the main elements
of snowshoe culture occur, but at the same time there is plenty
of evidence that there is not far down to the ice-fishing stratum.
More or less sporadically we meet with elements pertaining to
the latter.

Among the Algonkian Indians south of the Great Lakes agriculture has entirely upset the principles of economic life, but
when eliminating the latter we find an old hunting foundation
evidently corresponding to the ice-fishing culture. In the southeast outside the Algonkian area elements of the ice-fishing stage
may also be found, but they do not occur under such circumstances that it is justifiable to regard them as constituting a joint

complex. This is also true of the culture preceding the Algonkian occupation within this area, so it seems probable that south
of the Great Lakes the ice-fishing culture was introduced by
the Algonkians.

In the west the state of affairs has a different aspect. On the
coast of California there are great numbers of shell-heaps the
age of which has been estimated at about 3000 years, but nevertheless their contents of artifacts show an astonishing similarity
to the historical culture of this area. The same primitive basis
on which Californian culture has been built we meet again in
the Great Basin. Of course ice-fishing is precluded for purely
geographical reasons, but on the other hand the culture has
so many other elements in common with the ice-fishing complex
that the general aspect is essentially the same. It is an interesting question whether there are any relations to the Basket
Makers. So far it has not been investigated. It is true that we
do find some northern elements in the Basket Maker culture,
but the problem is sufficiently important to deserve a more
careful examination than we can offer here.

So far only North America has been considered. It is, however, a fact of no little interest that we find both snowshoe
and ice-fishing cultures outside North America. Erland Norden-
skiöld and Krickeberg have called attention to the remarkable
occurrence of what may here be called North American culture elements not only among the more primitive hunting tribes
of southeastern South America, but also in the high civilizations
of the Andes. At present we are not in position to offer any fully
satisfactory explanation of this curious circumstance, but I may
mention that we seem to find a similar mixture of ice-fishing and
snowshoe elements there as among the Basket Makers.

As may be expected it is, however, in the northern parts of
Eurasia that we meet the closest parallels. Apparently the position is the same in the old world as in America: the ice-fishing

culture is for the most part obliterated in the woodlands of Siberia and northern Europe, where hunting on snowshoes and still later reindeer nomadism have developed. Only among the Yukagir have the ice-fishing elements survived to a remarkable extent. In the outer regions here we are, however, faced with the difficulty that they mostly lie within closer reach of still more powerful sources of culture influence than in America; China, Western Asia, and Europe. And yet some parallels can be seen here too.

In other words there are some reasons for believing that the ice-fishing culture at one time extended over the whole circumpolar region. When speaking of it as a unit we must, of course, take a certain reservation. It is incredible that an absolutely homogeneous culture should ever have prevailed over the enormous area from northern Europe to eastern North America. There will certainly always have been local differences. In so far a term such as ice-fishing culture is merely an abstraction, an expression meaning that a certain common basis must be assumed to lie under the building up of the culture everywhere in the circumpolar region.

After this brief survey of the early cultures from an ethnologist's point of view it seems appropriate to try the opposite way, taking our starting point from the archeological side. So far the American northwest coast and the northern woodlands are, archeologically speaking, practically a terra incognita, and this leaves a very serious gap in our knowledge. Even in the very few cases where scientific excavations have been made, the remains, e. g. the crude stone implements and pottery from the Bona Sila site on the lower Yukon, give no clue to the development of Eskimo culture. It is not till we arrive at the plateau area that we perceive a faint glimpse in the darkness. Dr. de Laguna has shown certain points of connection between the old Eskimo culture of Cook Inlet and the archeological remains known from

Harlan I. Smith's important researches in the Columbia basin, but, as has been stated before, the Pacific Eskimo culture is so divergent from all the rest of Eskimo culture that, even in this case, the meaning of this conformity is still obscure. The implements described by Professor Jenks from the Arvilla gravel pit in North Dakota may have been derived from an old culture of a somewhat similar pattern, but to the best of my knowledge the forms are too little characteristic to be conclusive.

If we turn to the eastern parts of the continent we notice some scattered examples of conformity between Eskimo and archeological types in northeastern Canada and the New England States. Brinton and others even considered them proof of an early Eskimo occupation here—which, however, is going much too far. W. Duncan Strong, on the other hand, has advanced the hypothesis that they are evidence of a common basic culture. It is of very great importance that the whole problem be taken up again.

If really the ice-fishing stage originates in a Paleolithic or epi-Paleolithic culture we cannot leave the Folsom culture out of consideration, because the latter seems to be the only North American culture to which a later or at least post-glacial age can be ascribed with some degree of probability. But here again we are left in the lurch, for the Folsom remains consist of nothing but stone artifacts, and we know really nothing about the stone implements and stone technique of the ice-fishing stage.

From North America we now pass over to Europe. The early attempts to connect the Eskimos with the Paleolithic peoples all took their starting points there. At present only one systematic investigation has been carried out regarding this question, that of Dr. de Laguna who has undertaken a very thorough comparison between Eskimo and Paleolithic art. Her conclusion is negative in so far as the available material does not prove that Eskimo art is more closely related to the Paleolithic than are other arts of simple content; but she rightly assumes that this conclusion may not be final, because too little is known about the Siberian Paleolithic.

Here it should also be mentioned that among Scandinavian archeologists there now seems to be a general belief that the early Scandinavian Stone Age cultures should be regarded as epi-Paleolithic. It is now well known that the Maglemose culture is not the first in Denmark and southern Sweden. It was preceded by the so-called Lyngby culture belonging to the post-glacial tundra period, and this culture again is practically identical with the Ahrensburg finds in Holstein which, at least indirectly through the still older Hamburg culture, is connected with the late Paleolithic.

The earliest cultures of Norway are still much disputed. In Finmark, the northernmost parts of the country, and the adjacent parts of Finland there has been found a number of settlements containing a remarkably primitive culture, the so-called Komsa or Finmarkian culture. The origin has lately been looked for in the Paleolithic of Poland and Russia, and it has been dated as far back as the post-glacial period. It is quite probable that this hypothesis will not remain uncontradicted, but at any rate the affinities to the Paleolithic seem beyond doubt. Here there seems to be a possibility of combining archeology and ethnology, and perhaps fill up the gap between the Paleolithic and the ice-fishing cultures. I am thinking of the Lapps. So far we have no knowledge as to when the Lapps immigrated into northern Scandinavia, but it is at least absolutely certain that their settlement goes back to very remote times. There is linguistic evidence that they lived on the coast before they had adopted their present, Finno-Ugrian language. Tanner even ascribes the Finmarkian to a proto-Lappish population, and it is probable that at any rate the late stone age finds in Finmark should be ascribed to them. A. V. Schmidt's discoveries on

Olenii Ostrov form a link between the latter and the Lapp iron age culture.

Perhaps we may be allowed to say that we are beginning faintly to see the path that may lead to results in the future. Of course it will be of utmost importance to obtain a better knowledge of the archeology of northern Siberia. As a single example of what may be expected I may mention Chernetsov's recent finds from an apparently very late but still pre-Samoyedic coast population on the Yamal peninsula. But also in North America and in Europe our knowledge is far from being sufficient. It is pleasant to record that the International Congress of Anthropological and Ethnological Sciences has taken up Knud Rasmussen's old plan regarding an international investigation of this important question and has organized a committee with a view to cooperation between the countries interested in this matter, and a corresponding committee was organized last year by the International Congress of Prehistoric and Protohistoric Sciences.

ORIGIN AND DEVELOPMENT OF THE EARLY PALEOLITHIC CULTURES

BY

OSWALD MENGHIN

Professor of Prehistoric Archaeology, University of Vienna

Most scholars of the time about 1900 claimed universal validity for the chronological system of the Paleolithic cultures which is tied up with the name of Gabriel de Mortillet. That is to say, it was generally accepted that the earliest human civilization developed everywhere in the same way; only chronological, no regional, differences were admitted. We know today that we must abandon this view. In a special pamphlet I[1] have explained in detail, how Obermaier and Breuil gradually approached the idea of two great currents of civilization, the flake cultures and the handaxe cultures, mixing in Western Europe during the Early Paleolithic Age, or, as I prefer to say, the Protolithic. Especially Obermaier pointed out that Europe was divided into two definite cultural areas in Early Protolithic times, an area of flake culture and an area of handaxe culture. Middle and Eastern Europe are free from handaxes of older type. All Early Protolithic finds of that region belong to primitive flake cultures of Clactonian and Levalloisian character. Acheulean handaxes have been found in Middle Europe, but in a limited number and of late Acheulean date. As far as we know, the handaxe does not exist anywhere in Russia, with exception of the Caucasus and Crimea, and these areas were influ-

---

[1] O. Menghin, "Zur Geschichte der altpaläolithischen Kulturkreiskehre." Wiener Prähistorische Zeitschrift XIV, 1927, p. 30.

enced by the handaxe region of the Near East. Also the Russian Mousterian shows no handaxe tradition. We may conclude from these facts, that at the time when cultural developments began, Middle and Eastern Europe belonged to an area in which only flake cultures flourished, whereas the Atlantic part of Europe was a stronghold of the handaxe groups. In my book "Weltgeschichte der Steinzeit" (Wien, 1931) I tried to draw general conclusions from this most important scientific inference. I examined all Protolithic stone industries of the Old World, as far as I was able to collect information from books and museums, dividing them into the two main groups, established for Europe by Obermaier.

Since that time research on the Protolithic Age has made considerable progress. The conception has gained ground that the separation of handaxe and flake industry has not only a technical but also a cultural significance. As for Western Europe, it was particularly Breuil, who, in a most excellent way, deepened the analysis of the Protolithic on that basis.[2] He pointed out that in France, three series of cultural groups are derived from the Clactonian: 1) the Langudocian, which is a prolonged Clactonian; 2) the Levalloisian, which is characterized by a special progressive kind of core preparing; and 3) the Tayacin-Mousterian, a mixture of the former two with handaxe influence. Moreover, we have in France, the Combe-Capellian or Mousterian of Acheulean tradition, which places itself just between the flake and handaxe groups. The handaxe series of France has to be divided, first, into the Abbevillian (a new name for the Chellean, which unfortunately does not occur at Chelles), second, into the Early Acheulean, and third, into the Late Acheulean or Micoquian. Breuil follows the distribution of the Clac-

[2] H. Breuil, "Les industries à éclats du paléolithique ancien." Préhistoire I, 1932, p. 125.

tonian all over Western and Middle Europe, and North and South Africa. This culture, discovered in England only a few years ago, is the oldest and most primitive kind of flake industry known so far. It may be considered as the starting point of the whole series of flake cultures. According to Breuil, it appears in the first Interglacial (Günz-Mindel), contemporaneously with the Abbevillian.

Our knowledge of the Protolithic of North Africa has likewise made great progress in the last years. The cultural development there took a course similar, but by no means identical, to that of Western Europe. The most characteristic feature of the Sahara-Protolithic is the Aterian, which is akin to the Mousterian of France, but distinguished by the very frequent occurrence of pedunculated points, a type foreign to Western Europe. Sites of this culture abound in the Sahara from the Atlantic to the Kharga-Oasis, where Miss Caton-Thompson[3] has found it in well-stratified layers. In the Nile valley, however, it is almost entirely lacking. This Aterian survived, as Vaufrey[4] has shown, during Late Paleolithic times and was mixed with the new oncoming cultures. In Egypt, after the period represented by hand-axe cultures and classic Levalloisian,[5] we meet a rather peculiar pebble industry which is most probably a local offspring of the Levalloisian.[6] This group also seems to have had a very long range overlapping the Late Paleolithic.

A most impressive series of Protolithic cultures has been estab-

[3] G. Caton-Thompson. "Kharga Oasis." Antiquity, V, 1931, p. 221 (and E. W. Gardner.) "The Prehistoric Geography of Kharga Oasis." Geogr. Journal LXXX, 1932, p. 369.

[4] R. Vaufrey. "Deux gisements extrèmes d'Ibero-maurusien." L'Anthropologie, XLII, 1932, p. 449.

[5] K. L. Sandford and W. J. Arkell. "Paleolithic Man and the Nile Faiyum Divide." Chicago, 1929. "Paleolithic Man and the Nile Valley in Nubia and Upper Egypt." Chicago, 1933. K. S. Sandford. "Paleolithic Man and the Nile Valley in Upper and Middle Egypt." Chicago, 1934.

[6] O. Menghin. "Palaolithische Funde in der Umgebung von Benisalâme." Anzeiger der phil.-hist. kl. Akademie d. Wiss. in Wien, 1932, p. 89.

lished by Wayland[7] and Leakey[8] in East Africa. In the early diluvial deposits of Uganda, Wayland found a very primitive pebble industry to which he gave the name Kafuan, which he divided into four stages. The last of them is probably identical with Leakey's Oldowan of Kenya and followed there by four stages of Chellean and six stages of Acheulean. Leakey's subdivision of the handaxe cultures is based on the marvellous series of layers in the Oldoway Gorge. Apart from handaxes, the Acheulean of East Africa contains also cleavers, implements which occur rather rarely in France, but more frequently in Spain, where they have been named Castillo axes, and in the Sahara region (with the exception of Egypt). They also occur in East and South Africa. Flake cultures also existed in Kenya and Uganda. Leakey speaks of traces of a rude flake culture, which he believes to be contemporary with the pebble industry. He found also some evidence for the existence of pure Levalloisian in these countries. At any rate there occur different mixtures between handaxe and flake industries in East Africa. One of them is Wayland's Sangoan, which apparently flourished at the same time as the Acheulean; it is a sort of Levalloisian under Acheulean influence. Similar groups are the Nanyukian and the pseudo-Stillbay, which run parallel with the latest Acheulean. Leakey mentions also an advanced flake industry of the same age which he calls Proto-Aurignacian. Related industries are also known from the Protolithic of Western Europe; they remind one of the "Precapsian" of France and Spain. Leakey finally speaks also of an East African Mousterian, but very little is known about it and the question of its relation to the so-called Aurignacian of East Africa is not yet settled.

The South African prehistorians blame Leakey because of his

[7] E. J. Wayland. "Rifts, Rivers, Rains, and Early Man in Uganda." Journ. of R. Anthr. Inst., LXIV, 1934.
[8] L. S. B. Leakey. "Stone Age in Africa." Oxford, 1936.

using the European cultural terms for African cultures. In their opinion the local assemblages of this continent, though related, are never quite identical with those of Europe, and should, therefore, be given terms of their own. Our South African colleagues I think are quite right. Both from a typological, as well as from a chronological point of view, it is dangerous, notwithstanding mutual affinities, to group different cultures under one name. Such procedure has very often proved to be premature and has prevented clear insight into the true nature of cultural evolution. We need, no doubt, comprehensive terms, but they must have a general character like the wide expressions flake culture and handaxe culture. There can be, however, as van Riet Lowe[9] rightly says, no objection against the use of European cultural terms for describing techniques, so that it is permissible to speak of Levalloisian technique in South Africa. Our knowledge of the Protolithic of South Africa has been enormously enlarged in the last years.[10] There seems to be present a very old pebble culture and a Clactonian-like group, but they are not as yet sufficiently known. In our present knowledge handaxe cultures dominate the South African Protolithic. They are known under the name of Stellenbosch culture, a long lasting group which can be subdivided into three stages. Stellenbosch-I connects handaxes of Abbevillian type with Clactonian flakes, Stellenbosch-II handaxes of a more advanced type with cleavers, Stellenbosch-III represents handaxes chiefly made of Levallois flakes. The Victoria-West industry is characterized by primitive cores of Levallois technique. It was first thought that an independent industry of the flake group, perhaps even a sort of

[9] C. van Riet Lowe. "Nomenclature of Paleolithic Finds." Man, 1936, 266.
[10] A. J. H. Goodwin and C. van Riet Lowe. "The Stone Age Cultures of South Africa." Annals South Afr. Mus., XXVII, 1928. A. J. H. Goodwin. "A Commentary on the History and Present Position of South African Prehistory with full biography." Bantu Studies, X, 1935, p. 292.

Proto-Levalloisian, might be present. However, sites with Levallois-like cores turned out to be only workshops of the Stellenbosch-III group, or at least of a variety of it. The end of the Protolithic series of South Africa is represented by the Faure-Smith culture, a mixed group, on the one hand containing fine Micoquian-like handaxes, and on the other, cores and flakes of Levalloisian technique.

Turning to Asia we must confess that, as regards the Paleolithic, this immense continent is very badly explored. This is a great pity, for we are entitled to infer that just this part of the world is the cradle of the evolution of human culture. There are only three regions of Asia from which we possess any information about their Protolithic past. During the last years much research work has been done in Palestine by English and American scholars, especially by Turville-Petre,[11] by Miss Garrod and McCown.[12] These investigations revealed an almost surprising similarity of the Protolithic evolutions of Palestine and Western Europe. Abbevillian, Acheulean and Levalloisian are documented. There can be little doubt that Clactonian will also be discovered in the future.

Absolutely new and most valuable material has been brought to light by de Terra and Paterson on their expedition to India.[13] The archaeological series starts there with a pebble culture like the Kafuan of East Africa and continues with five stages of

[11] F. Turville-Petre. "Researches in Prehistoric Galilee 1925-26 and Report on the Galilee Skull." London, 1927.

[12] Bulletin of the American School of Prehistoric Research VII-XII, 1931-1936. D. A. E. Garrod, "The Stone Age of Palestine," Antiquity, VIII, 1934, p. 133.

[13] H. de Terra, P. Teilhard de Chardin, T. T. Paterson. "Joint Geological and Prehistoric Studies of the Late Cenozoic in India." Science, 1936, p. 233. H. de Terra and P. Teilhard de Chardin, "Observations on the Upper Siwalik Formation and Later Pleistocene Deposits in India." Proc. Amer. Philos. Soc., LXXVI, 1936, p. 91.

industry, which were called Soan culture by de Terra. The earlier Soan industry uses pebbles, too, and shows strong similarity with the pebble industry of Egypt, but it is associated with handaxes and cleavers of Abbevillian and Acheulean type. The late Soanian reminds us of the Aurignacian of Europe and may be already of Late Paleolithic age. Before forming a definite opinion on the Soan culture, which probably will turn out to be a series of different industries, we will have to wait for Paterson to thoroughly examine all the material and also, perhaps, for new investigations in India. The Soanian, at any rate, apparently does not belong to the handaxe group, although it is somehow connected with, or influenced by, it.

In the Indian Peninsula there seemed to prevail rather different cultural conditions. The oldest stone implements we know from that region, especially from the Eastern Ghats, are primitive handaxes. According to Cammiade's and Burkitt's statements,[14] they are connected with cleavers and Proto-Levallois cores of the Victoria-West type. In the collections of de Terra, Teilhard and Paterson there appear early Protolithic handaxes from the Narbadda valley and from Madras. These indicate, in my opinion, that India was a stronghold of handaxe cultures.

In recent years, China has yielded Protolithic finds of particular importance. I not only refer to the remains of Peking man, but also to the artifacts discovered in different places in China and also near Choukoutien. It is one of the most surprising facts that real Protolithic handaxe industries have not been found in China or in Central Asia. Flake technique is absolutely predominant in the Protolithic stone manufacture of China. It is important to note that the Chinese flake Protolithic differs rather

[14] M. C. Burkitt and L. A. Cammiade. "Fresh Light on the Stone Ages in Southeast India." Antiquity, IV, 1930, p. 324.

widely from that of Europe and Africa. It contains amazingly-advanced types which partly approach Late Paleolithic and even epi-Paleolithic workmanship. This observation would indicate that in China the cultural activity was much more vivid than elsewhere.

With such observations in mind, we now turn to the problem of the original homes of the two great cultural groups that have, so far, been dealt with. In my book "Weltgeschichte der Steinzeit" I put forth the theory that the handaxe cultures originated in Southern Asia, the flake cultures in the central portion of this continent. This view will be substantiated by the following paragraphs.

1. As shown above, we may establish in Europe a distinct cultural division into a flake and a handaxe area, the latter allied to the Atlantic, the former to the middle and eastern part of the continent.

2. The oldest stage of the handaxe culture in Europe, the Abbevillian or Chellean, is represented by nearly identical groups in North and East Africa. There can be little doubt that it spread from Africa to Europe.

3. Very primitive handaxes occur also in India. The question, therefore, arises whether Africa or India is the true home of the handaxe culture or if the whole range of countries from India to Africa might not be its cradle. The geographical and climatic diversity of this vast territory does not speak in favor of the latter conception, although it may be considered as an alternative. On the other hand, the present state of our knowledge does not allow us to decide about the other possibilities, for we know too little of India.

4. At any rate we may consider the southern origin of the handaxe cultures a certainty. This fact seems to me to be a most important result of research, for it enables us to answer the ques-

tion of the last background of the evolution and origin of the handaxe.

5. With reference to this problem I should like to emphasize that the origin of the different stone industries must, no doubt, be related to the necessities of life, which have been forced on mankind by climate, fauna and flora. The handaxe is particularly well fitted for dealing with trees and wood, digging up roots and cultivating the ground. Also, from this point of view, it seems to me rather obvious that the handaxe must have originated in a southern, tropical, or subtropical country, where forest and nutritive tuberous plants abound. After all, in contradiction to the general opinion and my own previous belief, even primordial stages of plant cultivation may have been carried on in the Protolithic handaxe culture. Professor Baumann, the well-known ethnologist of the Berlin Museum, has lately published a paper,[15] in which he says that one of the most primitive surviving cultures of Eastern Sudan is intimately connected with agriculture. Hence, one may well trace cultivation of plants back to the Protolithic; for our ideas of the cultural level of the Paleolithic can only be based on a comparison with the life of modern primitives.

6. There is, as we have shown, no Abbevillian in Middle Europe and not much Acheulean. There is none in Russia either. Hence, this region, as well as the middle strip of Asia, belongs to that part of the Old World in which the cradle of flake cultures has to be sought for. The greater cultural vividness of the East, as well as anthropo-geographic reasons, gives us cause to suggest that the earliest centers of the flake group lay somewhere in China or Turkistan.

7. As regards the different pebble cultures it would seem that even a provisional judgment of their cultural position and sig-

[15] H. Baumann. "Die afrikanischen Kulturkreise." Africa, VII, 1937, p. 129.

nificance is as yet impossible. Basing his opinions on the conditions of East Africa, Leakey seems to be convinced of a genetic connection between pebble and handaxe culture, the former being the ancestor of the latter. In Egypt, on the contrary, the pebble culture is nothing but a local variation of Levalloisian-Mousterian relationship under handaxe influence. The Soanian of the Indus region, too, inclines more towards the flake industries. It is, of course, possible that the different pebble cultures have nothing at all to do with one another. They may be products of local conditions and it is perhaps only the raw material which gives them a certain similarity.

So far we have only spoken of flake and handaxe cultures. But I believe that a third great cultural cycle should be distinguished, to which I have given the name "bone culture." I based my theory on the remarkable interglacial sites which have been discovered in the Alps of Switzerland and Austria since 1912. They are cave dwellings which were inhabited by cave bear hunters. These contain fireplaces and enormous quantities of cave bear bones which suggest ceremonial treatment. It is significant that the stone implements in these layers are rare, and, if existing at all, they are very primitive. In most cases they are nothing but split stone, which nobody would take for artifacts were they not found in connection with coal and ashes. The first discoverers of this culture, Bächler in St. Gallen and Hörmann[16] in Nüremberg, observed that a good many of these bones show artificial preparation or at least utilization. In these we may recognize an independent type of culture without any relations either to handaxe or flake industries. The supposition that the bone culture is only an industry which deteriorated in the mountains cannot be maintained, since it occurs also in the plains. Simi-

[16] K. Hörmann. "Die Petershöhle bei Velden in Mittelfranken, eine altpaläolithische Station." Abhandlungen d. Naturhist. Ges. zu Nürnberg. XXIV, 1933, p. 21.

lar sites were recently uncovered in Czechoslovakia[17] and Silesia,[18] indicating an extension to the northeast. These discoveries support my contention that the bone culture came from the northeast and that it had its source in the northern part of Eurasia, where, as in all later prehistoric periods, a strong predilection for bone utilization can be observed.

If my ideas are right, then we have three great belts of Protolithic civilization in the Old World: in the north bone cultures, in the center flake cultures, and in the south handaxe cultures.

How did the three cultural belts come into existence? Two possibilities present themselves. First, the three belts may have sprung up immediately from a wood stage following the distribution of mankind all over the world, and because of the necessity to adapt the implements to various uses. Or, the belts may have come into existence one after another in the course of the gradual occupation of the inhabitable part of our globe. Personally I am more inclined to plead for the latter conception. I should think that the primordial wood culture was first followed by a primitive bone stage.

While the bone culture advanced to a higher standard in northern Asia and occasionally spread to the south, the flake industries arose in the central belt of Eurasia, gaining an enormous extension over the middle and southern parts of the Old World. South American finds suggest that it also reached the New World.

Cultures of a more regional character did not arise before the very close of the Protolithic: such are the Mousterian, the Combe-Capellian, the Aterian, the Faure-Smith group, all of them being the results of different degrees of mixtures between earlier groups. The rise of such local industries towards the final

[17] L. Franz. "Die älteste Kultur der Tschechoslowakei." Prag. 1936.
[18] L. Zotz. "Die schlesischen Höhlen und ihre eiszeitlichen Bewohner." Breslau, 1934.

stage of the Protolithic was no doubt due to the increase in population and the cultural specialization connected with it.

I am perfectly aware of the theoretical nature of my ideas on the origin of the three great Protolithic cultures, yet I believe in the usefulness of such speculations which are apt to promote progress of knowledge.

EARLY MAN IN JAVA AND PITHECANTHROPUS ERECTUS

BY

EUGÈNE DUBOIS

*Curator, Paleontological and Mineralogical Department of
Teyler Museum, Haarlem*

Judging from the fossil skulls and especially the endocranial casts *Homo soloensis* (including the child *Homo modjokertensis*), discovered in Java, is really human, and proto-Australian. He is identical with *Sinanthropus pekinensis* and has nothing in common with *Pithecanthropus erectus*. Rhodesian man, another proto-Australian, closely resembles Solo-Man and is probably a near descendant of *Homo soloensis*.

In my opinion these are the most important of all known fossil men, because they represent the most primitive type of *Homo sapiens*, to which belong all the races of man living at present. The Australian aborigine has conserved much of the primitive somatic character, especially the fundamental and therefore most distinctive quality of any mammalian organism, the characteristic brain volume. Because of its great significance I have studied this quality of the Solo-man by means of the existant endocranial casts and skull measurements and by means of data concerning *Homo rhodesiensis* and the Australian aborigine.

From this it is apparent that the proto-Australian of Ngandong in Java, and the proto-Australian of Broken Hill in South Africa, had a somewhat smaller brain volume than the Australian aboriginal of to-day. Assuming for the average cranial capacities of the male and the female *Homo soloensis* 1,200 and 1,050 cc. respectively, we find a difference of 95 cc. to the benefit of the present Australian.

The average cranial capacity of the Australian aborigine we may assume to be, according to the best sources, 1,295 cc. in the male sex and 1,146 cc. in the female. To obtain accurate results for the Ngandong skulls I measured the endocranial length, breadth and height (the latter from the auricular height of the skull) and calculated by means of the formula of Froriep a volume of the cranial cavity of 1,143 cc. Comparing those internal chief dimensions with those of the cast of *Homo rhodesiensis*, I found 1,150 cc. for the first. We thus may safely assume 1,150 cc. for the cranial capacity of Ngandong Skull I. The features of this skull indicate a male. For the exceptionally large and certainly male skull No. V, I calculate 1,284 cc., rounded off to 1,295 cc. This gigantic skull has thus only a capacity equal to the average capacity of the male Australian aborigine. For Ngandong Skull VI, to all appearance female, I find 1,087 cc., rounded off to 1,095 cc. Assuming for the average cranial capacities of the male and the female *Homo soloensis* 1,200 and 1,050 cc., respectively, we then find those 95 cc. to the benefit of the present Australian race—a difference which may be easily accounted for as an absolute, not a relative one, by the influence of culture, by means of which the Australian could better provide for the necessities of life and hence somewhat improve his originally poor constitution. The brain increased together with the body, the cephalization remaining unchanged.

The recent very important reports of Franz Weidenreich on the formerly discovered *Sinanthropus pekinensis* skulls and the skulls which he recovered show that the cranial capacity in this race was generally low, the highest being hitherto c. 1,200 cc. In my opinion this fact is inconsistent with the consideration of *Sinanthropus pekinensis* as belonging to the neanderthal type of humanity.

From *Homo soloensis* we have two tibiae, which are by far too slender for a neanderthal type. The limb bones of *Homo rhodesiensis* are certainly of the *sapiens* type.

Pithecanthropus was not a man, but a gigantic genus allied to the gibbons, however superior to the gibbons on account of its exceedingly large brain volume and distinguished at the same time by its faculty of assuming an erect attitude and gait. It had the double cephalization of the anthropoid apes in general and half that of man.

It was the surprising volume of the brain—which is very much too large for an anthropoid ape, and which is small compared with the average, though not smaller than the smallest human brain—that led to the now almost general view that the "Ape Man" of Trinil, Java, was really a primitive Man. Morphologically, however, the calvaria closely resembles that of anthropoid apes, especially the gibbon. The name *Pithecanthropus* for the genus thus seemed fully appropriate. The name *erectus* was given to the species on account of the strikingly human-like essential features of the femur, which imply erect attitude and gait.

But in 1932, forty years after excavation of the first femur, I recognized in the old Trinil collection four more or less fragmentary and superficially corroded femora, which are similar to the type specimen. All five femora are unquestionably from the same species, though four were excavated in 1900.

Although fragmentary, these four new femora—I recognized a fifth new fragment in 1935, from Kedung Brubus, where a mandible, which can only be from a *Pithecanthropus*, was found —are extraordinarily important, because on them, natural corrosion, by removing the superficial or periosteal bone layer, has laid bare the internal structure of the shaft wall. This deeper shaft structure is entirely different from the human one (and also the deeper shaft structure of the anthropoid femora), and betrays a muscular function and a locomotion, which although facultatively erect and human-like on the ground, was also arboreal and perhaps on uneven ground a perfection of the semi-erect gait of the gibbon. Thus the evidence given by those five new thigh

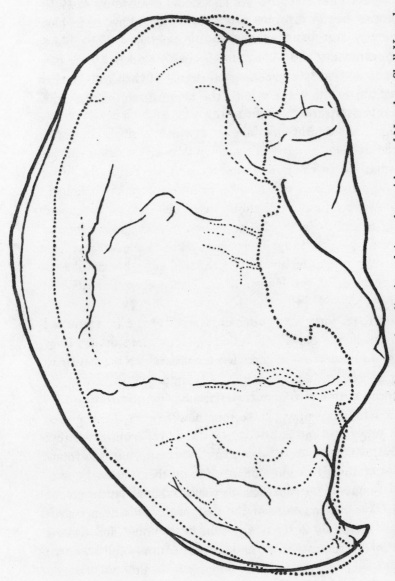

FIG. 49—Diagrammatic drawing of left norma lateralis view of the endocranial cast of Ngandong Skull V, made to equal length with right norma lateralis view (reversed) of the endocranial cast of *Pithecanthropus erectus* Skull (dotted line). Telephotographs in subfrontal (orbital)–suboccipital cerebral plane orientation.

bones of the morphological and functional distinctness of *Pithe-canthropus erectus* furnishes proof, at the same time, of its close affinity with the gibbon group of anthropoid apes. The gibbon-like appearance of the "Ape Man" is clearly evident by the general form and many morphological details of the skull. A close comparison in this respect with the chimpanzee, on the other hand, reveals great differences.

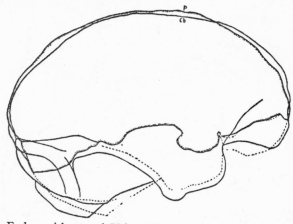

FIG. 50—Endocranial cast of *Pithecanthropus Erectus* (P) × ½, and chimpanzee (*Ch*) made to equal length. Both figures are diagrammatic drawings (Telephotographic outlines) of right norma lateralis views. Subfrontal (orbital) —suboccipital cerebral plane orientation. (*Proc. R. Acad. Amsterdam XXXVI,* 1933, *Pl.* III.)

In a paper read at the meeting of the Royal Academy of Sciences, Amsterdam, on April 29, 1933, entitled "The Shape and the Size of the Brain in *Sinanthropus* and in *Pithecanthropus*," I tried to prove the existence of a fundamental difference between these two organisms. The first one possessing a parietal vertex of the brain is apparently human the other lacking such a parietal accumulation of brain mass is distinctly anthropomorphic, in so far as regards brain form. See *Pithecanthropus* compared with Chimpanzee in Fig. 50, with *Hylobates agilis* in Fig. 51, and Man with apes and monkeys in the latter illustration.

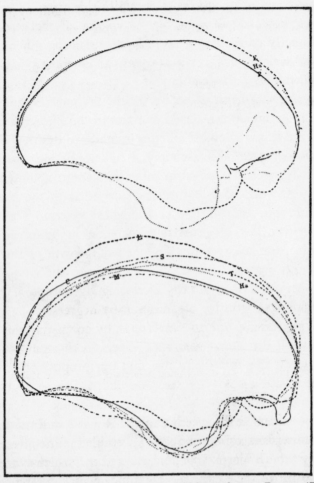

FIG. 51—*Upper Figure:* Endocranial casts of *Pithecanthropus Erectus* (P) × ½, Mesocephalic man (E), and *Hylobates Agilis* (Ha). Made to equal length.
   Lower Figure: Endocranial casts of Mesocephalic Dutch man (E), chimpanzee (T), orangoutan (S), *Hylobates Agilis* (Ha), *Cebus* (C), and *Midas* (M). Made to equal length with P of the upper figure. Both figures diagrammatic drawings (telephotographic outlines) of right norma lateralis views. Same orientation as in Fig. 50. (*Proc. R. Acad. Amsterdam, XXXVI,* 1936, Pl. IV.)

The strongest evidence of the gibbon-like appearance of *Pithecanthropus*, and of its near relationship to this group of anthropoid apes, however, is given by the volume of the cerebrum. This is exactly twice that of an imaginary siamang gibbon with the body weight of *Pithecanthropus*, as computed from the chief dimensions of the femora.

This surprising brain volume is indeed the most conspicuous, and the most important, distinctive feature of *Pithecanthropus erectus*, and it was to obtain a better insight into this new organism, that soon after the discovery, I undertook the search for laws which regulate cerebral quantity in mammals, and entered into studies, which should furnish evidence as to the place of *Pithecanthropus erectus* in the zoological system. They led, finally, to the law of progressive cerebration by great leaps (mutation), the law that the phylogenetic growth of the cerebrum proper was automatically discontinuous, the volume and the number of the nerve cells increasing by abrupt doubling, which implies progressive organization by degrees.

Applying this law to *Pithecanthropus*, by comparing this fossil Primate with the anthropoid apes, especially the gibbons, and with man, on the other hand, we find our proposition entirely confirmed.

This comparison more than confirms the opinion of Marcellin Boule, prominent sixteen years ago, that *Pithecanthropus* may have been a large gibbonoid species, distinguished from its congeners by those important particular characters which at the time were known to Boule.

Finally it may be remarked that *Pithecanthropus erectus* may well have been submitted to transformation towards human organization, needing only a slight modification of the function and corresponding form and structure of the femur, and these with the other parts of the lower limb, correlated with a similar, but not greater, modification of the function and form of the upper limb.

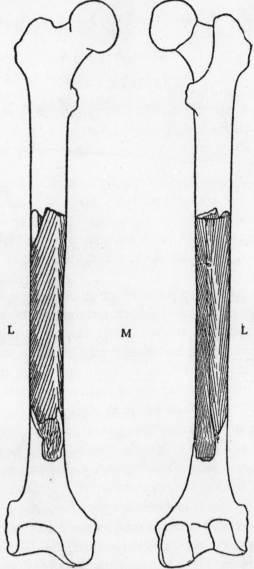

Fig. 52—Diagram of the fifth *Pithecanthropus* femur, from before (left) and from behind (right). The fragmental shaft, located in the outlined entire right femur: One-third natural size. (*M*), medial side; (*L*), lateral side.

EARLY MAN AND GEOCHRONOLOGY

BY

GERARD DE GEER

Geochronological Institute, Stockholm

As far as I have been able to find out after having studied the subject for a long time, there is scarcely any other way to get reliable datings of Early Man than that of bringing his relics into relation with such series of annual layers as are registered by nature itself, or, in other words, with geochronology.

How this new branch of investigation has brought together its exact datings by means of a direct counting of annual layers or varves without any conjectures or suspect calculations, has been reported in quite a series of papers, published mostly in the periodical Geografiska Annaler, Stockholm, during the last decade and in the reports of several international geological congresses, the last of which was in Washington.

By means of this natural time scale it has been found possible to identify and refer to historic time especially all melt-water clays from ancient glaciers, registering that part of the melt-radiation from the sun received every year by our planet, which for thousands of years has been found, in a marvellous way and within all the continents of the globe, to register the annual variation of the melt-temperature, though, of course, actualized only during the immediately associated summer times of the two hemispheres. But both of these in fact have exhibited such a minute similarity that, by comparison of a long varve-series in Argentina with the time scale in Sweden, it once was stated in print that a few single annual varves from exactly reported years must have been overlooked, whereupon these missing links by a new investigation in nature were rightly re-found at their indicated places.[1]

In the same way geochronological measurements of annual varves had indicated that the most detailed former estimates concerning the age of Niagara Canyon were about four times too long, and at the same time it was suggested in print that one reason for this over-estimate might be that a certain part of the canyon, above the Whirlpool, may only have been reexcavated out of till from the last glaciation. Soon afterwards this was confirmed by the discovery of considerable till-deposits exactly in that part of the canyon.

Such illuminating facts may, perhaps, lead to a really careful comparison of our already published comparative diagrams of thousands of annual varves confronted from many different parts of the globe and showing the most convincing correspondence, even in striking details. The distances between several of the localities are often considerable as reckoned in miles, but quite irrelevant in comparison with the enormous distance from the sun, the source of the melt-radiation.

Now, by considering the very varying thickness as well as mode of appearance in different regions, exhibited by those quaternary deposits which conceal the remnants of Early Man, it is evident that it should be very desirable to acquire, at least in certain instances, really reliable datings of some leading finds.

[1] De Geer, Gerard. "Gotiglacial broadmapping, Sweden—New York—Manitoba." Report of the 16th Intern. Geol. Congr., Washington, 1899. Washington, 1936, Vol. 1, pp. 192-202.

As far as it was the only possibility, archaeological correlations had to follow the analogous method generally available for geology in using more or less marked typological similarity of fossil types as an indication of about the same age. But this implies often a rather rough estimate with great possibilities of error, perhaps irrelevant as to long epochs, but rather serious with respect to the short history of Man. Here it is by no means sufficient with chronologic assumptions based only upon such similarities, as they may represent not identical time, but only analogous stages in evolution of implements or zones of climatic or biontic migration.

Of course it will not be easy to get good connections between archaeologic remnants and exactly datable varve-deposits, but it is no doubt worth while trying to do so.

As to deposits from the last archaeologic stages, or the Nordic Iron-Bronze, and Neolithic Stone-Age, the possibilities are of course the best, and even as to the Aurignacian and Magdalenian there seem to be chances, especially when the time scale will be extended through Poland over the Daniglacial subepoch until the limit of the last glaciation, which probably represents a marked and recognizable climatic vertex.

If Early Man immigrated into the valleys of the Alps at the same rate that the last glaciation receded, there may be possibilities of connecting relics of Man with datable annual melt-varves from late Glacial deposits.

Already dated are Gotiglacial varves in British East Africa with human relics of Aurignacian type.[2] This will be of special interest when direct determinations are acquired concerning the dating of the Aurignacian type in different parts of Europe.

[2] De Geer, Gerard. "Equatorial palaeolithic varves in East Africa." Geogr. Ann., Bd 16, Stockholm, 1934, pp. 76-96.

For such determinations it is of importance to remember that annually datable varves have been found in British East Africa as well as in Russia, which have been deposited in ordinary, not glacigene lakes, and these facts greatly widen the possibilities of reliable datings with respect to Early Man.

SOME OBSERVATIONS ON THE REMAINS OF A PLEISTOCENE FAUNA AND OF THE PALAEO-LITHIC AGE IN NORTHERN MANCHURIA

BY

A. S. LOUKASHKIN

Harbin Museum of the Manchuria Research Institute

In 1933 I submitted to the XVIth International Geological Congress at Washington a paper on "The Post-Tertiary fauna of Northern Manchuria contemporary with Primitive Man," in which I enumerated the discoveries made to that time of the remains of a chiefly mammal Pleistocene fauna. In the following years, new discoveries were made in different parts of Northern Manchuria, thanks to which it may be assumed that the country during the Pleistocene Age was thickly inhabited by many species which at present are either extinct everywhere, or survive only in other countries of Asia situated more to the South and possessing a milder climate. We may say without any exaggeration that nearly at every point of Northern Manchuria we encounter some remains of a long vanished fauna: from the steppes and semi-deserts of the Barga in the North to the shore of the Liaotung Peninsula in the South, in the mountains of the Great Khingan and in the wide fertile Manchurian Plain watered by the Sungari and its mighty tributary, the Nonni.

Richest of all in remains of the Pleistocene fauna is the Manchurian Plain with its deposits of loess-like loam. True, a great part of the recorded places where bones have been found are those in which casual discoveries of single detached bones, or even only parts of them have been made.

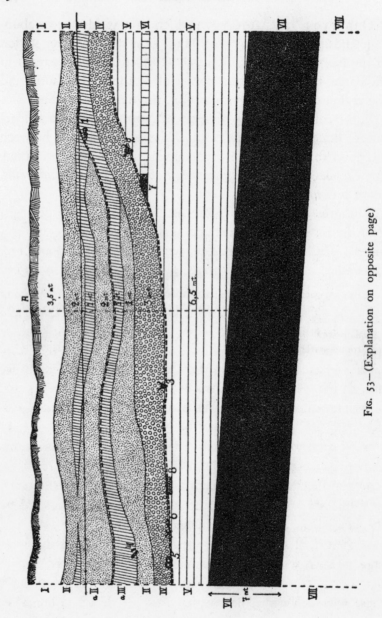

Fig. 53—(Explanation on opposite page)

Only two regions are known which have yielded more abundant finds, viz: the brown-coal mines near the Chalainor station of the North Manchurian Railway (former Chinese Eastern) in the Barga, the northwestern corner of northern Manchuria, and the region of the br·ckyards at Kuhsiangtun near Harbin.

In the collection of the Museum of North Manchuria at Harbin, of bones of mammals from Chalainor, brought in between 1923 and 1927, remains of the following species are represented, viz: *Elephas namadicus, Rhinoceros tichorhinus, Bos primigenius, Bison priscus, Antilope* sp., etc.

The greater part of these bones, according to the geologist Prof. E. E. Ahnert, were found at depths of from 8.5 to 13.5 meters. The strata enclosed between the depths mentioned are: the washed-out surface of early Quaternary deposits, then a bed

---

FIG. 53—A geological cross-section of the bone-bearing layer of Pleistocene Mammals at the Chalainor Brown Coal Mine of the North Manchuria Railway (former Chinese Eastern Railway), Barga, North Manchuria.

Explanation:

A. Ground surface.

   Layers:
   I. Chestnut-brown soil.—Modern deposits.
   II. Dry quicksand.
   IIa. Wet sand.
   III. Compact silt.   } Washed-out surface of early Quaternary de-
   IIIa. Frozen silt.   posits.
   IV. Small river pebbles.
   V. Argillaceous slate (thawed). } Washed-out surface of coal-bearing
   VI. Thin tier of sandstone.   deposits.
   VII. Brown coal.
   VIII. Grey clay.

Figures in the contact between IV and V layers:
   1. Skull of *Rhinoceros tichorhinus*.
   2. Skull of *Bison priscus*.
   3. Skull of *Bos* sp.
   4. Tibia of *Rhinoceros*.
   5. Pelvics and ribs of *Rhinoceros* and *Bison*.
   6. Other small bones.
   7. Petrification (?).
   8. Willow Wattling.

Layers included between two dotted lines—Eternally frozen ground.

(After V. P. Vodenikov, Aug. 1927.)

of eternally frozen ground, beneath which follows a stratum of washed-out argillaceous slates, which is richest in remains of a fossil fauna. The accompanying schematic sketch of a cross-section illustrates more fully the order of stratification of these beds.

The accumulation of bones of Pleistocene mammals at Chalainor is characterized by the simultaneous presence of implements of primitive Man. The same holds good regarding the second place, viz. Kuhsiangtun. But on this more later, after consideration of the Pleistocene fauna contemporaneous with the ancient dweller of Northern Manchuria.

The Kuhsiangtun deposits of bones of a fossil fauna proved to be the richest of all recorded thus far in Manchuria and perhaps in East Asia. They were quite casually discovered in 1931 in consequence of the activity of the inhabitants of Kuhsiangtun, making bricks for Harbin from the loess-like clay which composes the ancient terrace of the right bank of the Sungari River, on which stands the town of Harbin with its numerous suburbs.

In 1931, the author undertook excavations in this region together with the palaeontologist of the Peking Geological Survey, Dr. T. N. Yin, and the archaeologist V. V. Ponosov. As a result of this work an immense collection of bones, skulls, and teeth was gathered, which is now in the Museum of Harbin. Another large collection was gathered in 1933 and 1934 by the expedition of Prof. S. Tokunaga and N. Naora, which is now in the Vaseda University of Tokio.

At Kuhsiangtun, as I have written before (1932, 1933), the rich bone-bearing stratum lies at a depth of six to eight meters and lower in a thickness of loess-like clay, which consists of a few sub-strata little differing from each other, but in general more or less alike. Outcrops of these strata appear in two deep gullies, cut by the Wen-chuan-ho stream and flood-water torrents.

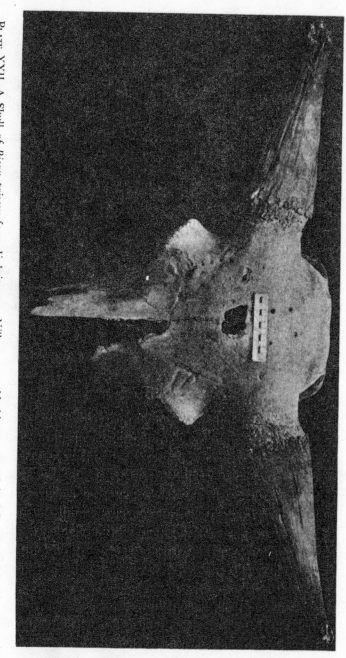

PLATE XXII—A Skull of *Bison priscus* from Kuhsiangtun Village, near Harbin, excavated in July of 1931 by the author and Dr. T. H. Yin from the wet greenish silt of the main ravine, eroded by the Hotsiagow River. Preserved in the collections of the Museum of Manchuria Research Institute at Harbin. (Upper view.) Photo taken by the Author, 1932.

After the excavations by the Scientific Research Institute of North Manchuria in 1931, partly continued in 1932 in excursions of the author and V. V. Ponosov, large-scale excavations were begun in 1933 by Prof. Tokunaga and Naora and concluded in 1934. Many private collectors of Harbin after heavy rains have secured, and continue collecting, bones washed out from the strata, so that at the present time many thousands of detached bones, horns, teeth, and skulls have been gathered.

As a result of the exploration of the bone deposit of Kuhsiang-tun during the past six years the list of recorded species of the Pleistocene fauna of Northern Manchuria has grown greatly.

According to the preliminary determinations by Drs. T. H. Yin, S. Tokunaga, N. Naora, Prof. Henry Breuil of Paris, Père Teilhard de Chardin, and the author, we have the following list of mammals, viz:

1. *Canis lupus* L.
2. *Canis* sp.
3. *Vulpes* sp.
4. *Hyaena ultima* Matsumoto.
5. *Hyaena* sp.
6. *Felis* sp.
7. *Tigris tigris longipilis* Fitz.
8. *Putorius* (*Mustela*) sp.
9. *Meles* sp.
10. *Ursus* sp.
11. *Tamias* sp.
12. *Pseudosciurus* sp. ?
13. *Arctomys* (*Marmota*) *sibirica* (Radde).
14. *Microtus* sp.
15. *Myospalax epsilanus* Thomas.
16. *Citellus dauricus* Brandt.
17. *Chaliodomys* sp. ?
18. *Arvicola* sp.
19. *Ochotona* sp.
20. *Lepus* sp. (*tolai* Pall. ?)
21. *Rhinoceros tichorhinus* Cuv.
22. *Rhinoceros* sp. (*sinensis* ?)
23. *Rhinoceros* sp. (*mercki* Jäger)
24. *Equus hemionus* Pall. (Var. ?)
25. *Equus caballus* L.
26. *Equus* cfr. *ferus* Pallas.
27. *Moschus* sp.
28. *Capreolus mantchuricus* (Noack).
29. *Capreolus* sp. ?
30. *Cervus canadensis xanthopygus* A. Milne-Edwards.
31. *Cervus* (*Euryceros*) *pachyosteus* Young.
32. *Cervus* (*Euryceros*) *ordosianus* Young.
33. *Cervus elaphus* L. (?)
34. *Cervus* sp. ?
35. *Megaceros* sp.

36. *Rusa* cfr. *elegans* Teil.
37. *Rusa* sp. ?
38. *Pseudaxis grayi* Zd. (var. ?)
39. *Pseudaxis* sp. ?
40. *Sika nippon mantchuricus* Swinhoe.
41. *Palaeotragus* sp. ?
42. *Alces* sp.
43. *Rangifer tarandus* L. (?)
44. *Gazella* sp. (*gutturosa* Pall.).
45. *Gazella* sp. ?
46. *Nemorhaedus raddeanus* (Heude).
47. *Saiga tatarica* (L.) ?
48. *Capra* (*Spiroceros*) *kiachtensis* Pavlova.
49. *Bos primigenius* Boj.
50. *Bos* cfr. *taurus* L. ?
51. *Bibos* sp.
52. *Bison priscus* Boj.
53. *Bison* sp.
54. *Bubalus teilhardi* Young.
55. *Probubalus* sp. (*triquetricornis* Rutimeyer?)
56. *Camelus* sp.
57. *Giraffidae* sp. ?
58. *Elephas primigenius* Blum.

Besides remains of mammals at Kuhsiangtun have been found a bone and egg-shells of the ostrich (*Struthio* or *Struthiolithis*), bones of the soft-armored turtle (*Amida maacki*), and fin-bones of the swallow-fish (*Pseudobagrus* sp.).

Of the enumerated finds the most interesting are the remains of the giant deer, *Megaceros, Euryceros;* of the fossil buffalo, *Probubalus triquetricornis;* of the ostrich; the deer, *Rusa, pseudaxis;* the giraffe; the screw-horned antelope (*Spinoceros kiachtensis*), etc.

Of the discoveries made lately in other parts of Northern Manchuria, particular attention is warranted by that of the upper part of the skull with the horns of a wild sheep, *Ovis* sp., which in the summer of 1934 was brought up by fishing nets from the bottom of Lake Dalai-Nor (Barga), not far from Chalainor station; it is now in the private collection of Archimandrite Nathanael Lvov of Harbin. This discovery and that of horns with part of the skull of the screw-horned antelope explodes the assertion of some zoogeographers to the effect that Manchuria has always remained outside of the area of representation of the members of the families of the wild sheep and goats. (Nasonoff, N. V., 1919).

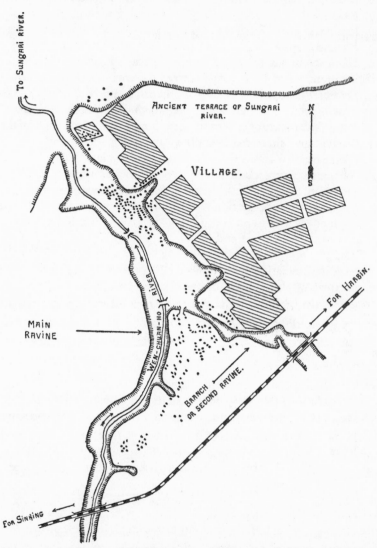

FIG. 54—A sketch plan of the Kuhsiangtun Village, suburb of Harbin (Northern Manchuria), where fossil bones of Pleistocene fauna and Palaeolithic bone and stone implements were excavated during 1931-1934.

Summing up and analysing the fossil fauna of the Pleistocene I take the liberty to repeat the formerly (1933) published particularities and characteristics of the latter.

1. From the point of view of contemporary zoogeographers, the Pleistocene fauna of Northern Manchuria is represented by various forms which give it an unusually complex and special character. Together with the representatives of the north, such as the elk, mammoth, and hairy rhinoceros, southern forms, such as the buffalo, hyena, and tiger, flourished. Another interesting peculiarity of the varied mixture of forms is that it comprised animals differing exceedingly in their characteristic habitat-typical plains forms, such as the hare, bison, antelope, and ostrich, and even typical desert forms, such as camels, existing side by side with typical forest forms, such as the ox, elk, reindeer, bear, and many others related to inhabitants of the high mountain regions of today.

2. The second striking feature shown by the remains found is the existence, in association with typically Pleistocene animals, of forms characteristic of the Tertiary fauna. To this category among others belong buffalo (*Probubalus triquetricornis* ? Rutimeyer) and a second species of rhinoceros (*Rhinoceros* sp., possibly *R. mercki* Jäger). This association indicates that in Northern Manchuria these animals existed considerably longer than in other localities and survived into the Pleistocene. Several lines of evidence indicate that, favored by the absence of a glacial epoch in Manchuria, numerous forms probably survived into relatively recent times. In Chinese chronicles are preserved several references to oxen and rhinoceros contemporary with men.

3. In the fossil remains of the ancient fauna of northern Manchuria we also find forms that exist in other countries at present—for instance the camel, hyena, and ostrich—and some that are still living in Manchuria, the long-haired Manchurian tiger (*Tigris tigris longipilis* Fitzinger, the wapiti (*Cervus canadensis xanthopygus* Milne-Edwards), the roe deer (*Capreolus mantchuricus* Noack), the antelope, and others. Not without interest is the finding, in Kuhsiangtun, of the bones of the soft-shell turtle (*Amida maacki* Brandt), which lives at the present in the ravines and lakes of Manchuria. All these facts put together confirm the existing opinion that

the contemporary fauna of Manchuria is a relict fauna preserving many animal and plant forms surviving from the far past of the country.

Proceeding now to the Palaeolithic Age of North Manchuria I must say that already in 1931, when I was at work excavating in the bone deposit of Kuhsiangtun together with the archaeologist V. V. Ponosov, I took notice of two circumstances calling for attention. Notwithstanding the richness of the bone deposit we did not find one single complete skeleton. Even the skulls were without lower jaws. All the bones were scattered and mixed up. The second circumstance, most astonishing to me, was the abundance of small fragments of bones, a great percentage belonging to the hollow ones rich in marrow, which for the greater part proved to be broken lengthwise.

All this taken together gave me the right to advance, in 1932 in my article "Recent Discoveries of Remains of Pleistocene mammals in Northern Manchuria," my query,— are not the bone deposits of Kuhsiangtun kitchen refuse of the Palaeolithic hunter of North Manchuria? This conclusion was reached, after, during our excavations, we chanced upon small lumps of charcoal. As a corroboration also served the discovery by Prof. Breuil on some bones in the collection of the Museum at Harbin of traces of fire and even of notches and scratches, not produced by natural wear and tear, but more likely by the hand of Man. Just then V. V. Ponosov found the first stone implement, made of rock-crystal in a very rough way, similar in type to the quartz implements of the *Sinanthropus pekinensis* from Choukoutien.

According to F. A. Velevskiy (V. J. Tolmachoff, 1932), among the bones of mammoth, rhinoceros, and others which were fished out of the Sungari River off the town of Harbin (derived from the banks below the mouth of the Wentsunho rivulet), there was one stone distinguished by its particular shape, which apparently had been given to it artificially. Unluckily, this implement was lost afterwards.

In the course of the excavations of Kuhsiangtun in 1933 and 1934, Prof. S. Tokunaga and his assistant N. Naora gathered an extremely large collection of bone fragments showing traces of having been worked by Man, also some implements and working refuse.

To judge from the photographs accompanying the reports of the savants mentioned, but very few of them may be considered as true bone implements. The first place among them is doubtlessly occupied by a wonderfully preserved object of bone which is well and neatly polished. This implement looks like a prick or stylet of oval cross-section, from which the peduncular part has been struck off. The length is 140 mm., the width at the base 14 x 8 mm. It is distinguished by a high polishing technique. Three other implements are of considerably coarser workmanship than the first, but they deserve attention. They are all made of mammoth tusks. A halberd-shaped implement is 217 mm. long and 51 wide, a scoop-shaped one 230 mm. long by 120 wide, and a spear-handle-shaped implement has a length of 120 mm.

The stone implements of the collections of Messrs. Tokunaga and Naora are for the greater part fragments and working refuse rather than finished implements.

Regarding quality of workmanship, first place among them is taken by a tiny curved scraper of bluish-grey opal, measuring 30 x 26 mm. and showing careful retouch at the working edge. Then follow larger scrapers of basalt and measuring 52.5 x 32 and 50 x 20 mm. of liparite having a length of 28 and a width of 53 mm. We note three other implements, which the savants mentioned classify as "willow shape" implements. Two of them are made of chert and have dimensions of 42 x 27.5 and of 34.5 x 26.5 mm., respectively, while the third one, of quartz, measures 61 x 25 mm. Thus we see that all these implements are of small size. The only large stone object is a lump of basalt of an irregularly triangular shape, measuring 126 x 98 mm., which shows traces of working on two of its borders.

In 1934, Archimandrite Nathanael Lvov and the archaeologist V. V. Ponosov also collected some stone implements, two of which are very interesting; one of them is a medium-shaped scraper-nucleus, the other one an elaborate little scraper-lamel.

The excavations by the Scientific Research Institute of North Manchuria in 1931 and by the expeditions of Prof. S. Tokunaga and N. Naora in 1933 and 1934, were conducted in the main gully, at the bottom of which the Wenchaunho flows, i.e. on that spot where the banks of the rivulet and of the gully have suffered most of all, both from the river itself and from the activity of the brickmakers of Kuhsiangtun. The bones and the stone and bone implements accompanying them were washed out by the river from the strata in the mass of loess-like clay and buried again in a disturbed order in its bed in the silt.

Prof. S. Tokunaga and N. Naora think that the bone-bearing stratum examined by them at a depth of one to three meters below the bottom of the gully "shows absolutely no sign of its having even been disturbed either by human hands or by the forces of nature, but it remained entirely as a natural deposition."

Personally I am of a different opinion, particularly since in the autumn of 1934 V. V. Ponosov and I found an undisturbed bone-bearing bed in the comparatively recently formed second gully (to the right) where it is marked at a depth of six to eight meters (according to a measurement by Ponosov). As the places of the excavations of 1931, 1932 and 1934 are considerably lower than this stratum, it is evident that all the bones and implements occurring there were washed out by the river from the bone-bearing horizon in a comparatively recent past, and they cannot be considered, of course, as undisturbed natural depositions.

In all probability even the whole bone-bearing stratum within the thickness of loess-like clay at Kuhsiangtun does not represent in itself the place of the original deposition of the bone, but rather one of secondary deposition. The bones, together with masses of the loess-like clay washed out somewhere upstream, migrated downward and formed the present deposits where Kuhsiangtun is now standing.

Thus, the place of the primary burial of the bones, and the traces of the Palaeolithic encampments, is to be looked for somewhere higher up on the ancient terrace, towards the East.

The second gully, in the bone-bearing stratum from which the stone implements were taken by Archimandrite Nathanael Lvov and V. V. Ponosov, having suffered less from natural conditions and the brickmakers, ought to draw the attention of explorers to more careful excavations, which may lead to interesting and valuable results and give us an idea of the remote past of Manchuria. I am not afraid of exaggeration in stating that to the deposits of Kuhsiangtun is reserved no small part in unfolding the archaeology of this country.

Comparing the stratigraphical conditions of the deposition of the bones and stone implements near Kuhsiangtun with those in the Palaeolithic encampment on Verholenskaya Gora near Irkutsk, we may say that they are identical; both belong to the type of the loess camps.

The implements collected by Prof. S. Tokunaga and N. Naora have been referred by these savants, in comparison with the chronology of the European Palaeolithic, as "Moustie" or "Orignan." The archaeologist Ponosov likens them on account of the type of their workmanship to the "Magdalen."

Conceding to Kuhsiangtun first place in importance for its rich remains of the Pleistocene fauna and the occurrence of implements of the Paleolithic type, the second place belongs to Chalainor, about which I have spoken above.

Though it has already frequently been pointed out in literature, I would repeat once more that at Chalainor in a stratum containing bones of the mammoth, bison, rhinoceros, and other mammals, at a depth of from 8.5 to 13.5 meters, human artifacts were discovered which preliminarily are to be attributed to the Palaeolithic rather than to the Neolithic. In 1927, P. A. Pavlov brought thence the butt-end of an axe made of a filed round piece of a deer's antler with a T-shaped cross-opening bored through it. This butt-end is rather well worked, and polished by use. Its size is 95 x 85 x 30 mm.

There also was found another piece of deer's antler 600 mm. in length with the tines struck off and a ring-shaped filing in the middle which for some reason has not been finished. Both these objects, as well as the fossil bones of mammoth and rhinoceros found together with them, are in an equally complete state of preservation, and covered with the same dark patina, being at the same time equally silicified, i.e. petrified.

At the same approximate depth, but in another place, a wattling of willow twigs measuring 500 x 2000 mm. was found, of the same type used by fishermen for closing a river. Not far from the wattling a fragment of a tree was found, rudely worked into a board measuring 400 x 1000 x 70 mm.

Unluckily, both these finds became lost to science forever, for the administration of the mine left them at the working place without taking photographs of them or protecting them.

In 1934, in the same mine, a human skull was discovered, apparently a female one, but it is unknown from what depth and from which stratum. In structure it is *Homo sapiens*. Its whereabouts at the present time are unknown.

In the Museum at Harbin is a part of the upper part of a female human skull, secured by Mr. Pateleyev in 1927 from the mouth of the Urshun River, where it was brought up from the bottom. This locality is on the eastern bank of Lake Dalai Nor, about one hundred kilometers west of the Chalainor mines. This skull is very old and has rather strongly developed eye arches. Perhaps it belongs to the later Palaeolithic.

Of other localities "suspected" as Palaeolithic, we may mention Hailar (Barga), where on a sandy blow-out, during the explorations of Neolithic encampments in 1928, working refuse and half-worked river pebbles of medium size were discovered, which by the shape of their finish and a more ancient aspect were distinguished from the typical Neolithic implements of this region. At the same place a vertebra of a rhinoceros was found, on which were preserved traces of scrapings with some sharp tool like a chisel, clearly not caused by the teeth of some beast of prey, as was thought first.

In 1934 the author discovered a fine natural cross-section in the diluvial sediments of the ancient terrace of the right bank of the Argun River near Hailar station, where he collected some bones of rhinoceros, mammoth, fossil horse, ox, bison, and deer. This place is still waiting for exploration, which perhaps may produce traces of the Palaeolithic there.

In conclusion we may say that the first steps in the realm of the exploration of the Palaeolithic Age of North Manchuria have led the explorers to concrete results in that the existence of this most ancient human culture may be considered as proven. Traces of human activities in the shape of implements, though not numerous, have been discovered. It is still left to discover Man personally. We hope that this second and concrete problem which is still before us, will be solved, too, by the united efforts of interested persons and scientific institutions, perhaps in a not so remote future.

THE CONFINS MAN—
A CONTRIBUTION TO THE STUDY OF EARLY
MAN IN SOUTH AMERICA

BY

H. V. WALTER, A. CATHOUD, AND ANIBAL MATTOS
Academy of Science of Minas Geraes, Brazil

THE highlands of the State of Minas Geraes are particularly rich in limestone formations, which geologists have determined to be of Silurian origin, and numberless caves exist which were carved out of the rock during pluvial periods of Pleistocene times. Many of these caverns were explored by W. P. Lund, the Danish naturalist, a century ago, and his collection of fossil mammals and human remains now forms part of the Copenhagen Museum. Since his days until the present, practically no exploration of a scientific nature has been carried out, and one of the objects of the Academy of Science of Minas Geraes is to continue this very interesting and important work.

Excavations have been carried out in the Lagôa Santa region of the Rio das Velhas valley during the past four years, the principal locality being the Confins Cave (also called locally the Mortuario Cave), a distance of five miles from the small town of Pedro Leopoldo, and about eight miles from the village of Lagôa Santa.

The Confins Cave is in a limestone rock, completely isolated, rising to a height of about one hundred and forty feet above the ground level, and the entrance to the cave is about half way up, access being obtained by climbing a winding path up the east side.

The entrance to the cave had been sealed with immense blocks of sedimentary conglomerate and rocks during pluvial times; but of relatively recent years (possibly at the time of the conquest) tribes of Indians had used the protection of the rock-shelter as a camping ground, and there had buried their dead. From time to time villagers from Confins would find human bones lying on the ground surface beneath the rock-shelter, exposed by erosion, so that the site came to be known as an Indian burial ground.

In 1926 Dr. Padberg-Drenkpol of the Rio National Museum visited the place, and undertook an initial investigation of the site. During excavations he was fortunate in unearthing the remains of many Indian skeletons under the rock-shelter, and while removing the conglomerate and blocks of fallen stone, the entrance to the cave was gradually exposed to view. Many tons of material were then taken away until the opening was perfectly clear, and the cave accessible. During this preliminary work a few molars of a young mastodon were recovered a few feet beneath the surface of the cavern floor near to the entrance.

Dr. Padberg returned to Rio after spending two months in the Lagôa Santa region, and the site remained abandoned until the year 1933. In this year work was recommenced under the supervision of a member of the Academy of Science of Minas Geraes, and earth and rock material were slowly removed from the cave and dumped outside. The Confins Cave is twenty-five feet wide at the entrance, tapering to five feet in width at the far end, which is at a distance of sixty-five feet from the opening.

During four years of exploration of the cavern interior no vestige was found of human remains; in fact, with the exception of rats and bats, no remains of existing animals were recovered from the alluvial deposit of the floor.

As the work progressed, to a depth in some places of fifteen

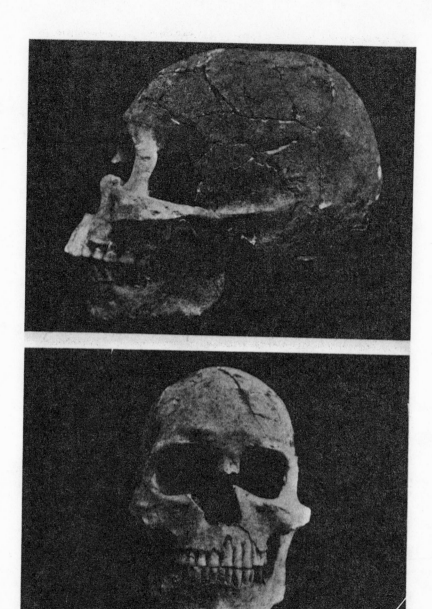

PLATE XXIII—The Confins Man.

feet, large blocks of decomposed calcareous rock were found often embedded in hard cemented earth, which contained few fossils, suggesting possibly great inundations, when the cave was completely flooded. Other epochs of perhaps little rainfall were represented by strata containing considerable quantities of gastropods, and it was in these beds that the remains of fossil mammals were mostly recovered.

Various layers of stalagmite were observed at different levels, indicating depths of the cavern floor in past ages.

Fossil remains of Pleistocene mammals which occurred during excavations include *Ursus, Auchenia major* (llama), giant capybara, *Equus, Smilodon, Mylodon* (giant sloth), *Dicotyles,* tapir, *Mastodon,* and other remains which still have to be classified.

In February 1935 while excavating beneath a layer of stalagmite which extended over the floor at the end of the cave, at a depth of a little over two meters, the skull of a horse in a fragmentary condition was recovered, and at a short distance three molars, one pre-molar and part of a limb bone of a young mastodon. A few days later, while continuing excavations at the same level but nearer to the wall, a partial human skeleton was exposed. This find was totally unexpected, for during the whole period of exploration by members of the Academy no sign of human habitation had been seen while removing the alluvial deposit which contained remains of fossil mammals.

The skeleton was lying in an extended position, and several bones were missing. Unfortunately on removing the skull it fractured into several pieces, but with care it was possible to make an almost complete reconstruction.

The conditions under which the skeleton was found clearly indicate that the man had a natural burial. The position of the remains differed from those found in Indian burial grounds of the Lagôa Santa race and other native tribes of Brazil. The Indians always buried their dead in drawn-up contracted positions, which is still a custom among native races of the East.

We can affirm that the Confins Man was found in an extended position. Furthermore, the left side of the skull and some limb bones show the claw marks of rodents, which supports the theory that the man was not buried artificially, but lay exposed on the surface of the cave until water carried in sediment, which gradually silted until he lay under a depth of over two meters of alluvial soil. Later a layer of stalagmite was formed as if to seal his sepulcher, and so his remains were preserved until they were exposed again in 1935.

Admitting that the Confins Man received a natural burial it is reasonable then to assume he lived towards the end of the Pluvial period, when the upper floor of the cave was being laid down. It is known that the only faunal remains which were found in this stratum were composed of extinct kinds, so it would appear that he survived and was a contemporary of the mastodon, horse and other mammals of the upper Pleistocene or Pluvial Age. At a later period the entrance became sealed with fallen rocks and sedimentary conglomerate, and the cave was left high and dry above the level of the Confins lake, which is nowadays thirty yards distant from the limestone rock.

The earth which covered his remains was similar to that found everywhere in the cave associated with fossil bones, and the general appearance of the skeletal parts was similar to that of extinct animals.

It is interesting to note that in historic times it is impossible for the Confins lake to flood the cave and carry sediment inside, as its elevation is sixty-five feet above the present level of the lake, and erosion has lowered the latter's bed one hundred feet below the rock-shelter.

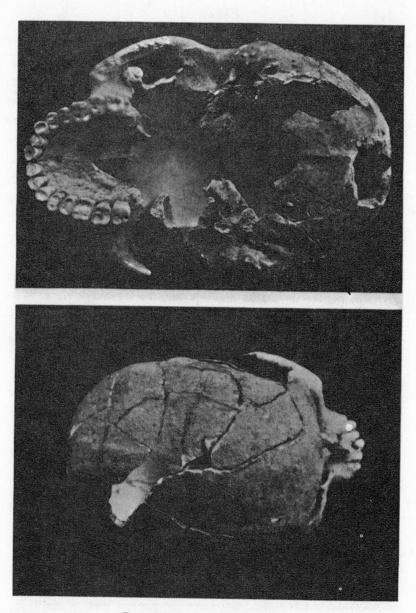

PLATE XXIV—The Confins Man.

No human artifacts were found together with the skeletal parts of Confins man.

Practically no evidence exists in Brazil from which it is possible to determine when the transitional period of the Post-Pleistocene (or Pluvial) commenced. Although it is generally assumed that many forms became extinct during or at the end of that period, it is not yet possible to compile a chronological order.

The fact that in our belief Confins Man was contemporary with animals now extinct, does not infer that he is of great age. From palaeontological studies made elsewhere in this region it is not at all unlikely that certain Pleistocene mammals became extinct in relatively recent times, and still survived when man first appeared in the Rio das Velhas Valley.

From these considerations we conclude that the Confins Man, who is a dolichocephalic type of "*Homo sapiens*," lived a few thousands of years ago, when the floor of the cave was two meters lower than at present, and when the ground level was such that heavy rain could flood the cavern and deposit sediment. We can only place this at the end of the Pluvial, or during the Post-Pluvial period, during which epoch there is every evidence of immense precipitations.

MEASUREMENTS OF THE CONFINS SKULL

Diameter antero-posterior maximum .... 178 mm.
Diameter transverse maximum .... 123 mm.
Diameter bregma-basion (obtained by calculation) ...... 141 mm.
Diameter biauricular .... 110 mm.
Diameter bitemporal .... 126 mm.
Diameter bistephanic .... 105 mm.
Diameter bifrontal minimum .... 94 mm.
Diameter asteric .... 107 mm.
Diameter biparietal .... 123 mm.
Length and breadth of the left glenoid fossa of the temporal. 25x15

Curves of the skull:

From the nasion to the ophryon .... 25 mm.
From the nasion to the bregma .... 125 mm.
From the bregma to the lambda .... 127 mm.
From the lambda to the opisthion .... 112 mm.
Biauricular curve .... 305 mm.

Face:

Interorbital interval .... 26 mm.
External biorbital distance .... 103 mm.
Internal biorbital distance .... 92 mm.
Maximum height of the orbit .... 33 mm.
Maximum breadth of the orbit .... 35 mm.
Depth of the orbit .... 5 mm.
Diameter bimalar maximum .... 114 mm.
Diameter bizygomatic (obtained by calculation) ...... 131 mm.
Distance from the nasion to the nasal spine .... 49 mm.
Maximum breadth of the nasal cavities .... 24 mm.
Total height of face .... 96 mm.
Height alveolar point .... 20 mm.
Distance from the alveolar point to the nasion .... 70 mm.
Distance from the alveolar point to the basion* .... 117 mm.
Distance from the nasion to the basion* .... 110 mm.

Inferior Maxillary:

Angular inclination of the ascending ramus .... 112°
Minimum breadth of the ascending ramus .... 37 mm.
Distance from the base of the sigmoidal slope to the gonion   52 mm.
Distance from the gonion to the gnathion .... 91 mm.
Distance from the external edge of the incisors to the mid-
  dle of the condyle .... 107 mm.
Distance from the intercondyle (taken from its center) ... 107 mm.
Height of the maxillary, between two pre-molars .... 31 mm.
Maximum thickness of the maxillary .... 18 mm.
Major diameter of the condyles .... 25 mm.
Minor diameter of the condyles .... 14 mm.
Breadth of the ascending ramus in its narrowest segment.. 37 mm.

---

* Obtained by calculation.

Nasal-malar angle of Flower 143,0
Angle of prognathism (method of Rivet) 66,30

Indices:

Cephalic 69,1
Nasal 48,9
Orbital 94,2
Height-length of the cranium 80,0
Height-breadth of the cranium 114,0
Strength of the mandible 358,0
Cranial capacity .... 1,281 cm.

From the accompanying photographs it will be observed that the basal parts of the skull are missing.

When measuring the skull the position of the basion was determined by calculation, considering the length of the occipital orifice as 3½ cm., which is the average in _"Homo sapiens."_ Also the diameter of the bizygomatic was estimated as one of the arches had been reconstructed artificially.

From morphological evidence it is apparent that the skull is masculine.

The measurements point out that it is dolichocephalic, hypsicephalic, prognathic, mesorhinic, with megasemic orbits and elliptical rather shallow palatine arch. The prognathism is essentially sub-nasal.

In consequence of the height of the zygomatic arches and the medium development of the fronto-parietal, the skull can be considered phrenozygic as can be seen in the photograph.

The frontal region above the superciliary arches is slightly salient developing posteriorly, however without any accentuation.

The forehead is low, and the skull although hypsicephalic does not possess the pyramidal aspect generally noted in the skulls of the Lagôa Santa race as defined by Rivet, Soren, Hansen, etc. The view in profile is impressive because of the submaxillary prognathism, and in the accompanying photograph the claw marks of rodents can be seen.

In view of the conditions under which the remains occurred, and for future reference, we have resolved to designate the skull as "The Confins Man" recognising him as one of the most primitive types of *"Homo sapiens"* of the paleo-American race of Asiatic origin yet discovered in South America.

THE PLACE OF HOMO SOLOENSIS AMONG FOSSIL MEN

BY

W. F. F. OPPENOORTH

Zeist, Holland

SEVERAL authors have, since my preliminary publications[1] on *Homo soloensis*, expressed as their opinion that this fossil man should belong to the group of *Homo neanderthalensis*. Among these authors are Weidenreich,[2] who believes that *H. soloensis* is perhaps the *Homo primigenius asiaticus*, all the skulls showing the same particularities, a question of race. Von Koenigswald[3] changes this name for reason of priority into *H. neanderthalensis soloensis*. Vallois[4] considers it like the man of Rhodesia, or closely related, instead of *H. neanderthalensis*.

I suppose that these opinions result from the incompleteness of my first descriptions, for there are several typical differences between *H. soloensis* and *H. neanderthalensis* as I already have had opportunity to explain in an address before the Netherlands National Bureau of Anthropology.[5]

But let us first look for the features, as far as they are present

[1] W. F. F. Oppenoorth, "Homo (Javanthropus) soloensis, Een plistoceene mensch van Java." Meded. Dienst v/d. Mijnbouw in Ned. Indie no. 20. 1932. "De vondst van palaeolithische menschelijke schedels op Java." De Mijningenieur, Juni 1932. "Ein neuer diluvialer Urmensch von Java." Natur und Museum, Sept. 1932.

[2] Fr. Weidenreich, "Ueber pithecoide Merkmale bei Sinanthropus pekinensis u. seine stammesgeschichtliche Beurteilung." Z. f. Anat. u. Entw. Gesch. 1933, Bd. 99.

[3] G. H. R. von Koenigswald, "Zur Stratigraphie des javanischen Pleistocän." De Ing. in Ned. Indie 1934, IV. no. 11.

[4] H. Vallois, "Le Javanthropus." L'Anthropologie, t. 45, 1935.

[5] Read at Amsterdam on May 2, 1936.

in the Ngandong man, that determine *Homo neanderthalensis.*
Boule[6] gives the following diagnostics:

"Corps de petite taille, très massif. Tête très volumineuse. Indice
céphalique moyen. Crâne très aplati; arcades orbitaires énormes for-
mant un bourrelet continu; front très fuyant; occiput saillant et com-
primé dans le sens vertical. Orbites très grandes, rondes. Une attitude
bipède ou verticale moins parfaite que chez les hommes actuels.
Jambes très courtes. Capacité céphalique moyenne d'environ 1400
centimètres cubes."

Boule remarks, however, that several neanderthaloid skulls
have been found that show only some of the characteristics of
the Neanderthal type, but that they are false Neanderthalers.

Some of the Neanderthal features still appear with recent man,
e.g. the Australians have a bar of bone above the eyes, a torus
supraorbitalis, but they are by no means Neanderthalers.

So with the Ngandong man, *Homo soloensis,* several features
are of the Neanderthal type, e.g., the flat forehead, the heavy
eye-brow ridges, but there are also many others that do not
agree. It is remarkable that in this respect there is a great conformity with another fossil skull that has given much trouble
concerning its relation to other fossil types and to recent man, the
Homo rhodesiensis.

All the Ngandong skulls show the same peculiarities of
shape, so there can be no doubt that they belong to the same
type, a type with primitive features: a flat forehead with a very
decided protrusion along the supraorbital region, forming a heavy
torus supraorbitalis; a considerable postorbital narrowing and,
in a vertical sense, a compressed occiput with a torus occipitalis
transversus. There are also typical features of Neanderthal man,
but when studied more exactly it becomes evident that all these
particularities are more or less different from those of the real

[6] M. Boule, "Les Hommes fossiles." 1912.

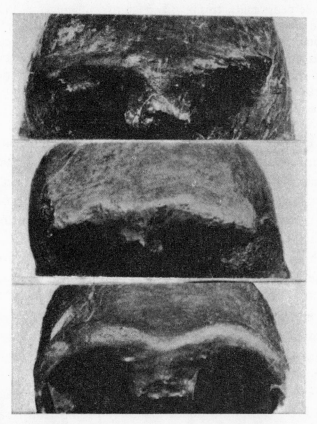

PLATE XXV—Above: Torus supraorbitalis of Ngandong VI, original. Middle: the same of Ngandong V, cast. Below: the same of Neanderthal man, cast of Neanderthal-Düsseldorf skull.

Neanderthaler. Moreover there are some very important differences.

I have made craniograms in the Frankfurt orientation of the skulls, I, V and VI; of skull IV (only the frontal bone of a female) the mid-sagittal contour has been made with the aid of a cast. When the mid-sagittal contours of these four skulls are placed together, all orientated on the *or-po* plane with the *po* coinciding, then will I, IV and VI nearly cover each other; V however is much longer and higher (Plate XXV). Of this skull, the biggest one ever found, the development of both tori is much stronger, also the places of attachment for the muscles are more developed, especially in the nuchal area; the forehead is flatter. So I think it correct to say that V is a male and that I, IV and VI are female skulls.

These skulls belong to adults, but there has also been found the frontal bone of a child (skull II) between 3 and 7 years old and this bone has neither a torus supraorbitalis nor a linea temporalis.

With all skulls the face is lacking; the remains belong exclusively to the neurocranium. Hence of the facial characteristics there can be made only suppositions, the more so as we did not find a mandible nor a single tooth.

The only limb bones found are a fragment of a tibia and a damaged right one, and this tibia shows no affinity with Neanderthal man and thus corroborates the conception that the two forms are different.

I have mentioned that the neanderthaloid (as we can call them) characteristics of *H. soloensis* deviate from the real Neanderthal features. One of the striking neanderthaloid features is the heavy bar of bone above the orbits. In Neanderthal man we see two arcs connected by a slight depression; on the Ngandong skulls the structure of the torus is quite different, more chimpanzoid. Though in all skulls not absolutely the same, the torus is a nearly straight, continuous bone ridge. Only on skull VI is there a slight depression and the torus gives an impression of arc shape above the orbits, but the upper side is a straight line (Plate XXVI).

Although immediately under this torus the orbits are broken away and so their shape is not known, it seems impossible that the orbits should have had the round shape of the Neanderthal type. In my opinion, and I have tried it by reconstruction with wax, the only possible shape must have been more rectangular, like that of Cro-Magnon man. On this consideration I compared the orbits of other fossil and recent skulls and found for the height with Obercassel 30 mm., Wadjak 33 mm., Goea lama (Java) 31 mm., recent Javanese 33-35 mm.; so I estimated 30 mm. as about right for *H. soloensis* females and used this measure for orientation in the craniophor.

On the Neanderthal skulls there is a fossa supraglabellaris that is lacking on the Ngandong skulls; here the torus supraorbitalis passes away imperceptibly in the frontal bone with a fluent, hardly curved, line. The frontal bone has a slight crest, which is lacking on Neanderthal skulls and gives to the Ngandong skulls in some degree a roof form.

The occiput of the Neanderthal skulls can be compared with the form of an egg with a ridge, the torus occipitalis transversus, but on the Ngandong skulls it has quite another shape. The nuchal plain is very flat, has a strong crest and is nearly rectangular (about 100°) to the upper squama. Between the two parts of the occiput is a heavy torus and so the occiput has a striking resemblance to that of Rhodesian man.

I hope to have shown above that those neanderthaloid characteristics are more seeming than real as far as proof of the identity with Neanderthal man is concerned.

But there are also additional points of difference.

The cranial capacity is of great significance. For *H. neander-*

thalensis Boule mentions an average capacity of about 1400 cc. It is best to take for comparison separately the capacities of male and female skulls. For the male La Chapelle skull Boule calculated 1600 cc., for the young male Le Moustier skull Weinert estimated 1564 cc., for the female skull of La Quina, Henri Martin calculated 1350 cc.

The Ngandong skulls, even the gigantic male no. V, have all a smaller capacity than the female of La Quina. In my preliminary publications I calculated the probable cranial capacity for Ngandong (according to the method of Welcker) as 1140 cc., and according to the method of Manouvrier as 1215 cc.; for Ngandong V, which I measured with dry sand, about 1300 cc. After that, skull VI was found and this skull, being more complete and having the base intact, offered the opportunity of making more accurate calculations. Moreover it was possible with the aid of this skull to improve the calculations of no. I.

The two just mentioned methods of calculating the cranial capacity are intended for recent skulls, so fossil skulls with very thick bones—and this is the case with the Ngandong skulls—will always, with those exocranial measures, give results that must be too high, particularly when there are still heavy tori. Since after the complete preparation of the skulls I could measure the thickness of the bones of some skulls and there could be made some endocranial casts (I, IV and V), I preferred the method of Froriep,[7] a method that has given very good results by comparison with measured capacities of skulls.

Cap—½ (LxBxH), in which

L—internal length, B—internal breadth, H—total height (Virchow), from basion to skull contour.

Skulls I, IV and VI have median contours that nearly coincide; the thickness of the bones of I and IV, I could measure

---

[7] Aug. Froriep, "Ueber die Bestimmung der Schädelcapacität durch Messung und Berechnung." Zeitschr. f. Morph. u. Anthrop. 1911. Bd XIII.

directly, also the internal length and breadth of no. I; so it is possible, with a great amount of exactness, to estimate the internal length and breadth of VI. H. ext. could be taken from the sagittal craniogram in Frankfurt orientation; H int. is about 10 mm. less.

With this method, one of the most accurate possible, I find for the cranial capacity of Ngandong VI, 1189, in round numbers 1190 cc.

In applying the method of Froriep to Ngandong I, we miss the total height, the basion being lost, but the opisthion is present. So by constructing in the sagittal craniogram the diameter of the foramen magnum from the data of skull VI, it is possible to find the basion with only a very little possible error; and the error in the total height will be still smaller. In this way the calculated capacity is 1158, in round numbers 1160 cc.

So I find for these two female Ngandong skulls capacities of 1160 and 1190 cc., giving an average of 1175 cc.

With the large male skull V the basion is also missing, but can be estimated in the same way as has been done for skull I; the consequent calculated cranial capacity is 1316 cc.[8]

The difference in cranial capacity between male and female

[8] Dubois in a recent paper ("On the fossil human skulls recently discovered in Java and *Pithecanthropus* by Prof. Eugène Dubois." Man, 1937, I) made the same calculations, with a somewhat different result. He measured the internal length, breadth and height on an endocranial cast of Ngandong I and calculated the height from the meatus acusticus on the skull cast. According to Froriep the total height can be obtained by multiplying the porion height by 1 −1/6. That this manner of obtaining the desired height is a little less exact than mine, is evident. Dubois found for Ngandong I a capacity of 1143 cc., only 17 cc. different from my calculation. But for Ngandong VI, which he too considers a female (while in his opinion Ngandong I is a male), he finds 1087 cc., a difference of about 100 cc.

I would still remark that most methods of calculating the cranial capacity are very sensitive to small differences in the measures taken; so by this method a difference in the height of 1/2 mm.—and how often this is the case with different investigators—will give a difference of about 50 cc. in the capacity.

Dubois points also to the exactness of the method of Froriep by comparing the calculation of the Rhodesian capacity with the measured one.

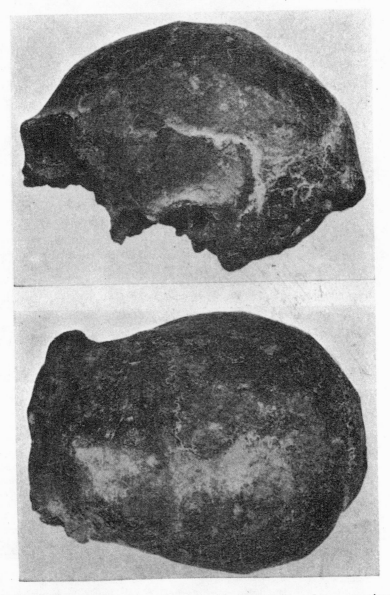

PLATE XXVI—Ngandong skull VI in norma lateralis, orientated on or-po plane, original.

skulls of *Homo soloensis* is thus about 140 cc., an average amount among fossil and recent man.

The cranial capacities of *H. soloensis* males and females agree remarkably well with those of the most primitive of recent man, the Australian aborigine. The shape of the endocranial casts, however, is very primitive. The brain specialist, Ariëns Kappers,[9] who could study the endocranial casts of Ngandong I, IV and V, considers the general shape even more primitive than that of Neanderthal man. His conclusion is: "Taking all together, there seems no doubt that of all endocranial casts hitherto available, the *Homo soloensis* group belongs to the most primitive, approaching in some respects the *Sinanthropus* cast."

So we have found that the cranial capacity of *H. soloensis* is considerably less than that of Neanderthal man and the endocranial casts indicate that the shape is more primitive, two important differences.

As in recent man the maximum breadth of the Neanderthal skull is rather high on the skull; on the Ngandong skulls it lies lower and a little above that of *Sinanthropus*, a more primitive feature.

The temporal bone has a strong disparity compared to that of Neanderthal man. Here the mandibular joint shows distinctly simian traits; the glenoid cavity is so shallow that its deepest part lies level with, or below the mid-point of the ear passage and an articular eminence is only just visible. On the Ngandong skulls, however, the articular fossa is deep and reaches up almost to the level of the roof of the ear passage; in front of it is a well marked articular eminence to which the condyle of the jaw mounts, when the mouth is opened (Plate XXVI). This is the typical modern human form of the joint. The tympanic plate in Neanderthal man is also simian; that of *H. soloensis* is much bigger

[9] C. U. Ariëns Kappers, "The endocranial casts of the Ehringsdorf and Homo soloensis skulls." J. of Anat. V. LXXI. p. I, Oct. 1936.

with a sharp crest that divides it into two parts, an anterior with a convex and a posterior with a concave surface.[10]

The direction of the long axis of the elliptical porus acusticus externus is neither forward as in Neanderthal man, nor backward as in Neolithic and modern man, but about vertical. The processus mastoideus of Neanderthal man is small and has a simian trait; that of *H. soloensis* is a real pyramidal process, quite as in modern skulls. The distance of its apex below the Frankfurt plane is, in skull VI, 33 mm., whereas in Neanderthal skulls the measurement is much less, varying from 15-25 mm. (in the young man's skull of Le Moustier, about 21 mm.)[11] and in skulls of modern man, 25-35 mm.[12] The length of the mastoid process in *H. soloensis* skull is thus far above the limit of Neanderthal length.

In connection with the strong torus occipitalis and the well developed places of attachment for the muscles on the nuchal area, we may assume a strong neck and a poise of the head not unlike that of Neanderthal man. But this poise must have been otherwise more like that in modern man. The foramen magnum lies more forward and so the head is better balanced. The central angle (angle between bregma-basion and glabella-lambda lines) that in Neanderthal skulls is about 80° (La Chapelle 80°, Le Moustier 81°)[13] is in skull Ngandong VI 88°, thus nearly as in recent man (90°). In this regard there is again a great agreement with Rhodesian man, in which that angle is 89°.

[10] Dubois ("Racial Identity of Homo Soloensis Oppenoorth [including Homo modjokertensis von Koenigswald] and Sinanthropus pekinensis Davidson Black." Proc. Kon. Akad. v. Wet. Amst., 1936, V. 39, no. 10) sees in the tympanic portion of the temporal bone the conclusive proof of the racial identity of *H. soloensis* and *Sinanthropus pekinensis*, while Weidenreich, on the contrary, emphasizes the primitivity of the form and the great difference from all *Homo primigenius*.

[11] Hans Weinert. "Der Schädel des Eiszeitlichen Menschen von Le Moustier." 1925, abb. 14.

[12] Arthur Keith. "New Discoveries relating to the Antiquity of Man." 1931, p. 335.

[13] Hans Weinert, *Op. cit.*, p. 26.

Considering the above mentioned features of the Ngandong skulls, we must conclude that the structure of these skulls has such modern traits that the resemblance with Neanderthal man is only seeming. And yet considering the only limb bone found, a right tibia, the characteristics of it will strengthen this conclusion.

The tibia has been found in the same excavation—I have made four excavations at Ngandong in different parts of the terrace, but only in one have been found human remains—as the skulls and in the same stratum, so there is no doubt that they belong together. This tibia is not short and robust like that of Neanderthal man, but rather slender, and the shaft is particularly straight. The proximal end is badly damaged, but there still remains a small area of the medial condyle, so the retroversion can only be less than in Neanderthal tibiae, perhaps about 10°. The length between the upper surface and the lower point of the malleolus is 365 mm., the front-to-back diameter towards the middle of the shaft is 29 mm., the bone is mesocnemic. A peculiar feature is the absence of the sharp crest, the crista anterior; in its place is a small rounded anterior surface. In the mid-section across the tibia both sides are convex, the medial more than the lateral.

Estimating the height of *H. soloensis* from the length of the tibia we obtain by using Pearson's formula a stature of 166.2 cm., if the tibia was that of a male, and 161 cm. if it was that of a female. With Manouvrier's formula are obtained nearly the same figures, viz. 165.2 and 163.4 cm. So we see that *H. soloensis* was taller than *H. neanderthalensis*, the male of Ferrassie being about 160, the female 145 cm., and the man of La Chapelle-aux-Saints was not more than 155 cm.[14]

But if *H. soloensis* does not belong to the group of Neanderthalers, where is he then to be placed? To consider this it is de-

[14] M. Boule. *Op. cit.*, p. 225.

sirable to look for another form that has given the same difficulty and that has as many traits in common with the Ngandong skulls; a skull of which the affinity till now was doubtful, viz. *Homo rhodesiensis.*

Hrdlička gives the following opinion:[15] "It is a most remarkable specimen of which the age, provenience, history and nature are still anthropological puzzles. Morphologically the skull is frequently associated now with the Neanderthal type of Europe. This may be fundamentally correct, but only to that extent. In its detailed characteristics the specimen in some respects is inferior, in others superior to anything known as yet of the Neanderthal man:"

and again: "It is not a Neanderthaler; it represents a different race, a different variety."

Keith[16] also considers the Rhodesian man as different from Neanderthal Man and places him, "at or near the base of the stem which afterwards branched into all types of modern man—*homo sapiens*—living and extinct."[17]

The discovery of the Ngandong skulls has been a treasure trove, for it elucidates the nature of the mysterious Rhodesian man. It proves that the Rhodesian skull is not a casual variant but belongs to a distinct kind of man.

In my first publications I proposed to unite *H. soloensis, H. rhodesiensis, H. wadjakensis,* all proto-australian forms, into a separate subgenus, *Javanthropus,* but—and I completely agree with Dubois that they all belong to this group—that name was not well chosen and it is better to drop it. Yet we have in *Homo*

---

[15] A. Hrdlička. "The skeletal remains of early Man." 1930, pp. 116, 129.

[16] A. Keith. "The Antiquity of Man," II, 1929, p. 416.

[17] Dubois in his recent publication in Man (1937, I) writes "Solo Man and Rhodesian Man—another proto-Australian, which closely resembles Solo Man, though discovered in South Africa—are representatives of the most primitive of the species *Homo Sapiens* and well distinct from *Homo neanderthalensis,* the other human species."

soloensis the oldest at present known representative of *Homo sapiens fossilis.*

There is still one thing to remark, viz. that the culture of *H. soloensis* is different from that of Neanderthal man. Together with the skulls a big collection of fossil animal bones has been gathered among which are many pieces that must have been worked by man.

A striking difference between the two civilizations is that the Neanderthal civilization is characterized by stone implements, that of Ngandong by implements of bone or stag horn; the only stone implements found are some stone balls of andesite, well known from European and South-African Mousterian sites.

The most important objects are horn pick-axes, antlers that have been roughly broken at the second branch, while the point of the first branch has been cut away so that a sharp section is obtained. This is quite different from what proceeds by rubbing along trees. Such implements are known from the Northwest European mesolithic and younger civilizations. In another specimen the first branch has been cut away obliquely and thus an object is obtained that can have been used as a cudgel. With a third kind of working, a small piece of the first branch is saved and then split, probably with the intention of fastening therein a stone axe. This implement resembles a neolithic axe of the Lake of Neuchâtel in Switzerland.

The many broken pieces of bone with sharp edges that exclude a long transport by river, give the impression that these bones (true of a great many long bones) have been broken to pieces intentionally to obtain the marrow. But among those broken bones are several that have been shaped into weapons.

The artifacts from Ngandong appear to be of a young civilization and do not agree well with the primitive shape of the skulls, but it must be kept in mind that with the certainly older *Sinanthropus* also many bone and horn implements have been found.

From a short description by Breuil,[18] one may conclude that the implements of antlers and long bones have a great resemblance to those of Ngandong but are found there together with quartz implements.

Yet there is not much known of the old premstoric eastern civilizations. Those of Chou Kou Tien and Ngandong, one found shortly after the other, are valuable contributions and they give the impression of an independently developing civilization in the Far East, which is not in accord with the contemporaneous civilizations in Europe.

[18] H. Breuil. "Le Feu et l'Industrie de pierre, et d'os dans le gisement du *Sinanthropus* à Chou Kou Tien." L'Anthropologie, 1932, t 42.

ON THE STONE AGE OF JAPAN

BY

R. TORII

Dean of Faculty of Literature, Sophia University, Tokyo, Japan

IN JAPAN there has not yet been found any vestige of primitive man of the Paleolithic age (Old Stone Age). We will have to wait for eventual discoveries in the future. The first vestiges of man appear in the Neolithic age, viz. the New Stone Age. We have found them everywhere, everywhere we meet with shell mounds.

The New Stone Age in Japan may be divided into A or Pre-Japanese and B or Japanese proper. A is of the aborigines of our country, the Ainu, Pan-Ainu; B is the age of our own ancestors. The stone age of our ancestors begins with the prehistoric and is followed by the protohistoric and historic ages.

In the stone age of A man lived on hunting and fishing. He was a pit-dweller and made stone and bone implements. He was specially skilful in making pottery, earthenware and human figures of clay. These figures give us an idea of the costumes and methods of clothing; we recognize the way of making up their hair and of adorning their clothing. Judging from the way they dressed they resemble the Eskimos, Aleutes, Chukchee, Koryaks. Like these they also tattooed their faces. Specially noteworthy is their use of the bone harpoon in the Eskimo way. Moreover their fire drill is the bow drill.

Summing up, it may be said that the mode of life of Stone Age A seems to be that of the Arctic Culture man belonging to the Paleo-Siberians. My studies have led me to believe that Hokkaido, Chishima, the Bering Strait and America belong to this Stone Age A. Therefore a comparative study of these regions is of the highest importance.

Stone Age B, that of our ancestors, is intimately related to Korea, Manchuria, eastern Siberia. Their stone implements and pottery show great resemblance.

In conclusion may I express my earnest hope that American Archaeologists and Anthropologists will lend their help to a close and comparative study of the remnants of Stone Age A.

GEOLOGICAL DIVISIONS

QUATERNARY	HOLOCENE OR RECENT	POSTGLACIAL
	PLEISTOCENE	V GLACIAL WISCONSIN
		4 INTERGLACIAL PEORIAN
		IV GLACIAL IOWAN OR FIRST PHASE WISCONSIN
		3 INTERGLACIAL SANGAMON
		III GLACIAL ILLINOIAN
		2 INTERGLACIAL YARMOUTH
		II GLACIAL KANSAN
		I INTERGLACIAL AFTONIAN
		I GLACIAL NEBRASKAN
TERTIARY	PLIOCENE	CLOSE OF PLIOCENE

NORTH

ROYAL BISON